Video Playtime

The 1980s saw an explosion in the use of the domestic video cassette recorder (VCR), arguably the most significant new form of home entertainment technology since television.

In *Video Playtime* Ann Gray investigates what women themselves felt about the VCR, both in terms of the way these entertainment facilities were used within their households, and what kinds of programmes and films they themselves particularly enjoyed. The ages, social, economic and family circumstances of the women differ, but almost all live with a male partner, and the book draws heavily on verbatim quotes from discussion to provide a rich description of different types of household microcultures and to give readers more direct access to the women themselves and the ways in which they accounted for their own experience. This particular method of research reveals the importance of first exploring the social and cultural context of a new piece of technology in order to understand its significance.

Video Playtime addresses questions of domestic technology as well as those of taste and cultural preference, particularly in relation to class, addressing the dynamics of power within existing social and cultural relations and thereby setting the analysis within a much wider social context.

Ann Gray is a Lecturer in Cultural Studies at the University of Birmingham. She has published related articles in a number of journals including *Screen* and *Marxism Today*, and has contributed to *Boxed In: Women and Television* (1987), edited by Helen Baehr and Gillian Dyer.

Comedia
Series editor: David Morley

Video Playtime

The gendering of a leisure technology

Ann Gray

A Comedia book
published by Routledge
London and New York

First published 1992
by Routledge
11 New Fetter Lane, London EC4P 4EE

Simultaneously published in the USA and Canada
by Routledge
a division of Routledge, Chapman and Hall, Inc.
29 West 35th Street, New York, NY 10001

Phototypeset in 10 on 12 point Bembo by Intype, London
Printed in Great Britain by Clays Ltd, St Ives plc

British Library Cataloguing in Publication Data
Gray, Ann
  Video Playtime: The Gendering of a Leisure Technology
  I. Title
  306.4

Library of Congress Cataloging in Publication Data
Gray, Ann
  Video playtime : the gendering of a leisure technology / Ann Gray.
  p.   cm.
  1. Video recordings—Social aspects.   2. Video tape recorders and
recording—Social aspects.   3. Television and women.   I. Title.
PN1992.945.G7   1992
302.23'45—dc20   92-13309

ISBN 0-415-05864-3   ISBN 0-415-05865-1 (pbk)

For my parents, Edna and Colin Johnson

Contents

Contents

Acknowledgements

I wish to thank all the women who participated in this research and who gave me so much more than their time. My thanks also to Andrew Tudor, Sue Plummer, Marie Kirwin, Jim McGuigan and John Johnson for their help and encouragement in the early stages of this research, to Joke Hermes and Charlotte Brunsdon for invaluable discussions and personal support during the writing of this book, and to Dave Morley, a patient and supportive editor. My especial thanks to Nick Gray for his love and friendship.

Introduction

The main focus of this book is the domestic video cassette recorder (VCR) and in particular how women use, and what they think about, this piece of entertainment technology. The VCR was the subject of a consumer boom in the early 1980s and was quickly established as *the* major innovation in home entertainment since television. The VCR was taken up across the social spectrum, this being made possible by existing networks of distribution for television sets which enabled rental contracts to be entered into, thereby eliminating the necessity for the large capital investment unavailable in lower-income households. The VCR offered the novelty of being able to record off-air and view broadcast material at alternative times and to hire pre-recorded tapes, mainly movies, from an increasingly large number of varied retail outlets. The VCR or 'video', as the vernacular would have it, rapidly entered the culture, exciting consumers, entrepreneurs and the self-appointed 'moral guardians', all of whom, in their different ways, were responding to an innovation in 'mass' culture. The present study does not deal explicitly or in any detail with the video industry which mushroomed as a result of the wide take-up of the domestic hardware, as its point of departure is the household. It is true, however, that the industry, its products, marketing styles and image, and the public debates which surround the viewing of 'unsuitable' material, have an effect on people's perceptions of the video culture, and these issues are taken up as and when they appear during my analysis.

The recent emergence of the VCR means that very little social research has been carried out into this phenomenon in this country, although some research has been undertaken in other European countries (Baboulin *et al.* 1983; Gubern 1985; Roe

1987). An exception to this in Britain is the study by Mark Levy and Barry Gunter undertaken for the IBA: *Home Video and the Changing Nature of the Television Audience* (Levy and Gunter 1988). Predictably, perhaps, this kind of institutional research is likely to produce 'evidence' which is of use to broadcasters and advertisers (one of the major worries for the commercial broadcasters was whether VCR use was disrupting advertising schedules) rather than social researchers (see Ang 1991 for a critical account of institutional 'audience' research). This seems to be the case from the way that the research material has been organized in their study. The concept of gender is avoided altogether, for example, in the statistical analysis, although there is a section entitled 'The social context of video use'. The questions posed were: (1) Who watches the video and with whom? (2) Is the social context of video use different from that of viewing off-air television? (3) Does the social context of video use affect the kinds of material viewed? (Levy and Gunter 1988: 37). This is a very limited understanding of the term 'social' in relation to home viewing. Mark Levy's collection, entitled *The VCR Age* (1989), attempts an 'overview of the VCR phenomenon' with studies from North America, Israel and Britain on topics under the headings 'Using the VCR'; 'The VCR and the individual' and 'VCRs, groups and societies'.

Whilst a small number of these studies identify gender differences in the use of the VCR, they do little to explain why gender differences might be of significance in the use of domestic entertainment technologies. One reason for this is that most of these studies are placed within mass communication studies frameworks which are predominantly concerned with impacts, attitudes and behaviours, using standard survey techniques out of which patterns of use are established and identified through a number of statistical correlations. Nowhere is the question of 'meaning' introduced, except in the weakest form of a question raised by Gunter and Wober about 'interest and enjoyment', where 'Responses from the sample audience for each program are transformed by calculation to a position on a 100-point scale, in which 100 denotes extremely interesting and/or enjoyable and 0 corresponds to not at all interesting or enjoyable' (Levy 1989: 61). Similarly, in all of these studies, categories used such as individual, gender, family, social are never questioned, but are simply taken and used as self-evident. Gunter and Wober criticize studies which are based on data provided by 'open-ended evidence during face-to-face interviews [which] may be tarnished by failure of memory or by the wish to project a particular (favourable) social impression', thereby revealing complete ignorance of developments in this kind of qualitative research and what it might be about, but also their complete faith in correlation of a variety of standard audience measurement techniques: questionnaires, diary reports, and different studies to produce, in their words, 'a full . . . accurate picture of VCR use' (Levy 1989: 50).

My main argument here is that, in order to understand women's use of VCRs, the social and cultural dimensions of households must be explored. Therefore, the present study straddles several previously separate areas of social and cultural research; the study of home-based leisure, television audience research, textual analysis and work on domestic technology. To a certain extent these have already been linked under the umbrella of cultural studies, but the nature of this research requires a combination of elements of all of these traditions in one project. What follows is an outline of the specific elements, drawing on particular pieces of research which have relevance for my study.

HOME-BASED LEISURE

Golding and Murdock have pointed out that the home is increasingly becoming the place for leisure and entertainment and the VCR is often looked upon as yet another piece of entertainment technology which offers an alternative to going out for the evening (Golding and Murdock 1983). Whilst accepting Golding and Murdock's argument, it is important to remember that for women in particular the home is also a place of work. Research suggests[1] that women are still largely responsible for household work and it would therefore seem that they may well be particularly affected by these developments in home-based leisure, as Deem reminds us:

> The home for most women, employed or not, is a workplace in a way that is true for few men, except those that do paid work from home and even in this case it is not the same thing as being a place for unpaid work
>
> (Deem 1986: 80)

This differential positioning has a major effect on the amount of time available for home leisure activities, as well as the nature of those activities. Rosemary Deem points to the relatively scant attention that has been paid to women's leisure in existing research, with gender often used as a 'bolt-on' category. However, more recently, feminist work into women's leisure has been undertaken, and it is this small body of research that is relevant here.[2] The results of these and other surveys have shown that married women's leisure time is more likely to be spent in the home than is that of her male partner, particularly if she has young children or other dependents. In order to explore women's use of the VCR, we must set our understanding within the context of her work, both outside and inside the home; her responsibilities and obligations to others; and the amount of spare time that she is able to organize for herself. The problem of defining what constitutes women's leisure is raised by Deem and others, and in order to overcome this any study must enable the women themselves to define their 'leisure'. Indeed, this may involve not using the term at all, as it has connotations of 'official' leisure, or 'going out and doing something', rather than referring to those non-obligatory activities which are carried out in the home. This idea of what constitutes 'leisure' suggests the extent to which women's non-work activities are marginalized, if not rendered invisible, to mainstream research.[3] We need to find ways of attending to those activities that women choose to do within the interstices of their domestic routines, and to assess the degree of control they have over the organization of spare time. This obviously requires an understanding of the domestic division of labour within households and of the decision-making processes informing family leisure activities. This can then form the context within which questions about non-obligatory activities can be raised.

TELEVISION AUDIENCE RESEARCH

Obviously the VCR is very closely related to television both in its domestic use and in the ways in which it might be conceptualized for the purposes of research. It is therefore necessary to consider certain forms of television audience research which are relevant to this study. In this respect the most significant move in television audience research occurred in the 1960s with what came to be known as the 'uses and gratifications' approach. This was developed from studies carried out in the 1930s in America

(Berelson 1949; Herzog 1944; Katz and Lazarsfeld 1955; Lazarsfeld and Stanton 1949), which sought to approach radio and the press from the perspective of the audience. Research into television and its audience in the intervening years had been dominated by 'effects' studies which assumed on the one hand an all-powerful form of mass communication – television – and, on the other, a passive audience, upon whom the various messages of television had effects.[4]

There is a wider social, political and cultural context within which we could place the various developments in research into television, which would take account of changes within the research community as well as funding agencies, but this is not necessary here. What is significant is the dominance of the 'television as problem' mode of thinking which constantly runs through the 'effects' tradition. This focus both reflects and produces attitudes towards television and its audience within the wider society. Furthermore, the academic discipline from which researchers drew their theories has been in the main, psychology, leading to a formulation of the 'problem' as behavioural, psychological, individual and measurable. One consequence of this was a failure properly to conceptualize the audience. Thus, the audience, in the dominant models of the 'effects' tradition, is seen as a mass of passive individuals who apparently bring nothing distinctive to the viewing situation but take everything from it.

The so-called 'modern' uses and gratifications approach developed in Britain proposed an active audience and, as such, made a break with the passive audience posited by the dominant mainstream tradition. Briefly, this approach suggested that what should be investigated is what people do with the media, rather than what the media does with people. However, one difficulty with the various manifestations of this tradition[5] was their lack of sociological discrimination. All too often these studies saw the audience as aggregates of individuals using the various media products to satisfy particular needs. Differences were conceived in terms of individual needs and 'uses' and were not related to a socio-cultural context. As Elliott has pointed out, the intra-individual processes with which the uses and gratifications approach deal 'can be generalized to aggregates of individuals, but they cannot be converted in any meaningful way into social structure and process' (Elliott 1974: 252). The uses and gratifications approach starts from the point of the free-thinking individual and

stays with that individual. It does not raise the important
questions of *why* individuals have particular needs and how they
come to choose particular forms for their gratification. Elliott
again suggests that television, and, we might add, any form of
cultural consumption, is 'more a matter of availability than selection. The audience has easier access to familiar genres, partly
because they understand the language and conventions, and
also because they already know the social meaning of this type of
output with some certainty' (ibid.: 259). In concentrating on the
individual, the uses and gratifications approach ignores social and
sub-cultural groupings and fails to consider how audiences perceive
and interpret the content of messages carried by the media.

The question of interpretation and sub-cultural variation
formed the basis of the next significant shift in British audience
research. In 1980 David Morley published *The 'Nationwide' Audience* with the object of investigating

> the specificity of communication and signifying practices, not
> as a wholly autonomous field, but in its complex articulations
> with questions of class, ideology and power . . . This is to
> return to prominence . . . [questions] as to the structural
> conditions which generate different cultural and ideological
> competencies
>
> (Morley 1980: 20)

Morley conceived of a socially structured audience, consisting of
sub-cultural groupings, whose position within the socio-economic
structure would have bearing on individual members' meaning
systems and in particular on their interpretations of media messages. Morley used Frank Parkin's model of class-based meaning
systems which suggests that in western societies there are three
major frameworks through which different interpretations of class
inequality can be made: the dominant value system, the subordinate value system and the radical value system (Parkin 1973).
Adapting Parkin, Morley suggests that there are three different
positions which the receiver or 'decoder' of the television message
can adopt in relation to that message: the decoder may accept the
dominant or preferred meaning of the message; he or she may
accept the preferred meaning but may negotiate that meaning
depending on his or her social experience or position; the decoder
may recognize the framework within which the message has been
'encoded' and supply his or her own alternative reading.

Alongside this reconceptualization of the television audience Morley, with Charlotte Brunsdon, undertook a semiological analysis of the early evening magazine programme *Nationwide* (Brunsdon and Morley 1978). The aim here was to determine how, within the encoding process, a preferred or dominant reading was established. This was not an attempt to seek the 'true' meaning of the programme, but rather to suggest that although programmes such as *Nationwide* are open to different interpretations (as assumed by the uses and gratifications approach) they nevertheless are encoded within a structured polysemy and that the programme makers are concerned to encourage a particular reading by the viewer.

Video tapes of the two programmes analysed were shown to a range of groups from different social backgrounds, who were then interviewed in order to establish the extent to which they accepted, negotiated or opposed the preferred meaning in the decoding process. There were 29 groups in all, with various social and cultural backgrounds, taken from different levels of the education system, and trade union and management training centres. The groups existed as social entities prior to the research with established formal and informal networks of communication. Interviews were tape-recorded and were of approximately thirty minutes' duration, and they formed the basic data upon which analyses of interpretations were made. This project challenged the predominant passive and individualistic conceptions of the audience, which it reformulated as an active, socially constituted audience, and also those theories which privileged the text as the site of meaning, leaving no space for the active reading subject.

The *Nationwide* study privileges class as the major structuring factor in reading and interpretation. Morley and Brunsdon's work was undertaken at the Centre for Contemporary Cultural Studies, Birmingham, and concurrently other members of the CCCS were developing a feminist approach to cultural studies and using ethnographic methods of research.[6] Dorothy Hobson's work exemplifies such developments and is of particular relevance to my work. Her two major research projects share very similar aims and methodologies. In 1978 she published 'Housewives: isolation as oppression' (Women's Studies Group 1978) and in 1980, 'Housewives and the mass media' (Hall *et al.* 1980) both of which were extracts from her unpublished MA thesis, 'A study of working class women at home: femininity, domesticity and maternity'. The latter extract identifies radio as important for working-class women at home with young children, both in terms of timetabling and as a link with the outside world. She also suggests a gender division in television programme preferences, manifest mainly in a male preference for news and current affairs and female preference for entertainment and fiction, especially in the form of soap opera. As she states,

> the ideology of a masculine and a feminine world of activities and interests and the separation of those gender-specific interests is never more explicitly expressed than in the women's reactions and responses to television programmes. Here both class and gender-specific differences are of vital importance.
>
> (Hall *et al.* 1980: 109)

Hobson is able to explore gender-specific differences by attending to women's accounts of their own preferences and those of their male partners, but it is difficult to see how she can claim to have conceptualized class-specific differences. Her study was based on long tape-recorded interviews with young working-class women, and, as such, could potentially provide a picture of that class and its gender-specific culture. However, we have no information about the activities, interests and programme preferences of women in other class positions with which to compare her material.

In 1982 Hobson's book *Crossroads: the Drama of a Soap Opera* was published. This was based on research in progress for a doctoral thesis in which she had previously claimed to be

> looking at the production processes of various popular television and radio programmes, which involves interviewing and observing the programme makers in the encoding moment, and I will then move to the audience of those programmes to try to understand their decoding of the televisual texts.
>
> (Hall *et al.* 1980: 292)

Her investigation of the 'encoding moment' was traumatized by the sacking of Noele Gordon from what was then ATV's *Crossroads*; the resulting publication was aimed at a general readership because, as she put it, 'the public outcry of support for the actress and media coverage of those events seemed much more relevant to a book of wider appeal than to remain part of an academic thesis (Hobson 1982: 11).

This resulted in a vastly truncated version of her original plan for applying the encoding-decoding model. Hobson had intended to look at the encoding of a range of popular programmes made for television and radio, and to follow this up with an exploration of the 'decoding' audience. Her section on the 'decoding moment' in which she reports on the audience for *Crossroads* is rather impressionistic. The subjects of her study are distinct only in that they are fans of the soap opera. This particular viewing activity is foregrounded at the expense of important contextual factors. Information about the women, their class, age, family circumstances and employment, where it appears at all, is introduced in an unsystematic way, resulting in a collection of disembodied reports, organized around different forms of reported and observed viewing practices and pleasures. There is no attempt to relate these to wider social or cultural categories, and the study is almost a celebratory account of viewing pleasures associated with a soap opera.

In spite of the shortcomings of her *Crossroads* study, Hobson made a key intervention in the field of audience research in that she focused her attention on the domestic environment, the context of most television viewing, and employed the qualitative methods of interviews, observations, and tape-recorded 'long unstructured conversations' (ibid.: 105) with viewers:

> It is important to stress that the interviews were unstructured because I wanted the viewers to determine what was interesting or what they noticed, or liked, or disliked about the programme and specifically about the episodes which we had watched.
>
> (ibid.: 105)

The domestic context of television watching was identified by David Morley as a lacuna of the *Nationwide* study (Morley 1986). The groups had viewed *Nationwide* in a 'contrived' setting, their work place, and not in their 'natural' domestic viewing contexts. In his next project Morley wanted to explore this context and the possibility of contradictory decodings which subjects may make across different types of texts and within different contexts. He also wanted to investigate the preferred genres of particular audience sub-groups.

TELEVISION IN THE DOMESTIC CONTEXT   TVFP

Readings, then, must be understood within the context of viewing and in the recognition that people occupy and assume different
subject positions in their social relations. Individuals who constitute sub-groups of the television audience cannot be seen simply
as bearers of deep structures (class, for example) which can somehow be read off or matched up with their decoding strategies,
but must be seen as subjects crossed by a number of different,
and often contradictory, discourses. This is not to regard the
subject as 'spoken' by those discourses, but, as Morley suggests,
we require to 'see the person actively producing meanings from
the restricted range of cultural resources which his or her structural position has allowed them access to' (Morley 1986: 43).

The cultural resources which are available to individuals and
from which their particular cultural competencies are gained can
be seen as major determining factors in the kinds of choices of
popular genres which people make. Moreover, these 'resources'
and 'competencies' are unevenly distributed within our society.
Referring to the work of Bourdieu and others, Morley argues
that the possession of cultural competence is 'determined outside
the sphere of television – by family socialisation and education'
(ibid.: 44).

When Morley showed his groups the *Nationwide* programme,
the question of whether those groups would choose to watch that
programme in the first place was not considered. In order to
understand what types of material are relevant and to whom,

> we need to deal more directly with the relevance/irrelevance
> and comprehension/incomprehension dimensions of interpre-
> tations and decoding, rather than being directly concerned with
> the acceptance or rejection of particular substantive ideological
> themes or propositions
>
> (ibid.: 45)

What is involved here is a move away from considering the
ideological problematic of specific televisual texts towards what
Morley refers to as 'audience availability'. In addressing this kind
of audience competence and its distribution across the social structure, we open up the important inter-discursive space which
encircles the viewing subject and her or his relation both to social
structures and to particular popular genres. Eighteen families were

interviewed in an attempt to provide an 'ethnography of reading' (Morley 1981) of the 'politics of the living room'[7] and of the way in which television takes its place within the household culture.

The opening chapters of Morley's *Family Television*, outlined above, suggest an alternative conceptual model for television viewing in the domestic context, but he admits in an 'Afterword', 'in the later analysis I have been unable to operationalise effectively all the theoretical consequences of this model' (Morley 1986: 174). One of the major problems is, in fact, that his sample of families is dominated by those with a working-class or lower-middle-class background. Given that he wanted to explore the range of cultural competencies and related choices, this restriction is a limitation on the whole enterprise. This is not to argue that a wider range of family backgrounds would have produced a more representative sample, but that a more diverse selection would have permitted exploratory investigation of differences in cultural competence. Accordingly, as class slipped out of focus in *Family Television*, gender emerged as the strongest structuring element in viewing practice. Gender clearly has a major influence on viewing behaviour and other domestic practices and must play a central role in any attempt to address the social constitution of the audience. Class and gender, in particular, intersect significantly and small-scale qualitative research projects can hope to explore some part of the complexity of their interrelation.

In *Family Television* Morley draws on the work of James Lull and Jennifer Bryce, both of whom had explored the place and significance of television within family and household relations. Their work provided important insights into the social use of television and Lull distinguished between the structural and relational uses of television. The former implies environmental and regulative use and the latter the creation of practical social arrangements. This approach to television audience research emphasizes the importance of attending to the social dimension of television viewing and to the ways in which the dynamics of domestic life, and relationships of power within that environment, affect the practice of television viewing. It insists on investigating the microcosm of the household in terms of the ways in which its members, in different permutations, organize space and time within its geography (Lull 1980).[8] In a more recent collection of his work, Lull argues that we must focus on 'the family' as the 'natural' viewing group and relies on direct observation of families and in-depth interviewing for his data (Lull 1990). He argues, drawing on a number of research findings, that television viewing can, by and large, be thought of as an 'extension' of the patterns of family communication within households. In Lull's important work television is placed centrally within the dynamics of family life. Whilst recognizing the importance of this work, and especially his cross-cultural dimension, I would want to distance my study from the 'family viewing' strand of television audience research. What I am fundamentally concerned with is the significance of home entertainment technologies for one particular member of each household, the adult woman; furthermore I do not want to subsume her accounts of domestic viewing practices into those of her family, although her perceived relationship to, and responsibilities for, other members of her household will undoubtedly emerge. Women are far too readily seen as representatives of their families by researchers and the state alike, and my concern here is to address them as individuals occupying particular social positions, and not to lose sight of their own distinctive viewpoints.

Reference has already been made to Hobson's pioneering work on the domestic world of television viewing which, along with *Family Television*, recognizes the significance of the domestic context for television consumption. However, both pieces of research tend to conceive of a 'unified' context. In looking at the introduction of the VCR into various households, the present research suggests that this context is not unified but diverse, constituted by different household members and 'appropriate' texts, and furthermore that each context offers specific and distinct viewing experiences for the women in the study.

The idea that television and radio tailor their output to different audiences at different times of the day is not new. Much work has looked at the structuring of schedules and the forms of popular television, assuming that characteristic audiences, particular domestic timetables, and different modes of viewing are produced as a consequence of scheduling and programming styles. Richard Paterson suggests that the scheduling of ITV and BBC presupposes an audience composed of families. Their programming assumes a specific pattern of domestic life, for example: programmes for women at home during the day; children's television shown immediately after school; and the nine o'clock 'watershed' after which it is assumed that children will be in bed (Paterson

1980). The schedules are therefore seen as specific modes of regulation of domestic media. More recently, Scannell has attempted to analyse the 'unobtrusive ways in which broadcasting sustains the lives, and routines, from one day to the next, year in, year out, of whole populations' (Scannell 1986: 1). The way in which radio and television's output is punctuated by regular segments of, say, news, weather reports and commercials, as well as the daily and weekly programming schedules, begins to take the place of the domestic clock. This regulation of domestic time, Scannell suggests, can be extended to the regulation of a wider 'national' time which sustains the annual round of events and festivals, weaving these into private and domestic timetabling.

From a feminist perspective, Tania Modleski has considered the female audience for daytime television, suggesting that the scheduling and form of daytime output – soap operas, quiz shows, etc. – assumes a distracted domestic female viewer, unable to give full attention to the screen because of her endless domestic duties and responsibilities. Thus, programming fits into pre-established domestic rhythms and renders interruptibility and distraction pleasurable. Modleski focuses her account of daytime viewing on an analysis of soap opera and its 'ideal' reader (Modleski 1982), a topic which will be taken up in more detail in the later discussion of textual analysis.

The arguments put forward by Paterson, Scannell and Modleski are all based upon analysis of the television product, from which major inferences are made about the 'typical' audience. All three seem to suggest that audience members occupy the subject position offered by these regulatory texts or groups of texts. But, whilst recognizing the significance of television and radio in the organization of domestic time, it is also important to explore the audiences themselves, not simply presuppose their uniform behaviour from institutional and textual analyses.

Obviously, the presence of a VCR in the household offers the viewer the opportunity to disrupt this 'temporal regulation', something which this study will explore. In considering the social organization of viewing in different domestic contexts, however, it is the effect of the VCR on the 'modality of viewing' which first requires consideration. John Ellis suggests some of the differences in modes of viewing between domestic television and the cinema, which are summarized in terms of the difference between the 'glance' and the 'gaze' (Ellis 1982: 137). Unlike Modleski,

Ellis suggests that the whole of television's output assumes a distracted viewer who may be constantly interrupted by domestic diversions. Television is 'perpetually present' in the home and in its construction of immediacy, through conventions such as direct address, 'breed[s] a sense of the perpetual present' (ibid.: 134). Television is, Ellis suggests, almost too available. As a result, he argues, the form of broadcast television has developed into a constant flow of short segments which continually attempt to grab the attention of the distracted viewer, with sound used to secure a level of attention out of range of the screen. The cinema audience, on the other hand, is in a darkened auditorium in front of a large, dominating image and consequently can be relied upon to engage with the cinema narration at a much higher level of concentration. Compared with television viewing, going to the cinema is an 'event' for which money is paid before consumption. These different social viewing contexts have, according to Ellis, created two distinct regimes of representation. Now, there are obvious analogies to be drawn between going to the cinema and hiring a movie from the video library – the movie has been specifically selected and paid for – but the viewing context remains domestic rather than public. To what extent, then, is the domestic viewing regime altered by this activity? Does the capacity to time-shift broadcast material affect modes of viewing? These are questions to be addressed in this book.

TEXTS – SUBJECTS – CONTEXTS

Family Television is primarily concerned with the social use of television, its consideration of texts being confined to the expressed preferences of members of the various households in the sample, revealing evidence of 'the ways in which particular types of material can be seen to appeal particularly strongly to particular sub-sections of the audience' (Morley 1986: 45). This is an obvious shift from the earlier *Nationwide* problematic in which the text, and its ideological effect, was central to the enterprise, but it also marks a continuation of the shift which the *Nationwide* study itself had already made.

It was noted above that *The 'Nationwide' Audience* challenged existing conceptions of the audience. It also challenged an influential body of work which had developed throughout the 1970s within film theory. This has come to be known as '*Screen* theory',[9] as *Screen*, along with *Screen Education*, published much of such work in Britain. Although focusing on the analysis of film texts, their claims about the relationship between language, ideology and 'the subject' had far-reaching effects across cultural studies in general. Freudian and Lacanian psychoanalytic traditions provided the major tools of analysis, which were used to analyse textual mechanisms that interpellate the subject at the moment of reading.[10] Thus, a single, universal set of psychic mechanisms were used to 'explain' the text-subject relationship. This effectively removed text and subject from both history and society, and significantly, left no theoretical space for the subject constituted outside that relationship – through other discourses and other texts; thus, there was no point in investigating or accounting for the reading subject as 'all texts depend on the same set of subject positions, constituted in the formation of the subject, and therefore that they need be accorded no other distinctive effectivity of their own' (Morley 1980b: 163).

This is obviously an unsatisfactory state of affairs if we wish to investigate 'real' readers in their social and historical specificity. Indeed, for the present research it is crucial to conceptualize a 'gendered audience'. Annette Kuhn, in the course of exploring such a possibility, notes that work on the 'gendered audience' has developed within two different perspectives, one emerging from media studies and the other from film theory (Kuhn 1984a). This has resulted in two quite different approaches. The sociological emphasis of media studies has tended to conceive of a 'social audience', that is, an audience made up of already constituted male and female persons who bring (among other things) maleness or femaleness to a text, and who decode the text within that particular frame of reference. Film theory, on the other hand, has conceived of a 'psychological audience', a collection of individual spectators who are subjects constituted in signification and interpellated by the film or television text. As Kuhn suggests, these two perspectives give us a distinction between femaleness as social gender and femininity as subject position (ibid.: 24).

Putting it at its simplest, in the first case context is emphasized over text and in the latter text over context. The spectator-text relationship suggested by the psychoanalytic models used in film theory disregard differentiating features of social context involved in film and television viewing. Also, these models cannot easily include reference to the subject constituted outside the text, across other discourses, such as class, race, age and general social environment. The social audience approach, conversely, sees response to texts as socially predetermined, and thus does not allow consideration of how the texts themselves work on the viewers or readers. This would seem to be an unproductive conceptual dualism and one which the present study attempts to overcome. An important element in this work is gendered preference for different popular genres, a pattern confirmed by Hobson and Morley's empirical research (Hobson 1982; Morley 1986). It is therefore important to examine different attempts to account for this phenomenon. But first, we must recognize that there has been criticism of the shift away from attention to the individual text and its ideological effect apparent in the context-preference strand of audience research. It is therefore necessary to clarify what is involved in this shift and to consider the usefulness of the concept of genre for this particular study.

In an interview with Gillian Skirrow and Stephen Heath, Raymond Williams spoke of the status of the 'text' in media and mass communication studies:

> I think that the whole tradition of analysis has been of the discrete single work and while something can be done with that approach, it would be rather missing the point of the normal television experience.
>
> (Modleski (ed.) 1986: 15)

Williams here reiterates his notion of television as 'flow' that was originally introduced in *Television: Technology and Cultural Form* (Williams 1974) and indicates the importance of attending to *how* people watch television in the domestic setting. More recently, and from a postmodernist perspective, Grossberg has indicated the inappropriateness of the single text–reader model, calling for an approach which recognizes the ways in which subjects appropriate the multiplicity of texts available and articulate them within their own subjectivity (Grossberg 1988). Charlotte Brunsdon is concerned that these shifts, together with the attention given to the social and domestic context of viewing, has resulted in a tendency to treat all texts as being the same.[11] As Morley and Silverstone point out, it is not a matter of losing the specificity of the text, but of paying attention to the specific modes of viewing of different texts. Who is viewing what, with whom and at what times of the day (Morley and Silverstone 1988: 27)?

Television viewing is carried out, in the main, alongside domestic life and within social relations which have different effects upon the viewing or reading experience. Grossberg and Radway have criticized those studies, in Radway's case including her own, which look at 'the relationship between singular texts or genres and locatable audiences' (Grossberg 1988: 385). Radway states,

> No matter how extensive the effort to dissolve the boundaries of the textual object or the audience, most recent studies of reception, including my own, continue to begin with the 'factual' existence of a particular kind of text which is understood to be received by some set of individuals. Such studies perpetuate, then, the notion of a circuit neatly bounded and therefore identifiable, locatable, and open to observation.
>
> (Radway 1988: 363).

Radway's study of romance readers (Radway 1984) does, indeed, fall into the 'circuit' trap which she identifies, even though she explores the social act of reading as an important part of the pleasure for the women involved. Nevertheless, all we know about the women in her study is the nature of their engagement with a specific genre consumed through a specific medium. What Radway and Grossberg are now suggesting is that reception ethnographies should be studies of 'everyday life' that explore the plethora of texts encountered across different media *and* the ways in which these are constitutive of subjectivity, something which is, in their terms, always in process.

GENRE AND GENDER

In this context, the present study centres on an item of domestic entertainment technology rather than a specific text or generic group of texts, the aim being to attend to how respondents themselves accounted for their own use, choices and preferences. The study then works with a *concept* of genre, but not with an equation between specific genres and specific audiences. Stephen Neale suggests that 'genres are not to be seen as forms of textual codifications, but as systems of orientations, expectations and conventions that circulate between industry, text and subject' (Bennett *et al.* 1981a: 6). Audiences for television, cinema and reading matter possess generic knowledge and make use of this in their selections and choices of viewing and reading. Furthermore, genre knowledge is unevenly distributed across different social groups, but especially between men and women. These different generic competencies need to be explored if we are to understand the reproduction of gendered cultural consumption.

There have been attempts to link text with subject in context by examining the particular characteristics of popular genres which appear to be addressed to a female audience. Hobson's work on *Crossroads* has already been discussed, but there are two other influential pieces of work which, unlike Hobson's, draw upon psychoanalytic theories. Tania Modleski and Janice Radway have used psychoanalytic theories of the reproduction of sex, gender and familial organization in order to account for the psycho-social constitution of women, in particular in their role as mothers, and their relationship to and pleasures in their preferred popular genres (Modleski 1982; Radway 1984). Modleski analyses the 'female' genre of soap opera and identifies the subject position offered as being one of the 'ideal mother'. The female viewer is offered a maternal position in relation to the many characters in the serial, identifying with no one in particular, but empathizing and sympathizing with all, while having 'no demands or claims of her own'. The portrayed vicissitudes of family life have no satisfactory resolution in the never-ending world of the soap opera text. Thus, Modleski suggests,

> soap operas convince women that their highest goal is to see their families united and happy, while consoling them for their inability to realize this ideal and bring about familial harmony.
>
> (Modleski 1982: 92)

Modleski's 'spectator position' is that of the passive feminine subject, and her discussion of the villainess exemplifies her use of the Freudian model:

> The extreme delight viewers apparently take in despising the villainess testifies to the enormous amount of energy involved in the spectator's repression and to her (albeit unconscious) resentment at being constituted as an egoless receptacle for the suffering of others.
>
> (ibid.: 94)

As we shall see from the following analysis, there are problems in inferring the spectator position from a close textual analysis where, in Modleski's case, the feminine spectator implied by the text as the 'ideal mother' and the female viewing subject in her domestic role are collapsed one into the other. Janice Radway uses Chodorow's re-working of Freud, and as her insights would seem to have a very broad application to dimensions of the present study, it is necessary to examine these in more detail.

Chodorow's *The Reproduction of Mothering* represents an attempt to break with Freudian phallocentrism and its presumption of universality (Chodorow 1978). She focuses her attention on the pre-Oedipal phase of psycho-sexual development and on the quality of the mother-daughter relationship as compared to the mother-son and father-son relationships of the Freudian problematic. Chodorow also locates her theory within a patriarchal social and familial structure in which women's primary role is to mother. She sees 'relational potential' as a crucial distinction between the genders:

> The main importance of the oedipus complex, I argue, is not primarily in the development of gender identity and socially appropriate heterosexual genitality, but in the constitution of different forms of 'relational potential' in people of different genders.
>
> (ibid.: 166)

Chodorow argues that a girl continues her pre-Oedipal attachment to her mother for a long time because 'mothers tend to experience their daughters as more like, and continuous with, themselves' (ibid.: 168). The daughter's separation from her mother therefore takes longer to achieve. A boy, on the other hand, experiences earlier separation from his mother, but in order to achieve masculinity must repress the feminine. According to Chodorow,

> Denial of sense of connectedness and isolation of affect may be more characteristic of masculine development and may produce a more rigid and punitive super ego, whereas feminine development, in which internal and external object relations and affects connected to these are not so repressed, may lead to a super ego more open to persuasion and the judgements of others, that is, not so independent of its emotional origins.
>
> (ibid.: 169)

She concludes that girls and boys develop different relational capacities as a result of growing up in families where women mother. These families produce girls who have the nurturing and relational qualities required for mothering whilst boys are constructed with firmer ego boundaries, less dependent on relational factors: 'The basic feminine sense of self is connected to the world, the basic masculine sense of self is separate' (ibid.: 169).

Janice Radway's study of female romance readers uses Chodorow's theories of gendered development in two ways. First, to explain why the women in her study read romances, she suggests that, whilst women are brought up to reproduce and nurture others, in the patriarchal family of western society no one performs this reproducing and nurturing role for women: 'Men are socially and psychologically reproduced by women, but women are reproduced (or not) largely by themselves.'[12] In reading romances, Radway suggests, women are able to lose themselves in a book:

> It supplies them with an important emotional release that is proscribed in daily life because the social role with which they identify themselves leaves little room for guiltless, self-interested pursuit of individual pleasure.
>
> (Radway 1984: 95–6)

Radway concludes that 'emotional gratification was the one theme common to all of the women's observations about the function of romance reading' (ibid.: 96). Of course, this general account of reasons for reading does not necessarily explain why it is the romance genre in particular to which women turn for their gratification. Second, Radway, again using Chodorow, suggests that the basic narrative structure of the romance plots the woman's journey into female personhood 'as that particular psychic configuration is constructed and realized within patriarchal culture' (ibid.: 138). Initially, the heroine is plucked from an earlier relationship and thrust into a public world, a process reminiscent of the girl's break with her mother. The heroine's search for identity becomes synonymous with the promise and eventual fulfilment of her relationship with a male other. In the resolution of the narrative the heroine has successfully completed the female self-in-relation with a male who *is* capable of nurturing and caring for her.

Thus the romance is concerned not simply with the fact of

heterosexual marriage, but with the perhaps more essential issues for women – how to realize a mature self and how to achieve emotional fulfilment in a culture in which such goals must be achieved in the company of an individual whose principal preoccupation is always *elsewhere* in the public world.

(ibid.: 139, emphasis in original)

The magical resolution of a 'happy ending' in the gratification of female needs validates the very institution, heterosexual marriage, within which the reader herself is positioned and leaves her emotionally re-charged as she returns to her role.

Most of the women in Radway's sample were married, white, middle-class mothers, which is perhaps why Chodorow's theories appear to have such relevance, given their concern with gender reproduction within the same class and family unit. Chodorow, however, makes a wider and unqualified claim that the reproduction of mothering is achieved across all classes, and, indeed, all cultures where women are primarily responsible for child care. She further suggests that if men were involved more in parenting, then girl and boy children would be able to identify with both parents, thereby leading to a breaking down of the traditional gender divisions. This, of course, is a reductive argument which takes no account of the economic and social context within which 'the family' exists. Structures of work would have to change in order for male parenting to be achieved. In addition, gendered subjectivity is not only achieved within the family, but is constantly produced and reproduced through other institutions such as education and the media.

However, Chodorow's important observation of gender difference based in 'relational potential' does seem useful. Radway's study did not explore *differences* between women, however, and the present study, whilst bearing in mind Chodorow's fundamental premiss, seeks to explore areas of difference in women's responses to cultural products and their perceptions of their roles within their families. In this way we can incorporate other determining factors, such as education, class and age, which may challenge Chodorow's more extravagant claims.

Ien Ang has approached the text-reader problem from a rather different perspective, by setting out to discover why the popular American serial *Dallas* is so pleasurable (Ang 1985). She executes an impressive and useful analysis of *Dallas* as text, focusing on its strategies and mechanisms for generating pleasure, and examines interaction with the text as conceived by viewers. Ang's viewer data comes from letters sent in response to her advertisement in a women's magazine. From these letters she identifies the appeal of *Dallas* in its achievement of 'emotional realism' for its fans: 'More specifically, the realism has to do with the recognition of a tragic structure of feeling, which is felt as "real" and which makes sense for these viewers' (Ang 1985: 87).

Using written accounts is problematic in terms of the 'distancing' involved and because the respondents come across as disembodied voices, lacking in any kind of social context. However, she does not take the letters 'straight' but attempts a 'symptomatic' reading of them: 'the letters must be regarded as texts, as discourses people produce when they want to express or have to account for their preference for, or aversion to, a highly controversial piece of popular culture like *Dallas*' (ibid.: 11).

What Ang found was that the majority of letter writers, whether they hated or loved *Dallas*, framed their responses within a familiar ideology of mass culture: the view that *Dallas* is bad by virtue of its status as a product of commercial mass culture. Those who claimed to dislike *Dallas* could justify themselves by reference to its commercial nature, its use of stereotypes, and the fact that they saw it as 'rubbish', views which, Ang argues, reflect the dominant social attitudes towards products like *Dallas*. The majority of *Dallas* fans recognized this ideology, but managed to negotiate their own position within it. Ang argues that there is no readily available cultural framework through which lovers of *Dallas* can express their pleasure in the serial, although some of her respondents invoked what Ang describes as an 'individual right of determination' (ibid.: 113). These respondents speak from a position within the ideology of populism, a position summed up in the phrase 'There's no accounting for taste' (ibid.). This offers them the possibility of simply rejecting what is claimed to be 'good' and following their own taste. Ang suggests, 'There exists [then] a cynical dialectic between the intellectual dominance of the ideology of mass culture and the 'spontaneous' practical attraction of the populist ideology (ibid.: 115).

Ang makes the connection between populist ideology and what Bourdieu has called the popular 'aesthetic', diametrically opposed to the bourgeois 'aesthetic'. The latter adopts a distanced and analytical position in relation to a cultural artefact, judging it upon established and universal criteria. The former, as expressed by the French sociologist, Pierre Bourdieu, is marked by

> the desire to enter into the game, identifying with characters' joys and sufferings, worrying about their fate, espousing their hopes and ideals, living their life, [and] is based on a form of investment, a sort of deliberate 'naivety', ingenuous, good natured credulity.
>
> (Bourdieu 1980: 238)

In identifying the different ideologies which inform her respondent's letters, Ang is able to suggest the social definitions of cultural products to which people have access. However, because her analysis focuses on the text-reader relationship alone, we do not know which viewers evoke the ideology of mass culture and which the ideology of populism. What we do know about her sample, however, is that the majority of letter writers were women. This is not surprising given the location of her advertisement, but Ang goes on to argue that, although *Dallas* as a prime-time serial is aimed at a mixed audience, viewing data suggests that it is predominantly watched by women. This is significantly reflected in the present study, as are the ways in which different women account for their preferred texts and genres. The work of Pierre Bourdieu is of relevance here in that he points to the close relationship linking cultural practices to educational capital. Bourdieu is concerned to examine the unequal distribution of 'cultural capital' across class and the role which familial and educational factors play in this cultural appropriation. Gender is largely ignored by Bourdieu, but differences in cultural competence and the acquisition of cultural capital are not only defined by class, but also by gender. In 'The aristocracy of culture', quoted above, Bourdieu outlines the results of research into 'taste' and discusses this in terms of 'aesthetic disposition'. He does have something to say about women in relation to their responses to the question 'Given the following subjects, is a photographer more likely to make a beautiful, interesting, trivial or ugly photo?' (1980: 241). Amongst these subjects were a landscape, a car crash, a pregnant woman, a butcher's shop, and cabbages. He notes, 'The statistics . . . show that women are more likely than men to manifest their repugnance at repugnant, horrible or distasteful objects' (ibid.: 243). Bourdieu accounts for this by suggesting that traditional division of labour between the genders assigns

' "human" or "humanitarian" tasks and feelings to women and more readily allows them effusions and tears . . . men are *ex officio* on the side of culture whereas women (like the working class) are cast on the side of nature' (ibid.: 243).

The 'aesthetic disposition' demands a distancing of subject from cultural artefact, and a refusal to 'surrender to nature'. This, Bourdieu suggests, is 'the mark of the dominant groups – who start with *self*-control [and] is the basis of the aesthetic disposition' (ibid.: 243). This appears to be an essentialist argument about both women and the working class. However, in a footnote, Bourdieu indicates that the traditional divisions of gender roles tend to weaken as educational capital grows. Thus,

> Women in the new petty-bourgeoisie who, in general, make much greater concessions to affective considerations than the men in the same category, much more rarely accept that a photograph of a pregnant woman can only be ugly than women in any other category. In doing so, they manifest simultaneously their aesthetic pretentions and their desire to be seen as 'liberated' from the ethical taboos imposed on their sex.
>
> (ibid.: 243)

There are two important points to be extracted from Bourdieu's work which have relevance to the following analysis. First, the notion of distance and self-control required for the aesthetic disposition which he locates within the dominant groups (that is, middle-class males), positioning women and the working class as subordinate groups within the popular aesthetic. This is manifest in close engagement with the cultural artefact, emotional affectivity, and lack of self-awareness and control. Second, the fact that middle-class educated women are likely to resist their gender defined position and adopt a more distanced and self-controlled attitude, although they are still likely to be more emotionally affected than males in the same group. Bourdieu was primarily concerned to account for the reproduction of class through culture, but his work also suggests how we might think of class, gender and educational capital as relatively weighted determining factors in the formation of cultural preferences and competencies. He is not concerned to account for how 'traditional' gender attributes are reproduced but here we can return to Chodorow's work on the different relational potential of gendered subjects. It is possible to map this into Bourdieu's account of cultural reproduction as in Figure 1.

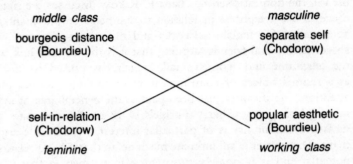

middle class
bourgeois distance
(Bourdieu)

masculine
separate self
(Chodorow)

self-in-relation
(Chodorow)
feminine

popular aesthetic
(Bourdieu)
working class

Figure 1   Class-culture and gender reproduction

By combining these accounts of reproduction we are able to conceive of the constitution of the subject in terms of both class and gender, but note that they both suggest the significance of the relational factor. In Bourdieu's terms this refers to cultural consumption as it relates to education and class, and for Chodorow to the differences in male and female sense of self and the extent of their dependence on others. This suggests that the 'aesthetic disposition' might more readily be attained by the 'separate self' of the masculine subject, and conversely, that the 'closeness' of the popular aesthetic lends itself to the feminine construction of self-in-relation. This study explores the different ways in which class and gender produce particular subjectivities and the extent to which a more complex account of the female subject will be required.

TECHNOLOGY AND THE DOMESTIC

Finally, it is necessary to raise one further cultural dimension, which has effects at many levels of relevance to this study: the VCR's status as technology within the household. Men and women have unequal access to technological knowledge within our society; this is generated through familial socialization, education and work-place experience, and has resulted in an ideology of female-related technical incompetence. Research has been carried out on gender and technology in the work place,[13] and there is a growing literature on aspects of domestic technology and information technology. There have, for example, been important insights by feminists into the gendering of particular technologies used in the domestic setting. Lana F. Rakow discusses the significance of the telephone in relation to women's employment and as a lifeline for female networks and maintaining contact with absent family and friends, arguing that it is the implicit link with the telephone and women's talk which has caused its neglect as a serious object of communication technology. Rather more attention, significantly, has been paid to the general area of information technology. Sherry Turkle's work on the computer and its latent masculinity is of particular interest here. Turkle argues that the computer is an 'intimate machine' in that it has a relational potential and is ultimately threatening to women in that it can replace 'authentic' human relationships. She makes a distinction between what is often seen as women's 'computerphobia', which she argues is merely transitional, and 'computer reticence' which is a more deeply held reluctance to engage with the predominantly masculine machine, offering, as it does, a powerful sense of mastery and control. This is an important distinction to bear in mind, indicating that it is not technical capability or skill which is being questioned here, but the culturally symbolic place which computer technology occupies in western cultures. Turkle argues for the creative potential of computers, suggesting that women do themselves and society a disservice by not overcoming their reticence and engaging with the technology. The question I want to raise here is the importance of considering the context of the use of any kind of technology, and the limitations and constraints which particular kinds of domestic settings have on differential access to technologies. These questions, and others, have been taken up by Roger Silverstone and David Morley in their study of the use and meanings of a very wide range of technologies which are now part of the micro-geography of households.

One aspect of my research is to examine the ways in which women relate to new entertainment technology and, where relevant, computer technology, compared with, for instance, new domestic technology, as each is inscribed with gender expectations disseminated through marketing and advertising. VCRs were marketed from the outset as hi-tech equipment which had to be mastered, thereby apparently addressing the male consumer. However, as Cynthia Cockburn points out, not all men are technologically competent (Cockburn 1985). It is relevant to this research, therefore, to explore the degree to which men were expected to have technical knowledge of the VCR and the extent to which women felt technologically incompetent.

The analysis which follows is structured so as to establish the social and cultural contexts of the households in which the VCR functions. Chapter 1 deals with research method and introduces the women in my study; chapter 2 examines divisions of domestic labour and organization of spare time within the household; chapter 3 looks at the different viewing contexts, their appropriate related texts and viewing modes; chapter 4 examines women's viewing and reading preferences, and those of their male partners as they were reported; chapter 5 looks at the VCR as technology in relation to other forms of domestic technology and reports on the decisions leading to its acquisition; chapter 6 deals with the VCR and its use for time-shift; chapter 7 reports on the use of video libraries and hiring of pre-recorded video tapes. By exploring VCR use within its wider social and cultural context it is possible to investigate to what extent those contextual factors determine the ways in which women use this new piece of entertainment technology and how, if at all, it disrupts those existing social and cultural patterns. These questions form the basis of the concluding chapter.

Finding an appropriate model for writing this kind of research is notoriously difficult. It is important, therefore, to outline my rationale in deciding to present as full an 'ethnography of reading' as possible which would form the core of this book, using chapter summaries and the final chapter to reflect on the ethnography. It seems that there is a delicate balance, which I do not claim to have achieved here, between allowing the subjects of the study to 'speak' in the text (based on a highly dubious belief in 'naturalism' and the status of these kinds of accounts) and, by virtue of sophisticated interpretation, losing their distinctiveness altogether under the weight of cultural analysis. I have therefore attempted to reproduce, within the organizing topics outlined above, as full an account as possible of our conversations, not simply because I feel it could well be used by other researchers into this field, but also because I feel that a major part of this book could be accessible to the subjects of my study in, for example, educational settings other than universities and polytechnics. I am thinking here particularly of Access courses and other less formal educational sites which, as long as they, hopefully, continue to exist,

appeal to a much broader constituency than the more narrowly
academic readership usually assumed by 'our' studies.

Chapter 1

Questions of method

As I have indicated in the introduction, audience research and reception studies are moving away from attempts to locate an identifiable audience group for a specific text or popular genre into a more general concern with consumption of a range of cultural products, via different communication technologies, set within the routines of daily life (Hermes 1991; Moores 1991; Morley and Silverstone 1988). When I embarked on this study in 1984, my intention was to carry out some empirical research on the significance of the VCR for women, using qualitative methods. What emerged from my conversational interviews with women, as the research progressed, was the need to extend the study in the very directions which now form the basis of the more recent studies indicated above. It is important to emphasize, therefore, that while the method I adopted has quite severe limitations it nevertheless has the potential to open up new and hitherto uncharted areas of study.

In the collection of working papers in cultural studies published in 1980 as *Culture, Media, Language*, the Centre for Contemporary Cultural Studies included a section entitled 'Ethnography'. The authors wanted to 'indicate the *presence* within Cultural Studies of a method – through shifting theoretical and substantive focuses – which continues to offer . . . an important mode of the production of concrete studies of the cultural level' (Hall *et al.* 1980: 73).

Setting this development of an ethnographic method within a general and reawakened interest in *verstehen* after the 'breakdown of the dominance of structural-functionalism' (ibid.: 73) in mainstream sociology, the centre saw it as a 'growing interest in methods capable of delivering qualitative knowledge of social relations, with all the rich distinctions and tones of living societies' (ibid.: 73). This 'search for a method' was important for the centre, given its emphasis on the significance of 'lived cultures' as a politically necessary area for study, particularly those of working-class youth (Hall and Jefferson 1976; Hebdige 1979; Willis 1977). However, such work was also carried out at the centre in relation to women, construed as an appropriate research method for investigating women's lives in the domestic sphere, their engagement with different media products, and the ideologies of motherhood and femininity which were seen to compound their oppression (Hobson 1978, 1980; McRobbie 1978, 1981, 1982b). My study is indebted to, and has much in common with, the work of the Women's Studies Group at the CCCS and bears the traces of what are now often regarded as 'early' feminist concerns. More recently there has been a developing critique within feminism and cultural and media studies (see Ang and Hermes 1991) involving what Susan Bordo identifies as the 'new scepticism about using gender as an analytical category' (Bordo 1990) in which 'any attempt to "cut" reality and perspective along gender lines is methodologically flawed and essentialising' (ibid.: 135). I stand guilty on this count, but would want to argue my case and insist that as long as our use of categories and indeed theoretical frameworks is sensitive to the particular research context, to our own political agenda and research practice, the social categories can and must allow us to say something about the wider social and cultural networks of power. I fear, like Bordo, that if we go down the road of a 'radically postmodern approach to feminist politics' (Ang and Hermes 1991), then gender becomes but one aspect of a 'neutral matrix' of subjectivity, along with class, race, age, etc. which seems remarkably similar to the methodological individualism against which much recent research into audiences and readership has pitched itself.

Bordo's article is interesting in that she locates the recent developments of feminist theory within the imperative of academic institutions – the pressure to publish, a competitive desire to be seen to be developing theoretical work – and points to the danger of the depoliticizing nature of these trajectories; she further notes that 'gender scepticism' could be operating in 'the service of the reproduction of white male knowledge/power'. For my part it is significant that in 1986, when I published my first research, paper, the only person with whom I had to argue the case for my concentration on women alone was a white middle-class male from a liberal humanist background; in general it was considered an important political dimension of my research, in that women had too often been subsumed into considerations of 'audience' with sparse attention being paid to the specifics of their daily lives and media consumption. I would therefore argue, along with Bordo, that many of these theoretical sophistications do not attempt to account for the actual reality of the lives of women and men; 'certainly the duality of male/female is a discursive formation, a social construction . . . but [this] duality has had profound consequences for the construction of experience of *those who live them*' (my emphasis; Bordo 1990: 149).

Whilst I agree with the postmodernists that crude generalizations using any social category can obscure and exclude differences, I would want to hold on to a category which enables not just differences to be revealed but also those profound and persistent commonalities which would seem to exist between women and which can form the basis of social critique. As I hope the following analysis will show, gender rarely reveals itself in pure form, but does intersect with other determinations, even within the most apparently traditional forms of household unit.

Taking gender as a key factor in the organization of domestic life, especially within familial relationships, I chose a sample of white women whose class, age, employment position, number of children and age of children differed, in order that I could explore the differential relevance of these factors in relation to television viewing, video use and ultimately the consumption of other texts. My sample consists almost exclusively of women who live with a male partner, in full employment, most of whom were married. The exceptions to this are a widow, living with her teenage sons and daughters, and two young single women living with their parents. The reason for including these women was to explore, to a limited extent, slightly different living units and to pay some attention to younger women. All the women shared the same ethnic background, for two main reasons. First I wanted to explore how factors such as age, class, employment and so on crossed gender within a broadly culturally homogenous group, and second because it is in the nature of this kind of research that the relationship between researcher and researched is a particularly delicate one. Quite simply, as a white researcher, I felt unqualified to establish the appropriate subject-to-subject relationship with women whose ethnic background I did not share. This requirement for homogeneity also accounts for my not looking at other kinds of domestic unit, where different relationships are lived out. However, in focusing my attention on 'families' I do not assume that 'the family' is somehow natural; clearly it is a socially prescribed way of living. But we must recognize that the ideology of the family as a naturally given, desirable 'institution' is a powerful force across different discourses within our society, especially for those living in that particular kind of domestic unit. Ownership of VCRs is most common in households with one male adult, one female adult and children of school age.[1] This group is not only the major user of video recorders, but it is also the group which is socially positioned as 'the family', both materially and ideologically.

Addressing more specifically the methods applied to related television audience research, it is clear that those television audience studies to date which are committed to qualitative research have not fulfilled the conditions necessary to be described as 'ethnographies'; Dorothy Hobson's work remains as the nearest example of an ethnography in television audience studies (Hobson 1978, 1980, 1982). However, what 'audience led'[2] research like Morley's *Family Television* has as its aim is to examine the way in which people live their culture; it insists that we must locate subjects in their social and historical contexts and develop ways of researching 'real' viewers. In this respect the study can be described as having ethnographic intentions. I chose to use a loosely structured but open-ended conversational interview, which I recorded in the women's homes, lasting for a minimum of one and a half hours.[3] An important dimension of this study is the way the women make sense out of their own experience. Other feminist researchers have noted that this open approach to the interview situation allows the respondents to raise issues and topics which they feel are important to the subject of the study, and in this way participate in the research (Finch 1984; Graham 1984; Oakley 1981). Graham goes further and suggests that in allowing women to recount their experiences through the telling of stories the researcher will gain a sense of the interrelatedness of certain aspects of women's lives, particularly in the domestic environment, thereby avoiding the tendency of more traditional survey methods to fragment women's accounts of their experience.[4] My ethnographic encounters certainly supported Graham's

suggestion, but not through my own design; many of the women
eagerly told me many stories about their family histories and their
present lives, enjoying the opportunity to talk about themselves
to an interested listener. Many of the conversations were fun and
certainly transgressed all notions of the 'ideal' research interview.

Although interviewing the women in their own homes has
many advantages for the accumulation of relevant data, they are
seldom places of uninterrupted peace and quiet. Small children,
dogs, telephones, husbands, callers and biscuits in the oven all
claimed attention at some time or another during many of the
interviews, and whilst they provide an insight into the various
demands on women's time in the home, they also disrupted the
interviews considerably. A great degree of flexibility was therefore required as each interview situation presented different problems, but I was conscious of the need to adapt and adjust my
own practice in order to facilitate discussion and make the women
feel at ease with me.

It is inevitable that this kind of data gathering is based on an
extremely limited form of actual 'observation' and relies heavily
on respondents' accounts and explanations of their own actions,
feelings and attitudes. It would, of course, be naïve to suggest
that this kind of interview or discussion is sufficient in itself.
However, through careful analysis, such material can be used to
investigate the wider structural and ideological frameworks within
which the respondents form their attitudes.

This research, therefore, does not take the 'centred' creative
human subject as its point of departure, but rather recognizes that
subjects are in part constituted by conditions which are external
to them. As Giddens says, 'The realm of human agency is
bounded. Men [sic] produce society, but they do so as historically
located actors, and not under conditions of their own choosing'
(Giddens 1976: 160).

What the women said to me does not directly reflect their
experience, but it is their way of articulating that experience. The
interview data upon which this project is based has therefore been
subjected to a double interpretation: the first is the interpretation
which the women bring to their own experience, and the one
which they share with me, whilst the second is the interpretation
I make of what they say. Their interpretations depend on their
subject position and the discourses to which they have access
and through which their subjectivities are constructed. My

interpretation depends on these things also, with the important addition of a theoretical and conceptual discourse, which constitutes the framework of my analysis.

It is important to say a little more about subject position and point of view. Some feminist researchers have argued for the importance of shared experience as women in this kind of research. This is reflected in some respects in studies of popular culture where the researcher declares herself a 'fan' of popular forms (e.g. Ang 1985). Whilst I would take issue with this notion of sharing, given that in the main the researcher, although a woman, has access to quite powerful institutions and intellectual capital, I want to declare something of my own history as it relates to some of the women in my study. I speak now as a woman who is an academic researcher and teacher, but my subjectivity bears the traces of past 'investments' through which I became firmly positioned as a feminine subject (e.g. working in an office from the age of 15, leaving my parental home to marry). I often feel that I am living and writing as a 'fugitive' from that particular social position and the fact that I have made this break would seem to lend weight to poststructuralist accounts of subjectivity; that is, that we can choose to occupy different discourses. However, I would briefly point out that my change was made possible through a variety of material encounters, including encouragement of the 'Educating Rita' type, class mobility through heterosexual partnership, economic support, not having had children, etc, and of course is deeply contradictory. My reason for this autobiographical note is not to join in the current trend for self-exploration through research (e.g. Walkerdine 1986), but to indicate a very particular level of identification which I had with the women in my study. I consider this shared position as quite crucial to the quality of the conversations I had with the women and that the talk that ensued was, in most instances, enriched by that shared knowledge. To put it quite directly, I am a woman in my study.

The problem of the 'status' of experience has concerned feminists,[5] many of whom believe that women's experience, unmediated by further theory, is the source of true knowledge. This, according to Chris Weedon, is a belief which 'rests on the liberal-humanist assumption that subjectivity is the coherent source of the interpretation of the meaning of "reality" ' (Weedon 1987: 8). We cannot rely unproblematically on 'experience' as the source of knowledge, but we must not deny subjective experience, since 'the way people make sense of their lives is a necessary starting point for understanding how power relations structure society' (ibid.: 8). What I have attempted to do in this research is to provide an 'ethnography' of a number of female subject positions, exploring the differences and coherences in those subjectivities and making sense of these contradictions and cohesions by constant reference to relevant structural factors. I have not, however, rendered the women, nor my presence as interviewer 'invisible' in my interpretation. Extracts from the interviews are quoted extensively throughout this book, not merely as examples in support of my interpretation, but in order to give the reader more direct access to the subjects of this study and the process by which the empirical data was obtained.

How I located the women

My initial focus for study was gender and the use of the VCR. The decision to interview only women was made for reasons already given, that is, my interest in how women account for their own experience in relation to gender and the VCR. Locating women to help in my research was not easy. This is always the case in this kind of research, but my problem was compounded by the fact that, at the time, there was some public anxiety about people enquiring into ownership of a VCR. This was due to large numbers of reported burglaries supposedly linked to the presence of a VCR in the household. The strategy I employed was to establish contact and win the confidence of the owner of a video library in Dewsbury, West Yorkshire. He agreed to my undertaking a questionnaire-survey of the people who came into his shop. This survey would provide useful information for him and respondents could be asked if they were willing to assist in further research. This produced a largely working-class sample of women. The middle-class women in my sample came from two separate personal introductions and selection of women appropriate to my sample 'snowballed' from them. There follow brief biographical details of each of the thirty women, in alphabetical order of their fictitious names, which I hope will facilitate identification throughout the study. The women are represented in a more traditional sociological table in the Appendix, which is largely based on socio-economic categories; this, although helpful as a summary, proved too rigid a classificatory system when analysing the interview material. I therefore found it necessary to group and re-group the women depending on the topic under discussion, and these formations are indicated in each of the chapters.

Alison

Full-time housewife. Aged 35. Living with a sheet metal worker, with his 12-week-old baby, and her three children from a previous marriage aged 15, 13 and 10. They own their detached modern house. She left school at 15, worked in Marks and Spencer doing office work until she had her first child. (C2/4)[6]

Audrey

Part-time doctor's receptionist. Aged 51. Married to a self-employed haulage contractor, with one son who is 27 and unemployed. They own a 1930s semi-detached house. She left school at 15 and worked as a telephonist until her child was born. Has held her present job for 10 years. (C1/4)

Barbara

Casual worker for her boyfriend who is a jobbing builder. Aged 38. Divorced, and lives with her two daughters aged 19 and 17 in a rented council house. She left school at 15 and worked in offices until she left to have her children. (E/2)

Beth

University lecturer and practising architect. Aged 37. Married to a lecturer; they run their own joint practice. Three children aged 11, 8 and 6. They own a large old semi-detached house. She has a degree in architecture and has had a continuous career. (A/4)

Betty

Evening hospital domestic. Aged 32. Married to a hospital electrician. Two children aged 7 and 4. They own a modern semi-detached house. She left school at 15 and worked in the textile industry before leaving to have her first child. (C2/2)

Brenda

Currently unemployed. Aged 30. Married to an asphalter. Three children aged 8, 6 and 3. They are buying their council house. She left school at 15 and worked as a machinist before having her children. Recently made redundant from her job as packer in the local biscuit factory. (D/2)

Caroline

Full-time research fellow. Aged 43. Lives with an architect, with her daughter aged 12 and their son aged 5 in a large Edwardian terrace house. She read English at university and after a post-graduate certificate of education year, taught in school, but took a break to have her first child. (A/2)

Cathy

Evening packer at the biscuit factory. Aged 21. Married to a maintenance engineer. One son aged 2. They own a modern terrace house. She left school at 15 and worked in the retail industry until she had her child. (C2/1)

Christine

Full-time supermarket assistant. Aged 21. Unmarried, living with her parents in their rented council terrace house. Left school at 16, since when she has worked in the same supermarket. (D/3)

Clare

Part-time college careers officer. Aged 35. Married to a secondary school teacher. Two children, aged 4 and 2. Degree in Celtic studies followed by full-time work as careers officer before leaving to have her children. (B/2)

Doreen

Part-time textile mender. Aged 48. Married to a warehouseman. Has two daughters living at home, aged 21 and 17. Renting council terrace house. Left school at 15 and worked in the textile industry on and off ever since. Has been made redundant 'several' times and has to travel to her present job. (D/4)

Edna

Newsagent. Aged 52. Recently widowed, but lives with her four children, two sets of twins aged 25 and 17. Left school at 16 and worked as a telephonist until having her children. She now runs her shop with some assistance. (C1/8)

Hilary

Part-time ESL supply teacher. Aged 44. Married to a university professor. They have two children, 16 and 13. Own their large Victorian terrace house. She has a degree in English and had been a secondary school teacher before having her children. (A/1)

Jackie

Unpaid lunch-time supervisor at her children's school. Aged 31. Married to an area manager of an oil company, with two children, aged 9 and 7. Owners of their modern semi. Left school at 16 and became a window dresser, which job she left to have her first child. (C1/9)

Janet

Full-time housewife. Aged 34. Married to an electrical engineer who often works abroad. Three children aged 12, 10 and 7. Owners of modern semi. She left school at 15 and worked behind the counter at Boots the Chemist. (C1/5)

Jean

Full-time teacher in a middle school. Aged 44. Married to a fireman. Three sons, 24, 23 and 19. The 23-year-old lives at home. They own their own semi. She left school at 17 and worked in the civil service until she had her first child. Qualified as a teacher as a mature student. (C1/7)

Jenny

Part-time research administrator. Aged 36. Married to a process worker. Two children aged 10 and 8. Rented council house. Read German at university and did a postgraduate certificate of education. Taught in middle school, but left the area. Had a break to have her children and is now employed in clerical administration on short-term contracts. (D/1)

Julie

Full-time housewife. Aged 27. Married to a fitter-engineer, shift-worker. One daughter aged 2. They own a small terrace house. She left school at 16 and trained as a nursery nurse. She left this job to have her child. (C2/6)

Kay

Part-time nursery assistant. Aged 39. Married to a pensions consultant. Three children aged 17, 15 and 10. They own a modern detached house. She left school at 15 and worked as an insurance clerk before having her children. (B/1)

Lesley

Part-time book-keeper for her husband. Aged 40. Married to a chef. Three children aged 22, 21 and 18, two of whom live at home. Left school at 16 and did some modelling work. Is now keen to establish her own business designing clothes. (C1/2)

Lynne

Part-time plant displayer. Aged 29. Married to a self-employed plumber. Two children aged 7 and 4. They own their semi-detached house. She left school at 15 and worked for a mail order company before leaving to have her first child. (C1/1)

Mary

Full-time nursery nurse. Aged 46. Married to a clinical psychologist. Two children aged 15 and 13. They own their detached house. She left school at 17 and worked as a receptionist in a psychiatric hospital. She had a break when her children were small and then trained as a nursery nurse. (A/3)

Maureen

Full-time housewife. Aged 25. Married to a company secretary. One 4-month-old baby. Left school at 18 and did a secretarial course. Worked as a pensions administrator and left when she became pregnant. (B/3)

Megan

Part-time supermarket cashier. Aged 34. Married to a self-employed sheet-metal worker. Two children aged 15 and 12. They own a modern semi. She left school at 15 and worked in the retail sector until she had her first child. (C2/3)

Michelle

Full-time primary school teacher. Aged 33. Married to an actor. They do not have children. They own their own Victorian terrace house. She trained as a teacher and has been employed since leaving college. (C1/6)

Rene

Part-time assistant in wine bar. Aged 50. Married to a leisure executive. No children at home. Owners of a modern detached house. She left school at 14 and worked as a comptometer operator, before having children by her first marriage. (B/5)

Sandra

Unemployed. Aged 19. Single, living with her parents in their rented council house. Has worked on YTS and at the biscuit factory. (E/1)

Sheila

Part-time clerical assistant. Aged 48. Married to a car sales executive. Two children, 20 and 18, living at home. Owners of large detached house. Left school at 15, trained as a secretary and worked for the Post Office until having the first of her children. (B/4)

Shirley

Voluntary tutor in English as a Second Language. Aged 36. Married to a solicitor. Two children, aged 5 and 2. Owners of modern detached house. Read French at university and worked as a bilingual secretary until she had her first child. (B/6)

Susan

Part-time hairdresser's receptionist. Aged 29. Married to a self-employed motor accessories distributor and expecting their first child. They own their modern flat. Left school at 15, worked mainly in retail fashion and hairdressing since then. Intends to leave her job to bring up her child. (C1/3)

Chapter 2

Organization of spare time

> I feel guilty, I feel as if I've cheated and taken something that's not mine, you know . . . I've taken that out of the day and that is not my time.[1]

> (Janet)

In this section I will discuss the organization of spare time in two separate areas, that of going out ('official' leisure) or leisure as it is perceived by the women themselves, and that of staying in, often seen as 'not leisure' but also as 'not work'. In general, these two uses of time were of major concern to the women, but tended to throw up contradictions. However, most of the women, when asked about leisure at home, replied 'what leisure?' Obviously the whole question of women's leisure in the home is linked to the division of domestic labour, and this therefore required some examination.

DOMESTIC DIVISION OF LABOUR

In this context it is important to determine which members of the household are responsible for day-to-day domestic servicing, for example child care, food provision and cooking, washing and ironing, cleaning of the house and maintenance of the garden (if applicable), and upon whom performance of particular tasks routinely depends. The person who is responsible for the completion of tasks bears a very different relationship to those tasks than does the person who 'assists'. Whilst it is true that many of the male partners in the sample performed some domestic duties, they did so from the position of 'assistant'. This confirms what Cynthia Cockburn refers to as the relatively autonomous relationship which most men have with the domestic environment in general and with domestic chores in particular (Cockburn 1985). Within the informal, unwritten constitution of domestic 'units' the responsibility is often unspoken and assumed. Domestic work is performed by the woman and goes largely unnoticed by her family. These responsibilities, pressures and demands, however, occupy her mind to a greater or lesser extent; whatever else she does in the day she must ensure that members of her family have food to eat, clean clothes to wear and that their house is not a health hazard. Within the ideology of 'the family', these duties and obligations are the woman's by 'natural' right; she carries them out for love of her family, her reward being their comfort and happiness. This has implications for the quantity, quality and individual understanding of leisure time spent in the home by men and women.

Because the division of labour has become embedded in the 'unconscious' of many of the households it proved difficult to elicit information about it. To overcome this problem a 'colour coding' strategy was employed whereby the women were asked to imagine different tasks and equipment as coloured either pink or blue.[2] This simple method revealed the gendered division of labour in the home to the women themselves, which they were then able to discuss, and there are references to this coding in some of the following extracts.

Out of the sample only three women reported that they shared responsibility for domestic work equally with their husbands. Two of these women, aged 29 and 33 years old, were full-time workers with no children, the third was 37 and a full-time worker with three children. Their initial response was not taken at face value and further questioning as to the nature and distribution of domestic tasks performed did indeed reveal a shared responsibility with their male partners. Washing, ironing, cleaning, shopping and cooking were all shared. It is worth noting here that in the case of the two younger women, their joint incomes and freedom from children gave them the choice of going out if neither had provided food for the evening meal. This option was not open to the majority of the sample, because of lack of funds, presence of children, or both.

I have organized the discussions of domestic labour in three main categories, which emerged from various accounts and descriptions of housework: 'Family histories and male careers';

'It's women's work'; 'Challenges to traditional roles'. It seems that social class is not a straightforwardly significant category in determining divisions of labour in the home and, furthermore, the ways in which women account for their role in domestic routines are indicators of the process whereby these routines become established, and are subsequently maintained.

Family histories and male careers

Caroline and Hilary offered an explanation for the ways in which their domestic worlds had been established; this was the important influence of their own and their partner's family background and upbringing. For Caroline, it was the influence of her mother in particular. She referred initially to the use of domestic equipment:

> I realize, though, that I bring to this erm . . . you know, as with women of my generation . . . our mothers were very poor on the domestic equipment and it was important to them to remain that way . . . that whole notion of feminine behaviour. And although my mother worked full time all her life: was a teacher, a graduate, my father likewise, my mother never learnt to operate the gramophone, never learnt to drive. There were a lot of things she didn't do. And he [father] used to say . . . she's a funny woman your mother . . . he was very wry, but yet, when she tried to operate those things, he would say 'oh, Nancy' . . . there were . . . real power things going on somewhere underneath there . . . but also her life was full, it was absolutely jammed full, so I bring that kind of pattern . . . you know how difficult it is to break those patterns . . . and I look at things like the electric drill and I think, well mm . . . I don't *need* to know how to operate this. (Caroline)

In a very similar way, Hilary reflected on her personal history and family background, but also set it within a socio-historic context.

> I mean, I'm not telling you I do lots of Women's Institute and knitting, you know. I'm not a sort of standard housewife. I think you are fairly subscribed, except I suspect people are a little . . . you see I'm a little bit old . . . you see I went to university in 1960, really the beginning of the explosion, and

> I suspect people that are ten years younger than me or those who were rather more avant-garde than I was . . . I mean I was the complete antithesis of avant-garde because I was very narrowly brought up, a very subscribed northern background which I found it difficult to break away from . . . I suspect that people ten years younger who also had the pill when they were younger, this is the thing . . . actually have more equal relationships with their partners whereas mine is really quite traditional. (Hilary)

She then went on to say that this was in spite of the fact of her being a graduate and both her and her husband being 'university people' and continued,

> I think that now I've got to my age I've become quite, as it were, limited in this way, and looking back it is rather difficult to see how it happened. I think it pre-eminently happened when I had children, but I also think it was because I had very deeply rooted into me very, very old-fashioned, rigid ideas about male and female roles which you never really break away from . . . I mean you just don't expect the man you're married to to make the tea, that's just not an expectation you have . . . I often think about this because I do wonder quite how one did arrive as limited as I am . . . I mean I'm really making a blow for freedom taking Sarah [daughter] away with me and that's only because I earn my own money, there's no way I could do that if I didn't. (Hilary)

This woman, aged 44, whose education and material circumstances placed her in a position of apparent privilege, reveals in her autobiographical account the complexity of her experience. The strong ideological pull of her family background with its assumptions about women and men could not be resisted through her university education. But there are also significant material factors influencing her life. Not having adequate contraception, lack of state provision for maternity leave and child care led almost inevitably to her adopting the role of full-time mother and housewife, thereby establishing a pattern of living which now seems impossible to change. Her domestic servicing undoubtedly enabled her husband's career to develop ('he never changed a nappy or thought of washing the children's hair') as he was always free of child care and domestic responsibilities. Her attempt to return to full-time teaching also demonstrates the vulnerability of women in her position and their dependence on the vagaries of the labour market. Financial autonomy, as she pointed out, is the key to her 'blows for freedom', to be able to do things on her own. Women in her position, married to successful and well-paid husbands, live within constraints which would not be immediately obvious.

Caroline, 43, a graduate and full-time Research Fellow, lives with an architect and has two children. She confirmed that the division of labour in the home fell into the rather traditional categories of blue and pink.

> I think they do actually, I think they do. And I have been subjected to considerable pressure from my more sorted London chum who says, you know, 'there are things here that you ought to be doing'. But I'm already doing . . . I mean it seems like the car . . . which I suppose is classic pink and blue, things like petrol, oil, tyres . . . she says 'you should do these'. And I say, 'Look, you know, I'm already doing an amazing number of things', and I think this matter of having your life very full already means that the entering of the blue territory is actually very difficult to achieve. (Caroline)

Hilary reported a similarly traditional division of labour and felt that there were some advantages in terms of smooth running of the household.

> And you do, of course, evolve a pattern, which in a sense works quite easily in many ways, you see, I mean it works quite well because everybody knows what they're doing . . . it sort of moves along. (Hilary)

Hilary's first child was born in 1971, before the 1975 Employment Protection Act which introduced six weeks' paid leave for women who had two years' service with their employers. She therefore had little option but to give up working to look after her children, but always assumed that she would be able to return to teaching.

> Once you give up work you tend to adopt a different attitude in the home . . . it didn't seem to me particularly sensible if Philip had been working all day that he should come in and do all the housework, if I'd been at home all day because I'd rather spend the evening pleasantly with him than hoovering

the floor. You establish a pattern of behaviour, whereas, fewer women now I think give up work when they have children. (Hilary)

At the point at which she was ready to return to the job market, it had virtually closed and she is now working as a part-time ESL teacher. In the meantime her husband's career developed.

I think the other thing that influenced us was that my husband became much more successful than we expected . . . because he's only got a white tile degree [laugh] . . . he never expected to end up as a university professor. So, far from being the relaxing job it was when he started, it's now a tremendously complicated job . . . It requires a . . . I mean it's not much good me expecting him to run the house . . . he hasn't got the time, he's working most evenings until 10 o'clock. I mean it does cause resentment, I'm not good about it all the time, I do get fed up and bitchy on occasions. I mean you can see how it happened . . . and it happens very slowly of course, over a period of about six or seven years. (Hilary)

Let me now turn to Shirley and Clare, two women graduates in their mid-thirties, both with children. Shirley described herself as a full-time mother. Clare had recently returned to her work on a part-time basis, but prior to this had also given her occupation as 'mother'. These two women offer a comparison with Hilary, being a decade younger and therefore having, as she would see it, a wider range of choices than she had. However, there is a similar pattern repeating itself here in terms of staying at home to bring up the children, here out of 'choice' rather than necessity. Also, in Shirley's case, her husband's career development takes priority over his involvement in domestic tasks. For both women we see the consequent breaking down of domestic labour into the 'traditional' patterns. Shirley finds herself totally responsible for domestic work and child care. The only truly 'blue' item in the kitchen is the coffee percolator.

I suppose that mostly it's [kitchen] pink . . . I mean he would work the dishwasher and the washing machine, but I'd have to give him specific instructions. The coffee percolator can be blue – he'll often make the coffee after a meal. (Shirley)

This is mainly because her husband works long hours, often

working at home until 9 p.m., but there was a sense in which she felt that the kitchen was her 'territory'.

> I'm not averse to anybody going into the kitchen and cooking a meal for me – that would be wonderful. But it annoys me sometimes; my husband . . . it's probably fair to say he's tidier than I am and occasionally he has these binges which extend to the kitchen cupboards . . . I do feel 'hands off' . . . he can clear up in the lounge as much as he likes, but I suppose it's because I'm the one that's got to go and use things and find them after that. (Shirley)

The garage, where all the tools are, was a blue area and very much her husband's territory. This woman had given up her work as a bilingual secretary when she had her first child (now aged 5). Her second child, aged 2½, had just started to go to a play-group, thus giving her some child-free time. She was, however, dubious about her return to the labour market, not because secretarial jobs have become scarce, but because they now demand some knowledge of word processors.

> I mean when I worked it was before the age of word processors . . . but I've sometimes thought about trying to keep up to date with word processors, you know, going on a course which would be quite a useful thing to do. (Shirley)

In the meantime she teaches English as a second language on a voluntary basis, one morning a week. As with Hilary, but for different reasons, employment opportunities have changed and women like these who are full-time mothers find that the labour market has shifted the jobs they left out of their reach.

Clare, married to a teacher at a boys' grammar school, had also decided to give up her career as a careers officer at a further education college when she became pregnant. She was asked if the roles within the house had changed since she gave up working full time.

> Yes . . . but partly from choice. When we both worked we shared things equally and, even to the cooking, we used to take it in turns to cook. But now when Colin comes home I find it much more relaxing to be able to shut myself away in the kitchen and cook a meal and for him to take over the children . . . we used to work it so that one cooked and the

other washed up, but again, I'm quite happy to wash up and he can wrestle with them in the bath . . . by the end of the day I'm quite happy to cope with inanimate objects . . . that stay put! (Clare)

For Clare, being at home all day with small children was proving extremely exhausting and when her first child was 18 months old she was offered some part-time careers advisory work back at her old college, which she took.

At first I thought, I won't be able to, my brain is dead . . . er . . . I won't be able to contribute anything and after a couple of weeks it did my confidence such a lot of good . . . I could think again . . . there was life beyond the nappy bucket. I hadn't planned to do it at all . . . I . . . it was . . . because I never thought I would go back to my job because I said that the children would come first, but this is a very good compromise. (Clare)

She can now fit in this job around her responsibilities for her children and other domestic work. It would seem that once a woman gives up her full-time work, then she will almost inevitably become more involved in domestic tasks, as well as having primary responsibility for child care. This is particularly likely when her partner is in full-time work and bent on career development. However, this can also apply for non-professional workers.

It's women's work

For many of the women there was an assumption that domestic labour was naturally women's work, which they did and with which they occasionally got help from their male partners.

Mostly me yes . . . Craig's not very good, he wasn't brought up to be domesticated . . . he's more or less useless. He will do it, if I say would you vac. up he will, and he washes up quite often . . . erm, but there again, he usually washes up the pans before the glasses and things like that [laugh]. (Lynne)

Cathy told me that they shared the housework. I asked about the washing and ironing.

I do that . . . but if there's anything he really wants desperately he'll wash it in the washer . . . but he's useless at ironing, so he doesn't bother . . . you've got to do it though haven't you?

What about the cooking?

Oh I don't mind doing that . . . I mean Michael will make some of his own things sometimes, he'll make sandwiches for work, and he does that . . . I don't ask him to, he just does it . . . I haven't to push him to do anything, he's good like that – he'll get up and vacuum and dust for me . . . he's good, and I don't think he did it at home . . . but I just think he sees how much ladies have to do, especially with David [son] and that, and working as well . . . I've got to clean up all the time after him, so I think Michael knows that sometimes I do get fed up. (Cathy)

This concept of 'sharing' is interesting. Her husband will wash his own clothes if he is 'desperate', and make his own sandwiches, but he will also help with *her* vacuuming and dusting. This reveals the extent to which domestic chores are seen to be women's work and the minimal participation required by her husband in order to qualify as 'good' about the house.

Betty, like Cathy, worked in the evening and I asked if her husband did some housework.

Well, he washes up after the tea. Well, I don't think he'd ever dream of getting a duster out or anything like that, but, like, he gets the tea ready . . . well I leave it ready but he sort of sorts the tea out, and then he washes up, gives 'em a bath, puts 'em to bed. So, yes, he does his share, though if I'm at home he wouldn't dream of doing anything. But when I'm out at work really he's got to. (Betty)

Alison, at home all day with a small baby, discussed the division of labour in her household.

We've had numerous fall-outs over that, because Brian says to me 'I hope you rest during the day' because as soon as he comes home it's . . . you know . . . 'I'd love a cup of tea' and he doesn't get off his backside from coming home to going to bed. When we first moved in together he did help a lot, he helped me make tea, and on occasion he helped me wash up, but . . . (Alison)

There is no doubt at all in this household whose washing up it is; she constantly referred to her partner as helping or not helping her.

For these women there was no real speculation as to how things had become the way they were, this being the 'norm' and the accepted way of living. Indeed all these women and their partners had gone straight from living in their parental home to their present marital home. What did emerge was some dissatisfaction with the role of 'housewife' in terms of the invisibility of the work, its repetitive nature and the fact that it can be undone as soon as the children come home from school.

> I can work hard all day doing their bedrooms, and then they're like a jumble sale next day . . . I mean they're not too bad, I must admit, like the eldest lad, he'll come and if there's any-thing out of place he's tidying up, but that's it . . . you know . . . whereas, if you go out and do a job, like I go to my husband, like, you know, he's going abroad and goodness knows what, you can say you've *done* something . . . some-times I think, well, I've done nothing . . . do you know what I mean? (Janet)

Challenges to traditional roles

Beth has managed to pursue her career as well as having had children. She is a full-time university lecturer and runs an architec-tural practice in partnership with her husband, who is also a university lecturer. Their professional equality is reflected in the domestic division of labour in that 'things are fairly evenly divided', and has produced some interesting role reversals. Her husband, for instance, would choose to bake at the weekend, whereas she would choose to do the heavy work in the garden.

> [domestic work] has always been fairly evenly divided, but I think because he's not expected to do it [cooking] he probably gets more enjoyment from doing it. In the same way that I get more enjoyment from building stone walls, because I'm not *expected* to be able to do it you see. So I think there's a trade-off there. You see the normal roles suggest that the man shouldn't be interested in doing cooking, so by being perverse, and doing it, he gets a kind of pleasure out of it. He thinks,

well, here's an achievement I wasn't expected to achieve, and I can do it.

What kind of pleasure do you get out of building walls?

It's the finished product. I think if I can make anything I'm happy . . . anything that exists slightly longer than a fruitcake . . . I mean it's very nice when you're cooking to produce something, but it disappears too quickly for me . . . I want things to be around a little bit longer. (Beth)

This couple's constant project was their large, old house which they were 'doing up' and she was asked about the division of labour in this area.

Well, building technology falls into the pink and blue categories: if it's rigid, George usually does it, if it's wet and floppy, it's left for me. So, I put a carpet down, anything that's slightly [hand gesture to indicate 'adjustment'] . . . there's a certain amount of division there. So when it comes to the tiling we do it together. I always do the painting . . . erm . . . but in using domestic technology, there isn't much distinction there. (Beth)

The other area of shared work was in their architectural practice and she discussed their occupational roles here.

Yes, there are distinctions in what we do. I tend to do the design work – I always do the landscape drawings. He tends to do the major structural sections and I will then come along and do all the schedules that go with those. So there is a division of labour within the practice that I think is quite interesting.

Did you consciously decide who was going to do what?

No, no, it just developed, it just happened that way, but you can see it's quite well defined, who does what. I always do the practice filing, I also do the accounts, but he always does the structural calculations, so it isn't that . . . both of us *can* cope with the mathematics, it's just again the division of labour, I don't know why it . . . just happened. (Beth)

This household is unique in the study, particularly in terms of the parity which exists between the male and female partners.

However, this case allows us to explore the extent to which male and female prescribed roles are subverted, and the point at which they are not. It is interesting, for example, that they both take pleasure in reversing their roles in what are largely considered to be 'domestic' tasks, in the cooking, gardening, etc., but that the nearer the work moves towards their professional practice, the more rigidly defined the roles become. She provides the office 'servicing' – a traditionally female function – as well as the land-scape drawings, whilst he does the structural calculations. He apparently does not find pleasure in doing landscape drawings, accounts or office correspondence in the way that he does in baking simply because he is not expected to know how to do it. What is perhaps the key point here is that the issue has never arisen, it has never been discussed: 'it just happened that way', suggesting, perhaps, that the professional ideology of appropriate gender roles and associated tasks is much more deeply ingrained than the domestic ideology. This may be to do with professional self-image on his part; whilst he feels his self-image or masculinity is not compromised by adopting the traditional female role in the kitchen, it probably would be if he were to adopt it in the studio.

Whilst Beth and her partner had organized their domestic lives taking into account both their careers, Jenny, a part-time researcher told me,

> He *does* do things . . . he does, I suppose, most of the cooking; he will help out all the time and he does quite a lot of constant stuff with the girls and things, but it's me who actually carries the first responsibility for seeing that they've got clean clothes for tomorrow, seeing that that's done . . . if you like the organizational approach to it . . . I can say to him, you go and do such and such and he'll do it, but I've got to say it . . . he won't take control of it. If something needs doing, therefore, I'll go and do it rather than sitting down and asking.

Is that mainly because you're here more than he is?

> Yes. We've talked about . . . things would have to change if I went into full-time teaching again, that would have to alter, but quite how you shift something like that . . . you know, I can say to him do such and such and he'll do it, erm . . . we did have a slight shift recently – apart from doing most of the cooking he actually took over quite a lot of the shopping –

they should go hand in hand, obviously, if you know what you're going to cook, then he should go and get the stuff in. You know, erm . . . but I think it would be something that we would work at very consciously if I got back into full-time work. And it wouldn't be easy, especially over areas like washing and ironing, getting stuff ready, are they organized for tomorrow . . . erm . . . I had a go at him recently about hearing the children read . . . and he just hadn't thought of it. He's quite happy to do it if I say it to him. I carry the awareness and he doesn't, but it would need really working at. Whether I could actually be bothered doing it . . . if I stayed in the present role, I don't know. Perhaps in niggling little ways as they occur to me, but I wouldn't make a major thing of it I don't think. (Jenny)

Of the other women who shared domestic responsibility equally with their partners, Michelle told me that *she* was the one who 'noticed' the dust and the dirt rather than her husband. It is interesting to note that one of the partners in each of these households had been married before. Both the males and one of the women had lived alone before the present arrangement, rather than, as in many of the cases under consideration, leaving the family or parental home to get married and tending to adopt similar household organization. For the majority of women the home is first and foremost a work place and it is therefore often difficult for them to find the time and space within their domestic environment to pursue leisure or non-work activities. They therefore consider going out as a more direct route to leisure and relaxation.

LEISURE OUTSIDE THE HOME

Although this aspect of the use of spare time is peripheral to the main concerns of the study, like domestic labour, it forms part of the context within which the organization of spare time at home must be placed. The purpose in introducing this topic, briefly, is to outline the significance of 'outside' leisure, the negotiations which precede and determine these activities and the constraints which might limit the possibility of such leisure. This material has been organized under headings which indicate the different types of outing embarked on by the women, largely defined by other members of the household involved, and the different perceived needs which they are meant to fulfil. These are: going out as a family, going out with their male partners and going out alone or with friends.

Family outings

Going on 'outings', especially for those women with young children, was of importance in terms of 'doing things as a family', a phrase which came up again and again. It is worth noting that in most cases the women themselves took the responsibility for agitating for and arranging these outings, for example,

> They are important to me yes . . . but I do enjoy them much more than he does, certainly as such. We have done a few but we've had very few that have been successful . . . he has us home again by three [laugh] . . . I don't think he finds that sort of thing at all relaxing. (Hilary)

> We go out quite often for Sunday lunch as a family . . . we just decide and then go . . . I really enjoy that . . . I usually say the Sunday before 'let's go out next Sunday'. (Kay)

> We do all sorts of things really . . . erm we go walking a lot, we like to go into the forests, we go swimming, which is very nice, we like that.

> *Do you consciously think about doing things together?*

> No, by we I mean the children and myself. (Jackie)

> If I say I fancy going out, and he says I'm not interested really, well we won't go out. (Cathy)

> Very often the family outings tend to be me. I don't think we do enough of it. I think I'm the one who instigates more of the family oriented stuff. But we do have separate areas of interest, you know. (Jenny)

Some of the women who had young children felt that television and video had taken over precious time which they would rather spend doing things as a family, whether it be going out, playing cards or board games, or simply having a conversation. For example,

> I go many days, 'it must have been nice in those days when there were no television, and just play cards, sit and talk' . . . we don't converse like they used to do, even when I were younger, I mean I can remember my Mum and Dad would think nothing of getting ready and going for long walks, you don't do that now, well we don't and nobody round here does that I know of. (Janet)

> Sometimes on a Saturday if I'm wanting to go anywhere . . . the weekends that are free . . . we'll get up and I'll do what I have to do with the kids and things and he'll sit and watch television [laugh] . . . I like to be doing something. (Alison)

Some of the women felt that their partners shared their concern to go on family outings. But this belief often concealed differential control of leisure activities. For example, Lynne and Jackie's family outings involved the pursuit of their husband's hobbies and leisure interests.

> He's more of an outdoor person than me, and he takes the girls out hiking and things . . . I go along with him to a certain extent, but sometimes . . . (Lynne)

> My husband likes car racing and things like that and we tend to watch a lot of that. (Jackie)

In the cases of Shirley and Alison, their partners usually decided if, when and where they would go out and this presented them with difficulties.

> The family drives, well . . . my husband decides. He looks at the map and says, how about going to Spurn Head, or somewhere . . . It's often at his instigation at the weekend, he does the driving on those trips, it's more his area. I find that once I've been shopping on a Friday, then he says 'why don't we go for a picnic or something' and I say, 'well, why didn't you say before?' (Shirley)

Most of the women quoted above seemed to have an ideal notion of the family outing and were keen to give this impression. This was particularly so in Lynne's case; she was quite upset about the length of time she had spent talking about her family's television and video viewing, pointing out, 'We do all sorts of other things, you know.'

What else do you do?

> What else do we do . . . well as I say Craig likes to go out and about, things like that . . . we go swimming and, er . . . Craig and the girls have got a bike as well . . . he's also into all sorts of daft pastimes on a Sunday afternoon . . . flying kites when it's windy, things like that . . . and so we have some barmy times over there . . . when it's snowing we go sledging and things like that . . . and we . . . er . . . (Lynne)

This image of the ideal family, unified in its leisure pursuits, was implicit in much of the women's conversation, and seemed best realized when including their partners' full participation in the activity.

The two women who were least concerned with projecting this image were Caroline and Beth. I asked Caroline if they shared any leisure activities with their children. She replied, after a long pause,

> No . . . [laugh] . . . erm . . . we don't appear to go out as a family the way that some people do. We've joined a local sort of sports centre and we go there at weekends and swim and play tennis, that sort of thing, but that's probably the closest we get to an outing with the children altogether. Now and again I'll occasionally, if I'm feeling particularly guilty, or rotten or something, I'll take them out to tea. (Caroline)

She felt guilty about not having sufficient leisure for herself:

> This is making me feel terribly bad because I actually realize that I have very little in the way of leisure, I allow myself very little in the way of leisure. (Caroline)

When asked about going out, Beth said,

> We go out to supper with friends, take the children for walks occasionally, but John [child] really hates that. We go tobog-ganing in the snow. Nothing on a regular basis. (Beth)

Both these women had full-time professional jobs and thereby experienced a blurring between leisure and work, and although they felt their family life was extremely important, expressed a sense of autonomy and distance which many of the other women did not have. The women who cared most about 'doing things as a family' were those who were at home full time, or who felt their family was their main concern in life. There would seem to be a strong identification and self-image linked with being a good mother and facilitating a 'happy' family.

Going out together

This varied a great deal and was to a large extent conditioned by economic circumstances or the presence of children, or both, and therefore the necessity to provide a baby-sitter. For those women who were full-time family managers, going out for the evening was an important part of their routine; getting ready to go out was often cited as part of the pleasure. However there is a more general feature of women's leisure apparent here, in that 'going out' was unequivocally defined as leisure.

> I think leisure for me is almost entirely about going out. Working full time means that when I'm in I'm generally doing the domestics. (Caroline)

This indicates the constraint felt by most women when at home: the responsibility for domestic work and demands made on them by children and spouse, as discussed above. Going out meant getting away from these demands and pressures, and a time to relax.

Going out for a meal was cited by many of the women as their favourite treat, but for some this was limited to 'special occasions', birthdays, anniversaries and so on. The financially better-off women went out regularly for meals with their partners and friends, and these outings were often spontaneous and unplanned. This was especially true of those women without children at home. Eating as an event – either out or in – featured quite strongly in their responses with 'conversation' often cited as an important feature of the pleasure.

The major obstacles to going out for the evening were economic, the presence of children under 14 and the unsociable working hours of one or other partner. This was the case right across the sample with the men or women in almost half of the households involved in some work-related activity in the evenings.

This ranged from vocational evening classes, working late, to evening jobs in the case of the women, and professional work at home to shift work in the case of the men.

All the women with young children were responsible for arranging baby-sitters and this, in most cases, was an extra expense to be added to the cost of the evening. The exceptions were those women who had parents living nearby who were usually asked to baby-sit. Indeed, some of the women didn't like leaving their children with anyone other than a parent or relative, an attitude which put even greater constraint on their freedom to go out.

These were not the only obstacles to going out; as in the case of family outings, there were reluctant males who preferred to stay in and enjoy their domestic surroundings. The women who felt this most sharply were, predictably, those who were full-time mothers and family managers. They felt they *needed* to get out, to have a change of scene and 'really relax'.

When it gets to night time I think, ooh, I could really just do with going out, just me and him by ourselves, and he says 'do you really want to go out?' and I say 'no it doesn't matter if you don't want to.' And then I think, well, he's been working and he might be tired so I'll say 'oh no it doesn't matter'. Then he says, 'well, if you really want to go I'll go' and that makes me feel guilty, you know. (Alison)

He goes out so much and goes to so many different things, to him it's just like being at work, where I think it's absolutely fantastic, to me it's a break from cooking and everything. (Jackie)

Clearly for these and other women in the sample who spent a large amount of time in the home, going out was invested with extreme importance. But we can also see that they were prepared to rationalize their partner's opposite desire, given the lack of time available to them at home because of their employment.

Going out with friends

About half the women who had reluctant partners, or whose partners worked unsociable hours, would go out with female friends, or, in some instances, alone.

Going out with friends served different functions. Often they were able to indulge in activities which their husbands did not enjoy, such as visits to the theatre, sporting activities, and in some cases, going out for a drink or a meal. But for some of the middle-class women it was also significant to maintain some separate interests from their husbands.

> I sing in a choir one evening a week and when we moved in here I looked around for a choir and joined it. I think it's important to keep up some interest, single ones rather than joint ones. That's my night a week, come what may. (Shirley)

Also, some felt strongly about the importance of doing things on their own, in spite of their husband's reluctance.

> I mean sometimes when I go to badminton, I see husbands and wives together and I think, ooh that must be nice, but my husband played once or twice, but he didn't enjoy it. But I feel that I'm doing something, you know, that because my husband doesn't like doing something, I'm not thinking, oh well, you know, he doesn't like to do it so that's that. I'm independent. (Kay)

It is important to note that going out with female friends often depended on a degree of financial autonomy and access to transport, as well as the approval of their partners. This was not always forthcoming, especially amongst the working-class women, who were also often limited by income and access to transport. The general rule in these households was that husbands and wives went out together, if at all, or that the husband went out on his own.

Regularity and routine in going out were prominent features in those households with a low budget for leisure spending. Regular visits to 'the club' or to the same pub with the same friends featured here, whereas the higher-income groups exhibited much less of a routine and considered spontaneity an important element in their leisure decisions, something they were keen to express.

> We don't like routine to that measure. There are probably about four or five public houses . . . erm . . . we are a member of a country club which is near so if we feel like a dance we

go there. Or sometimes on a Sunday we can go for a bar snack, a quiet bar snack and a drink. (Audrey)

We go out but we don't go anywhere every week or every month, not regularly. (Lynne)

A lot of what I do at work and at home is somehow about driving and controlling and sorting and it's important for the leisure to be spontaneous, but involving people and talking, laughing . . . I like the spontaneity of the jazz concerts, the fact that you never know what will happen, how good it will be, or who will be there. (Caroline)

Having described family outings, going out with partners and with friends, what these outings mean to the women and the various constraints involved, I will now turn to the organization and use of spare time in the home.

LEISURE TIME AT HOME

The most significant factor in the organization of spare time in the home appears to be engagement in paid employment outside the home. This is closely followed by the presence of young children. I will therefore begin this section by looking at some of the women who were full-time mothers and family managers.

I asked Shirley what she did at home when she had some time to herself; she replied,

You mean when the children are in bed?

Does spare time only come in the evening?

Well yes it does. It's only just been the last three weeks that the young one has started play-school when I've had this hour, for example. Otherwise it's not been practical for me to do things . . . I mean sometimes I would take them into town or something like that, but erm . . . my leisure is usually in the evening . . . it's more a case of fitting things in . . . you know, you've got to do this, that and the other before . . . especially with picking them up from school now that cuts into the afternoon . . . erm, yes, it's generally evening time.

She had a similar response to the question of spare time in the evening.

> I occasionally do some singing practice. This doesn't happen very often, but I can't do it during the day because my children tell me to be quiet and in the evening I get the same response from my husband. He plays squash so I usually do it when he's out . . . and then, reading . . . er . . . I must admit, I think this is one of the things I deplore about having children. The days when you actually sat and read a book from cover to cover are really hard to achieve now . . . occasionally I have a reading spell when I tell people to go away until I've finished, and I get it over with in two or three days, but it doesn't happen very often now . . . and then it's the television . . . I do watch television in the evening, often I feel I'm too tired to embark on something large, or a project that's going to take a while. (Shirley)

For women who do not go out to work, there are very few external constraints on their timetabling for the day. It is therefore their own responsibility to structure their days. In her study of housework, Ann Oakley points out that 'A lack of structure is intrinsic to housework; thus a psychological structure is imported to it. Women enter a form of contract with themselves to be their own bosses, judges and reward givers' (Oakley 1974: 112). Two of the women had very young children: a 3-month-old baby (Alison) and a 2-year-old (Julie); one of the other women's children were at school (Janet), although her husband worked away for quite long periods. During the discussions about 'spare' time during the day both Janet and Alison spoke of their feelings of guilt about taking 'time off' their household work.

> If I sit . . . my fault is guilt, because I think I shouldn't be doing this, I should be doing so and so, and I do actually feel guilty. Not because anybody's on at me, I feel guilty and I think to myself 'why do you feel guilty', and I just can't . . . I feel guilty taking any time out of a day for *me* . . . do you understand what I mean? Like I'll put . . . if it's anything for my husband or any of my three kids I will put myself out and do . . . but myself, I feel guilty, I feel as if I've cheated and taken something that's not mine . . . you know, I've taken that out of the day and that is not my time. Like, if Megan

were to come round and say, do you want to come and watch a video . . . I would be guilt-ridden to watch that video there and then, because I've not built the rest of my day round that.

You couldn't drop everything and go?

Well I could, but I'd feel guilty . . . you know . . . and I'd come in like a raving lunatic, charging round, as if I've stolen that hour or two out of a day . . . whereas if I knew I was going I could build the day round those two hours. I've got to be really busy in them other hours to give me those two hours, and then I wouldn't feel guilty . . . but just to go on spec. if I hadn't done what I have to do, I would feel guilty. (Janet)

This woman used particular television programmes to timetable her day in the house, making sure that she had done enough work to 'earn' *Falcon Crest*.

If I was watching television through the day, I think I would feel guilty . . . I mean it isn't that my husband's coming home saying . . . I don't mean for that, I'd just myself feel that I was cheating. I sort of look upon it as a job, you know, it is my work really . . . like you go out to work, but this is my job and I think if I'm sat I'm not doing my job, that is, just in my own mind. If I had television on all day and didn't do anything, I'd feel guilty, it may be silly I don't know, because I don't have to answer to anybody, but . . . I look upon that hour [*Falcon Crest*] as a treat . . . I can be working, and I've got that to look forward to, that hour, to sit down and relax and that hour's mine.

Alison had a small baby which imposed its own routine upon her, but she spoke of television watching in similar terms:

No, it doesn't go on during the day . . . I don't know whether it's because I feel guilty, you know, sometimes, I feel as though I should be doing something, I'm not here just to sit about. (Alison)

Ann Oakley suggests that 'a woman who declares a positive attitude to housework is likely also to have a high specification of standards and routines' (Oakley 1974: 108). This is certainly true in these two cases. Both spoke of their high standards in regard to housework, which often caused them problems. They were both accused by their partners of doing too much, of being over-fussy about cleanliness and tidiness. Being 'houseproud', therefore, does not necessarily have positive connotations, but it does produce feelings of guilt and other obsessive traits in the women who have a strong emotional involvement with housework. This is how Janet described her role at the beginning of our discussion:

> It might sound silly, but you know, when people say 'ooh, don't you get bored at home?' I don't. Because there's always something to do, you know, I mean, I don't dislike being, you know, a housewife and all that . . . you know, I've always liked that. (Janet)

Likewise, Alison told me about her attitudes towards housework and her role as housewife:

> For the eleven years I was at home before when my three children were little, I enjoyed every minute of it. I didn't want to go out to work, but actually I was more . . . I was overboard . . . it used to be a thing with me . . . I mean the house that I lived in there, you know, there wasn't a thing out of place, it was spotless, no dust anywhere, and it got to be a talking point in the neighbourhood . . . you know . . . 'God, you wouldn't believe she'd got three children'. . . you know . . . and I was too much. (Alison)

These two women were both employed in large retail outlets before leaving work to have their children. They had therefore chosen to pursue the 'feminine career'[3] and they both identified closely with their role as housewife and mother. They gained their self-worth from their excellence and their conscientious commitment to their work. The fact that they were often criticized for this, mainly by their partners, but also by neighbours and friends, put them in a rather ambiguous position in relation to their work and self-image. It also quite severely constrained their use of spare time.

One of the other full-time housewives and mothers identified herself much more with her role as mother than as housewife. She did her household chores with the television on, and didn't worry unduly if they didn't get done. She was a trained nurse and perhaps to some degree she brought this occupational identity to her role as mother.

Guilt can be seen as a severe constraint in the way in which the full-time housewife feels able to organize her spare time during the day. This, however, usually carries over into the evening period, when her children and male partner come home. She then has to prepare a meal, help with homework, etc. and often feels unable to demand help from her partner because 'he has been out at work all day'. The partner is, under these circumstances, free to relax or, as Alison put it 'sit on his backside all night'. She went on,

> And then, you see, he's bringing the money in . . . this came up last week, he says 'I'm bringing the money in' . . . not in so many words, and I just sat back and thought, well what do I do . . . you know, he's right, but sometimes I just feel as though he's taking me for granted. (Alison)

Their financial dependence is something else that these women have to cope with. Their partner's responsibility for providing for the household is used to justify them getting their own way in the evening.

Part-time workers

For Clare the major obstacle to spare time at home was her young children, who demanded constant attention.

> One of the things that I find most distressing at having children is the constant needing things to be done for them . . . the constant interruption. I can never even finish a school text without something happening . . . it is nice to get out and have a few hours away from that where I can think things through . . . I find that very peaceful and without interruptions.

> *Do you find that you need to get out of the house in order to get that?*

> Not always, but if I'm in the house I need to be on my own and one of the nicest things that can happen to me is for someone to take the children away for a couple of hours, so that I'm on my own – I find that very relaxing. Just to sit

somewhere tidy . . . you know, you're constantly picking things up; just to have a few hours when I can sit down and not get interrupted and not having to do things. It's lovely [laugh] it doesn't happen very often. (Clare)

When the evening came she often felt too tired to 'do' anything with her free time.

I don't have a lot of time for myself, this was the thing that surprised me . . . erm . . . when I gave up work I thought one of the advantages, apart from having the children, was that I would have lots more time to do the things I like to do and I was amazed how total having just one child is; it's a real 24-hour-a-day commitment. I find when I've got time I'm so tired that I'm exhausted trying to do anything.

So do you just sit?

Mm . . . [laugh] . . . and fall asleep. But it's getting easier now . . . I mean, I really like reading but I'm always so tired . . . I often fall asleep and I get very frustrated because I feel that the evenings are my time and I don't like wasting them by falling asleep. Because often I just flop and Colin says 'why don't you go to bed?' . . . you know, the children are settled . . . and I don't *want* just to go to bed because I feel that that's just a waste of my precious time . . . and then 'you'll only fall asleep on the settee' . . . 'I won't' [laugh] and I always do. (Clare)

Given this woman's energy level and tiredness, which she constantly fought in the hope of salvaging some time for herself in which she could do 'something useful', her evening activities were fairly gentle.

The first thing I would probably do once the children were settled, and we've got tidied up . . . er . . . is to finish off the paper. That's the first thing, and then possibly do some reading. Letter writing as well, I do quite a lot of correspondence. (Clare)

Even when young children were no longer a pressure, the women in the group had a clear idea of the division of the day, into 'daytime equals work' and 'evening equals leisure':

I never do any housework in the evening, never. I mean as

soon as the children come home at four I stop whatever I've been doing. I mean, I never knit in the day, I never read books in the day . . . I just wouldn't think to do anything like that . . . er. (Kay)

She then went on to explain the reason for this more fully:

I'm just not the sort of person who can sit down . . . that's why I work at housework. If I was contented and could sit down with a book in the afternoon I would, but I'm not because I've tried it . . . I've picked up a book in the afternoon and I'm thinking, I haven't done this, and there's that to do . . . and instead of thinking about what I'm doing – reading my book, I'm nattering inside about things that . . . you know . . . I mean when the children aren't here, it's a perfect opportunity, I've got the house to myself . . . but I love the house to myself doing my housework and I cannot do house-work when there's people in the house, because I've got some-one to talk to, I've got somebody to take my interest. And, as I say, I stop at half past three, when I've got the children home, that's me finished then. I'll sit on the settee and maybe daydream for half an hour. (Kay)

Kay cannot distance herself sufficiently from the demands of 'her' housework to enable her to concentrate on reading a book during the day. She then explains that she really loves having the house to herself to do her housework, although being on her own would also be a perfect opportunity for her to read. She finds it difficult, however, to read in the evening once the family is at home, because they all like to watch television in the main living-room. As she likes to be with them – 'I don't like being on my own, I like to be with everybody' – she does her reading for half an hour in bed, before she goes to sleep. Kay had brought up three children as a full-time mother and is perhaps still feeling the pleasure of having the house to herself – what Clare longs for. However, it does seem that her time is heavily prescribed both during the day and in the evening, when she largely goes along with her family's desire to watch television.

Her children come home from school for lunch, which she prepares for them, and they always switch on the television as soon as they get home. When asked if she ever watched television during the day, she confirmed watching the lunch-time news with the children, but as for other daytime programmes,

> Very, very rarely . . . if I'm not well, and I think now . . . because if I'm in I'm usually doing housework, and I think, now, you could do with just sitting down and forgetting about housework . . . so I'll sit down and put the television on and hope that something will take my interest. (Kay)

Rene, an older woman with no children at home, but with a part-time job in a wine bar, often watched television during the day, but chooses her programmes.

> I have the same routine, it's virtually housework, but I always stop to watch the one o'clock news. And something else I always watch during the day is *Sons and Daughters*, the Australian soap opera thing which I thoroughly enjoy. (Rene)

Rene also talked about reading.

> I feel very lazy reading, if I read during the day. No, if you weren't here, and I'd done my housework and everything . . . now I don't feel lazy sat watching television, isn't that strange? I think it's something to do with time, I get lost in a book, there's no way you can get lost in time on television because you always look at the clock and know that this programme's only on for an hour. But with a book, a book can take over, two hours have gone before you realize, so yes, I feel really lazy reading. (Rene)

Apart from this being an interesting inversion of the dominant values associated with television and reading, as expressed by some of the middle-class women in the study, it also indicates the usefulness of television's finite and regular programming in the structuring and control of spare time as against work time in the home. Reading does not have the inbuilt cut-off point, but requires active intervention by the reader to put the book down. As John Ellis notes, television demands and gets intermittent, less concentrated attention from the viewer than cinema (Ellis 1982) but also, in this case, reading. The point this woman makes also challenges Raymond Williams's notion of 'flow' (Williams 1974) in that the viewer does intervene to interrupt that flow and television programmes are thus used discretely in order to structure domestic routines. It is the intervention of the active viewer that is crucial here.

Reading was the one activity which all the middle-class women considered to be very important. Unlike listening to the radio, or music, or watching television, this is perhaps an activity which is not so easily combined with domestic responsibilities. It is important to emphasize in relation to spare time in the home the significance of the amount of available space, in particular, private space within the household geography. Those women who lived in larger houses or, indeed, had a room of their own, were able to escape to that room, or another level of the house when television was being watched by the other members of the household. This literal space is important in enabling them to pursue their reading, something not available to many of the women.

Although this was an important and valued activity for the middle-class women, spare time during the day was not generally used for reading, even when they were on their own in the house.

Can you tell me the sorts of times you read

Usually late evening, I normally work up until ten o'clock, so it would normally be late evening. I never read in the daytime unless I'm ill.

Why is that?

I think it's always at the bottom of the list – I think I have a slight feeling that I shouldn't be reading during the day and I've always got too much else to do. (Hilary)

She did, however, read a newspaper during the day.

Yes, I read *The Times*. I usually read it over lunch. (Hilary)

For this woman reading the daily newspaper was an activity which needed no justification, although it was combined with eating lunch. Reading a novel, however, was not considered a legitimate daytime activity, unless illness provided the excuse.

Cathy had no such guilt feelings about her reading and used Mills and Boon⁴ romances to fill in gaps during the day.

I read . . . once I start I don't want to put it down, I'm at it all the time. I can read one in two days, on and off . . . if David is playing out I can read a book. I'm still into it and I can watch him at the same time.

What stops you reading?

> David. I've got to stop and make his tea for him, or owt like that. Not because I get bored with it [reading] because I don't normally get bored with it at all. It's normally because I've got to stop to do something . . . then if I've any spare time I'll go back to it and finish it. (Cathy)

Mainly the women who did read would read in bed at night, sometimes going to bed early if they didn't like what was being watched on television by their partner. Occasionally they would read during the day if they were into a really good book.

> If I get a book that's . . . it can really tie me and I can't put it down. (Megan)

> Occasionally, if I'm really into a book I will read during the day. But I'd never pick a book up to start . . . you know, I'll be knitting or watching telly. (Julie)

Doreen shared her very small maisonette with her husband and two adult daughters.

> Well, I like reading actually, a lot. I'm in the library and I read because I'm not really interested in television. But, like, I wouldn't dream of coming in from work and reading a book [laugh], it's in the evenings when I read. (Doreen)

The evenings, however, were dominated by television and video, so she had to go into another room to read, although she never got away from the noise, which she found distracting.

> I suppose really when the girls leave home I shall probably start reading again, but at the moment either they're watching something they want to watch or the other one's got the records on upstairs, so it cancels me out. It's very rare that I can get one night that I can do what I want. (Doreen)

I have noted the ability of the breadwinners to relax at home after work, and also in an earlier part of this section, their relative autonomy in the domestic environment. Jenny talked about what her partner did when he got home from work, comparing this with her own practice.

> He will immediately make himself a cup of coffee, go and have a fiddle around in the greenhouse, put some music on or

go back to the record library. And I'll come in and start making the children their meal. (Jenny)

Jenny's partner's greenhouse was his hobby, and many of the men were 'hobbyists'; computers, astronomy, jazz clarinet were cited as well as participation in sports. Cynthia Cockburn points towards hobbies and sports as being an important area for men which is *between* work and home, between the 'masculine' world and the 'perilously feminine' world of home and family. Occupying this space enables an easier transition between these two worlds. 'For men, the negotiation between work and home is not only a matter of time (as it is for most women), but it is also a matter of reconciling conflicting cultures' (Cockburn 1985: 213). It must be noted, however, that this space does not necessarily need to be outside the home. It can be achieved by time spent in front of the television, in the greenhouse or garage, before fully entering into the domestic world.

The values accorded to different activities within the households are often linked to the person executing them. The 'invisible' work which women perform routinely, the recognition of which is often only hers, tends to be undervalued. However, something very interesting happens when men perform domestic tasks. Cooking a meal, for instance, if performed by a man, is usually a highly visible and remarkable event. As we have noted, Jenny's partner cooked their meal.

He'll wait for me to be finished and out of here before he starts our meal. But his immediate thing is always to sit down, to have some relaxing time. (Jenny)

He was not interested in the preparation of 'nursery food' like hamburgers and chips, but enjoyed trying out his skills on more adventurous grown-up food. We have noted that baking was also enjoyed by one of the male partners, his pleasure apparently coming from the fact that he was not expected to know how to do it. When the task becomes identified as a male task, then it has a much higher visibility and value in the household, thus confirming Margaret Mead's comment: 'Men may cook or weave or dress dolls or hunt humming birds, but if such activities are appropriate activities of men, then the whole society, men and women alike, votes them important' (Mead 1962: 157–8).

Full-time workers

For the full-time workers the notion of home leisure was quite a difficult one to define. In spite of three of them having paid help with the cleaning and ironing, they still had many domestic tasks to perform in the evening and at weekends.

> *Do you have any spare time when you do something you might do for pleasure?*

Yes, I'm sure I do, but it's difficult to bring it to mind. The notion of leisure is a very difficult one for me to deal with. What do I do? I listen to music when I'm at home, I read . . . I think I might do the garden but I actually never do . . . erm . . .

> *How do you listen to music?*

When the children have gone to bed in the evening, because the house is on three floors and we are able to separate ourselves off, and if James is doing something else and I am pottering below, we've got music on both levels and so I can . . . I put music on downstairs. Since I've been working full time I've been aware that I ought to give myself a bit more space . . . I'll sometimes actually sit down, just sit and listen, but very often I guiltily or puritanically co-ordinate it with something like ironing. (Caroline)

The distinction between what the women would choose to do and what they have to do is important.

> Some of the evening is sometimes taken up with work things that you've got to prepare for the next morning, or the practice, and if there's any time left over, I suppose the two things I would do are watching television, if there's anything on I want to see, or knitting. Erm . . . and various sorts of mending activities, but I don't enjoy that, but I class knitting as an activity in itself . . . it's something I would choose to do and I've usually got something on the go half-knitted. (Beth)

Television came rather low down the list of desirable use of spare time for many of the women, but in particular the middle-class women.

> I like to watch television when I'm washing my hair which

takes me about an hour to comb and so I usually try and do that on a Sunday evening when I think there's going to be a film on. (Beth)

Perhaps the major factor in choosing how to spend spare time was the amount of energy the women had left late in the evening. When tiredness was significant, then television was used as a reason to put up the feet and rest.

We both watch television if we're fed up; if we're both really exhausted, what you do is you come home, make a gin and tonic, and you sit and watch the telly and it's great; and you sit – that's how I think of the telly. It's there to absorb you when you just want to forget. (Beth)

If I'm tired I'd probably watch television, or perhaps I'd read if I'm in the middle of a good book. If I'm not tired I do something like baking or sewing. (Mary)

For other women in full-time work, their spare time at home was spent mainly in reading, sitting, and watching television. The two teachers relished 'peace and quiet' perhaps above anything.

When he's [husband] not at home I'll do sewing, I'll get the machine out and sew, just sit and relax, enjoy the peace and quiet. I don't have a radio on, I don't have television on and I enjoy my own company . . . I perhaps do some washing and a bit of ironing . . . I just love being on my own having peace and quiet. (Jean)

Sometimes I like to stay in and do nothing and sit and watch telly, and just sit and be a slob for a while (Michelle)

The young woman who worked as a hairdresser's receptionist had her day off during the week and enjoyed working in the house with the radio on. She would also watch television – a good film, or a recorded tape of *Dallas* or *Dynasty* – if she had some spare time during the day.

The overall impression given by the women in full-time work is that their work outside the home justified them in treating the domestic environment as a place to relax, and the lack of demands of young children meant that they had a wider range of choices as to what to do with their spare time.

TIME AS A VALUABLE COMMODITY

What is striking overall, whether the women were full-time or part-time workers, or full-time workers in the home, is the felt need for the women to utilize their spare time, that is, not to waste time. The times when they had some 'space' in order that they could do something for themselves were not to be squandered on valueless or unproductive activities. This often resulted in maximal use of such time, for example, knitting (a pleasurable activity for most of the women who chose to do it) would be done whilst watching television. Other activities which filled these spaces were often extensions of their roles as mothers or domestic workers. Baking and sewing came into this category, something which was not demanded of them but that they liked to do if they had the time.

The distinction between obligatory and non-obligatory activities was important in defining the use of spare time at home and the women in this group cited knitting, sewing and baking as activities which they would choose to do for their own pleasure. However, the time to indulge in these activities was not freely available. Betty worked as a domestic in her local hospital between 5 p.m. and 8 p.m. and was asked if she watched television on her return from work.

> If there's something that really appeals to me, then yes, I'll make a point and watch it, but I'd rather be doing something.

> *Do you feel housework is 'doing something'?*

> No. That's something that's got to be done [laugh]. You don't think about that, it's just something that's there, you do it.

> *But it's different, say, from making clothes for your little girl?*

> Yes, I do that through choice, the housework is there and it's got to be done, and I've got to get that done before I do anything else. There's no way I could settle down to do something else knowing that there's ironing waiting to be done. I've got to get the housework done before I think about doing any sewing, otherwise I just feel guilty. (Betty)

The routine household tasks have to be completed before she can 'indulge' herself in making clothes for her daughter. Obviously this activity is an extension of her domestic role and makes a contribution to the well-being of her child, but what is interesting for our purposes in this section is the way in which *she* defines and classifies different kinds of activity; in her terms 'doing something' does not include watching television or housework.

Audrey, an older woman with grown-up children, had the same attitude towards television.

> Well, I think I value my time to spend on something else, rather than watching [TV]. I like sewing. I like making my own . . . an odd skirt, or dress, or something like that. (Audrey)

Lynne, a younger woman with two small children, had to fit her sewing into the household routine. I asked her when she found the time to sew.

> I don't know really, there again, if I buy some material and I want to make something it depends how desperately I want to make it as to when I'll fit it in; it's surprising what you can do if you want to do it . . . I usually sew for the girls, sometimes for me . . . skirts usually, you make quite a good saving on them. (Lynne)

Cathy enjoyed baking when she got the time.

> I do bake . . . I enjoy baking, but I've got to be on my own because I can't do it with David [son] there because he's . . . so I wait until David has gone to bed and bake in the afternoon. It's something I don't have to do . . . only if I've time, but I enjoy it, I like seeing the results. I get pleasure out of that. (Cathy)

Knitting was an activity that was often combined with television watching. The women in this group rarely sat down and watched television in the evening without something to do: knitting, mending, or sometimes a book, as well as ironing.

SUMMARY

The main purpose of this section has been to outline the context, in terms of domestic labour, outside leisure and the organization of spare time in the home against which background use of television, the VCR, and the consumption of print-based media should be set.

It is clear that, from the women's accounts, they occupy a very different position (from their male partners) in their relationship to the domestic environment. This is evidenced in the unequal distribution of domestic labour and available spare time in most of the households under consideration. All the men in the study were in full-time employment and appeared to view their time at home as being at their own disposal. This meant that it could legitimately be spent in relaxation or in pursuing work-related matters or hobbies. The legitimacy of such practices appeared to be endorsed by their female partners, but as we have seen, some of the women expressed resentment at this apparent right to time.

For the woman with children, whether in full or part-time employment, or fully employed within the home, the domestic environment does not seem to offer this range of opportunity and choice. Once at home there are constant and persistent demands on her time and attention, making it difficult for her to find time to herself to embark on any project requiring long periods of concentration. Indeed, the domestic routines established during the period of maximum child dependency seem to become structural to the extent that the growth and development of the family members depend on them remaining in place. This is particularly the case where the male partner's career has been enabled through this kind of domestic support and servicing.

Many of the women spent quite long periods of time in the house on their own. But even during this time they did not feel free of the constraints of their position as wives and mothers. This manifested itself in their feelings of guilt at taking time off, whether it be to read a book or watch television, and many engaged in complicated 'reward' negotiations with themselves in order to justify this 'indulgence'.

The women in the study who were in a position of economic dependence used this as a justification for their partners having the right to relax in whatever way they chose, and also as an explanation for their own inability to challenge the status quo. This was explicitly stated by some of the women, but for many it was the implicit assumption behind the inevitably unequal access to time and relaxation in the home.

Indeed, the few exceptions to this division of labour along gender lines, and consequent restrictions on spare time at home came from those women who were economically independent or who had no children. The combination of these factors seemed to produce the most egalitarian households, and a clearer division between work and leisure for the women involved. In his study *Divisions of Labour*, R. Pahl found that women's employment status far outweighed the significance of social class in determining divisions of labour (Pahl 1985), and this would certainly seem to be confirmed by the present study. It is worth noting, however, that those women in the sample who were in full-time employment and had children or those whose household could afford it, would engage other women to clean their house or take care of their children. Although the labour was then displaced on to a paid employee, it was the woman's responsibility to engage and organize such help. Also, as we have seen, economic independence does not necessarily guarantee a release from obligation to household tasks and child care, or the sharing of these activities with the male partner. This was especially the case with women with children and older women whose traditional attitudes had been formed under the influence of their parents. Once a woman has children it seems that, under present social arrangements with regard to work and child care, she is mainly responsible for their care and therefore adjustments must be made to her life-style rather than to that of her male partner. She may inevitably find herself spending more time in the home, and thus spending more time on household work, which is then defined as her responsibility.

With regard to the actual use of spare time, the majority of women with children claimed to be the main instigators behind family outings. The importance of family-based leisure activities was most felt by those women who were full-time mothers, and we have seen that this commitment to the family encroached into their organization of time in the home. There is a felt need for such women to have time to themselves, but there are also contradictory pressures on them to satisfy their family's requirements before relaxing on their own behalf. They are therefore continually negotiating these contradictory 'pulls' even when their partners and children are not present. Watching television and videos during the day is often bound up with feelings of guilt. Many of the women claimed not to watch television during the day at all, and the majority of those who did would do so by building a favourite programme into their daily routine. In this way television provided a focus which enabled them to achieve

a certain distance from the distractions and demands of housework and children.

Tania Modleski has written about women watching television
at home. She sees, speaking of American daytime television, a
'fit' between the endless 'flow' of television programming and
the endless flow of domestic labour. Furthermore, she suggests,
the form of daytime genres assumes a distracted domestic viewer
who is constantly 'on call' and unable to devote her total attention
to the television set:

> The formal properties of daytime television thus accord closely
> with the rhythms of women's work in the home. Individual
> programs like soap operas as well as the flow of various pro-
> grams and commercials tend to make repetition, interruption
> and distraction pleasurable.

(Modleski 1983: 73)

Daytime television reinforces what Modleski refers to as the 'prin-
ciple of interruptibility' upon which basis the 'housewife' functions. Whilst the evidence of this study supports Modleski's
description of the nature of domestic labour and the decentred
female subject it inevitably produces, there is no evidence to
support the claim of a necessary 'fit' between this social circum-
stance and the formal properties of daytime television output.
Modleski's model of the rhythms of reception tends to leave no
space for an active female subject who might wish to resist both
flows. The women in the present study switched the television
on and stopped working to watch it. Also, the finite time of
programmes provided a natural end to their 'time off', compared
with, say, reading, which tended to result in time slipping away.

Thus we can see that organization of spare time in the home
is not a straightforward matter for women, and is a crucial influence on their use of television and video as well as other leisure
activities.

Chapter 3

Viewing contexts and related texts

> Sometimes I'll watch the portable in the kitchen, but it's damned uncomfortable in there.
>
> (Rene)

This chapter will explore different viewing contexts and their associated texts,[1] both for broadcast television and video tape rental. The intended context of viewing is an important consideration in determining choice of genre or programme, depending on which household members will be watching and at what time of day or night. The VCR is, in most cases, in the sitting-room and is used in conjunction with the main, that is, colour television set. Many households had more than one television, but as second sets were usually small black and white portables in the kitchen or one of the bedrooms, preference was for viewing on the main television set.

It is this one screen, therefore, which forms the focus of television and video viewing for all members of the household and here I shall explore respondents' accounts of the various permutations of household viewing groups and the extent to which there are related genres or programme types for these different contexts. Broadcast television scheduling itself carries implicit assumptions about the nature of the audience at different points during broadcasting hours, and Richard Paterson has suggested that these assumptions are predicated on a model of the family as the ideal viewing unit (Paterson 1980). The domestic context for television viewing has been, until recently, largely overlooked by television audience studies which have tended in their different ways to assume a direct relationship between viewer and text.[2] One of the early exceptions to this was Dorothy Hobson's work on *Crossroads* and its audience (Hobson 1982). Her audience research was carried out in her respondents' homes and took into account the domestic constraints involved in women's viewing. But she focused exclusively on the viewing contexts for that particular soap opera. What emerges from my broader study is that the domestic context is not unified, but diverse, and that each sub-context often has its own associated texts. My analysis determined important differences between households and these can be understood within three main groupings, which I broadly define as representing class position. Of course, this is by no means a self-evident category, but the material in this chapter can most usefully be discussed in relation to these differences. These differences are manifest in the actual practices of viewing, but also in the attitudes towards viewing in general. Details of the groups can be found in the Appendix: group 1 are A, B; group 2 are C1, C2; group 3 are D, E.

GROUP 1: A, B

Table 1 is a typology of contexts and related texts, using the respondents' own descriptions, which emerged through an analysis of discussions with this sub-group. Each context will be dealt with separately for this group.

Family together

Apart from Mary and Kay, watching broadcast television in this context was not a regular occurrence, although those women with older children said that their children did watch quite a lot of television. Attention has already been drawn to size of house and availability of extra rooms for alternative activities, and this is obviously pertinent in providing an opportunity for different members of the household to get away from the television if they do not wish to watch. However, Mary and Kay said that they watched *EastEnders* 'as a family':

> We watch *EastEnders*, we watch it as a family. It started off with Melanie [daughter] wanting to watch the first episode and it's the first soap opera we've ever watched and we've all got reasonably hooked on it. She sometimes misses it because of her Speech and Drama, but she will catch up on a Sunday.

Table 1 Group 1: A, B

Context	Film	Television
Family together	*Superman; Gremlins*	*EastEnders;* nature; Rolf Harris cartoons; *Great Languages of the World;* Shakespeare; *Dallas; Dynasty*
Children only	*Mary Poppins; Star Wars; Bed Knobs and Broomsticks*	*EastEnders;* children's TV; *Dallas; Dynasty; Top of the Pops; The Young Ones; Spitting Image; Grange Hill*
Male and female together	*Local Hero;* 'quality' films; Burt Reynolds; *Casablanca; Inherit the Wind; Company of Wolves*	*Paradise Postponed; First Among Equals; Minder; Hill Street Blues; Jewel in the Crown; Edge of Darkness; Fawlty Towers; Alias Smith and Jones; MASH; Star Trek;* news; *Juliet Bravo; The Bill; Coronation Street;* documentaries
Male only	*Brazil;* horror; cowboys; science fiction; war; spy films	'trash' to relax; news; sport; nature; *Question Time;* elections; *Tomorrow's World; Monty Python; Fawlty Towers*
Female only	*Woodstock; Slipper and Rose;* love stories; weepies; comedy	*EastEnders; Dallas; Dynasty; Princess Daisy;* 'quality' plays; *Coronation Street; Brookside; A Woman of Substance*

Are you surprised at your involvement in it?

No, not really, it's just that we've always avoided something that we've *got* to watch regularly because we never feel we can have that commitment to television. And if we're not in it doesn't matter, we can pick it up quickly, but I would say it's the one thing we do watch almost religiously if we are in . . . and I think that's because the children say 'oh, it's half-past seven' . . . probably . . . we tend to have had our meal by that time, so it's a convenient time to sit down. (Mary)

Kay said that all her family liked *EastEnders.* Did they make a point of sitting down to watch it?

Yes, because that's the one programme that all the family love. It's the one soap that we all love, so we all sit and watch that.

How did you get into it?

Well, we just started from the very beginning, it was advertised and we . . . I mean the children go in for these sorts of things. I don't think I watched the first one because I thought it would be a *Crossroads* type thing . . . and just listening to them talk about it, I thought 'oh, I'll watch' and I got into it and I liked it. (Kay)

These two women were interviewed in early 1986, when the audience for *EastEnders* was at its peak of 23 million. David Buckingham notes that *EastEnders* aimed to extend the traditional audience for soap opera, in terms of age and also gender, 'which (audience) is weighted towards women and towards the elderly . . . strong male characters would . . . serve to bring in male viewers who were traditionally suspicious of the genre' (Buckingham 1987: 16). It is increasingly necessary to re-assess popular genres and their audiences, and soap opera is a telling example. The late 1980s landscape of soap was changed fundamentally by the carefully scheduled and highly popular Australian soaps *Neighbours* and *Home and Away*, both of which appeal to a very young audience and would seem to have a certain cult following amongst students, both women and men, a group previously not considered to be part of the audience for soap. It has now become very difficult to sustain an argument which places soap opera as a female genre, unless we (a) attend to specific and different viewing pleasures and (b) make the post-structuralist move which refuses the *necessary* fit of feminine to the social category 'women'. The broader address of *EastEnders* is reflected in the responses of these two families. I cannot make any kind of generalization on these two examples, not least because *EastEnders* was launched between the two phases of interviewing, and therefore the earlier sample were not viewing it. But it is interesting to compare the watching of *EastEnders* with the family viewing of *Dynasty*, as reported by Kay.

Well I'm afraid the women in the family [laugh] really enjoy it, but the men, they watch it, and I think they like it really, but they . . . they just make sarky comments all the way

through, but they watch it, they wouldn't miss it [laugh].
(Kay)

There is no doubt that both male and female members of this
household found pleasure in *Dynasty*, but that they did so from
a different viewing perspective. Her husband and son seemed to
view with distance and a sense of irony, whereas Kay and her
daughter would seem to be much more closely involved. This
will be raised in the following chapter.

Beth reported that she wanted to watch television with her
children for a slightly different reason.

> George [husband] dislikes intensely quiz programmes, and the
> kids like watching Masterteam, it's on at half past five – the
> smallest child is absolutely hooked on that and I would be
> happy to just sit and watch it as well, but he really dislikes
> quiz programmes so I tend not to watch it and talk to him
> instead. Erm . . . but other than that I suppose we watch
> things that we both enjoy watching because it's more of a
> social event then. Somehow watching television on your own
> is like going to the cinema on your own, it's not as pleasurable
> as when you've got someone there to say 'oh', or have a laugh
> with. That's why I like watching with the children as well, I
> don't like to think of them on their own. (Beth)

Clare also tried to watch children's television with her son.

> The BBC programmes for children are on at lunch-time and
> Martin likes to watch those and I like, wherever possible, I
> try and watch with him, especially now when he talks a lot
> about what he sees, and I like to be able to share the experi-
> ences. (Clare)

The films watched in this context were often hired for a children's
party, or similar event: a special treat.

Children alone

There was an underlying anxiety about television in the households in this group who had young children. For example, Clare
was asked if she organized what her children watched.

> Yes, yes. He is very good actually, he will switch off at
> the end of a programme and . . . I got quite stroppy about

advertising, especially on children's television, and he's marvellous, because he doesn't watch a lot of ITV. I hope it
continues . . . I mean it's hard, it would be much easier just
to leave . . . and I have friends who video all the children's
programmes and, you know, great long tapes of *Thomas the
Tank Engine*, to keep them quiet. (Clare)

Caroline had a similar anxiety and didn't like coming home from
work to find her children in front of the television.

I think, why are they not doing something, why aren't they
outside if it's nice weather, why aren't they this, that and the
other. So the television is something that in my more extreme
and stressed moods I threaten to throw out of the window . . .
it is really an object of great revulsion to me . . . but obviously
it's not the thing itself, it's the way in which it's used and the
way it throws . . . our boy, who gets up before the rest of
us, has now got into the pattern of getting up – he sleeps on
the middle floor and the television's on the middle floor – and
he goes in and switches it on and watches it in the morning,
and that gets me down too. But James [husband] says, you've
got to make a choice here, if he's in front of the telly he is
not niggling at us to get up. It's a reasonable trade-off, but I
can't reach the point . . . it still gets to me. (Caroline)

The feeling that their children should be doing something rather
than 'just' watching television was a strong one and Beth felt that
her children shouldn't watch a lot of television.

I think it's important, not because of the content, or any of
the issues about television, but because they could be learning
to be able to be on their own and to generate their own
pleasures. How you generate your own pleasures, how you
do things together . . . and if you give them television, too
much access to television, then they never get the opportunities
beyond school to do that, I think that's important. (Beth)

The women with older children didn't have these anxieties,
although Mary gave the impression that this had not always been
the case. She had outlined her and her husband's use of television
as being very selective. She was asked if that was true of the rest
of the family.

Not the children, no [laugh], but we select for them in a way, not so much now as we used to, but they do watch quite a lot of the soap operas, and we're trying to read, so they tend to go into the playroom, there's another television up there, so they can do that when they want when we don't want it on, it can cause a bit of conflict. (Mary)

Hilary's 13-year-old daughter watched the most television in their household; she liked:

Dallas, Dynasty, all those.

Do you ever watch them with her?

I think I can honestly say I've never sat through an episode of *Dallas* or *Dynasty* or *The Colbys* or *Howards End* [*sic*], I've just seen bits of them. No, I don't think I've ever sat through one. (Hilary)

Hilary showed no concern about either the amount of time her daughter spent watching television, or what she was watching, believing that she was rational enough to recognize that such programmes were 'ridiculous'.

I think they're a group ethos. I think they do get involved with the characters, although they know it's ridiculous, but most children you ask say because they look very attractive, they like the clothes, the easy life-style and the glamorousness of it . . . they do get involved with the characters, but it is so ridiculous that they can't always take it seriously – I think they watch it for the glamour of it. They do get involved with the characters, but they know rationally it's ridiculous. (Hilary)

Her 16-year-old son often watched *EastEnders* with her daughter. Was there anything else they watched regularly?

She's been watching *Dempsey and Makepeace*, but he hasn't watched it regularly. He watches whatever is on television when he wants to watch television. Whereas she watches what she wants to watch when it's on. Totally different; he just uses it to unwind. She's selective, whereas I don't think he is at all. He usually watches just trash to relax – he moves channels to find the trash, but then he's doing very heavy A levels, so he just goes through the channels for the grottiest trash he can find [laugh]. (Hilary)

Mary described her son's viewing in a similar way:

> I think they're reasonably selective, erm . . . if they've got other things to do, like, she's got her music. Andrew's got his O levels this year, so I feel that when he wants to watch television it's his relaxation, it's the thing he enjoys doing apart from . . . if he's not doing sport, then he's just sort of lying around watching television.

Are you ever concerned about it?

> Not really because he does such a lot of physical things er . . . and it's not all the time, he is quite sensible with it, and his school work – but he breaks up his studying by coming and watching half an hour, so already he's selecting programmes he wants to watch; he's not as indiscriminate as he was. (Mary)

We can see for these two women that 'serious' school work is used to justify even indiscriminate television watching, but underlying all the responses is the fact that if their children are usefully employed at other times then they are perfectly justified in watching television. There is no doubt at all, however, that the 'television question' has been, and still is in some cases, an issue involving parental control and that television watching has to be earned or deserved as a result of hard work or other 'useful' activities.

Male and female together

Most of the women in this group significantly reported that, in general, they and their husbands shared the same taste in films and television programmes.

> There wouldn't be a big difference, they'd probably be fairly common, except that I would say sport would be added to his. We have a common nucleus, plus sport on his side . . . we probably both agree on other things. (Shirley)

These films and television programmes were often referred to as being 'good' or of 'quality' as opposed to being 'rubbish' and 'trash'. If we take their stated television selection in Table 1, perhaps the first thing to notice is the predominantly British origin of the programmes. The only American programmes are *Hill Street Blues, MASH* and *Star Trek*, all of which have a cult following, with *Hill Street Blues* being referred to as an example of American 'quality' television (Feuer *et al.* 1984). Rene reported on her husband's attitudes towards American and British programmes:

> Bill is certainly not a *Dallas* fan, and there's no way would he sort of sit here and want that on. He doesn't agree with the American soap operas, he quite likes our own, he loves *Coronation Street*, he thinks *Coronation Street's* fabulous, I mean . . . and *Emmerdale Farm*, he likes anything the British do, he just hates these *Dynasty* and *Dallas* and *Falcon Crest*. (Rene)

Although Rene and her husband enjoyed the products of the Hollywood film industry, this Britishness also can be seen in some of the film choices, with Caroline comparing them favourably with the American product:

> Well, I think the great saving humour that seems to distinguish a lot of stuff we make from the stuff they make, taking, say, *Letter to Brezhnev*, a wonderful sense of a wry undercurrent throughout that . . . and that wonderful film, *Local Hero*. (Caroline)

It is also notable that the television programmes which the women chose to mention were in the main prestigious series, and possibly the kind of programmes with which they would wish to be associated as viewers. Nevertheless, the fact that they chose to mention them as being watched with their partners is significant in itself.

The organization of television and video watching and the forward planning involved was often not achieved by some of the women in this group. Caroline, who was a full-time worker, explained that even if she had thought of watching a programme which interested her she hardly ever got round to it. Was this because someone else was watching a different programme?

> It's never that, it's just that I forget, or get a different priority. I watched the television the night before last for the first time in a long time, in weeks I think . . . quite randomly because I was doing some ironing and I watched the edited highlights of the royal wedding, compulsively and crossly [laugh] . . . yesterday. I try to watch *Hill Street Blues* and I try to watch *Minder*, there are one or two things that I try to watch, but I

realize I don't use the opportunities presented by television in any real way. (Caroline)

Beth was asked if they had watched any serials.

> We followed *Edge of Darkness* when they re-ran it because everyone said we should, and we did once watch a very good one on computing. But because we don't get the *Radio Times*, it is very much pick, and choose, and we don't get a daily paper. We know when the things we like come up, and when films come up [*How?*] Well, because you remember and you see occasionally we'd look in the Senior Common Room at the newspaper to see if there was anything on. But then, of course, there's always the review that you get in the *Observer* – we keep that for a week. (Beth)

Word of mouth recommendations and the *Observer* preview served as reminders or indicators as to what was worth watching for Beth. Other women in this group – Caroline, Kay and Shirley – took very little positive action towards planning their viewing. This is not to say that these women were not 'selective' but that viewing was a very low priority for them, and in all four cases, any planning was done by other members of the household.

It has been noted that many women in this group shared the same tastes in programmes and films as their male partners. They were asked what happened if there was a conflict of interest in this viewing context, and their replies revealed different kinds of negotiation:

> Well, in any relationship there's a . . . it's like in rural communities where you help each other – there's a sort of barter system, and you know very well when you are in credit and when you are in debt. In a relationship there's exactly the same thing; if I've watched something I wanted to watch previously, then it's somebody else's choice . . . and . . . you know . . . I mean, not consciously, but unconsciously, you are aware of where you stand. (Beth)

> Well, occasionally we both want to watch something at the same time. It doesn't often happen because I don't . . . there are not that many things that I really, really want to watch. What tends to happen . . . I would say that Colin watches more television than I do, so he usually gives in to me because

he says he gets his choice more often . . . so . . . there'll be give and take. If it is something I was very keen to see, then he would give way . . . and, he's different from me actually, he would probably sit and watch it with me. (Clare)

Well, we discuss it and decide, or one of us would watch it in black and white, which would normally be Wilf, he doesn't mind. But it doesn't happen very often, because we don't watch enough for that conflict to arise. He likes *Monty Python* . . . I just go to bed when that comes on and *Sportsnight* . . . he usually watches that with Andrew [son], so I go off to bed. But, I was going to say, I can do something else when the television's on, if I'm not interested in it, like read, or do some sewing. But he can't have television on as a background, it's either got to be off and reading, or vice versa, he can't have it as background. (Mary)

The VCR was seldom used to settle conflicts, the favoured option being to view on a portable or simply do something else in the same or another room. The VCR was more commonly used to record programmes or movies when viewing was not possible at all, and mainly for joint watching. This seems to indicate two things: that incidence of conflict was quite low, with neither partner being sufficiently bothered to get out a tape and record for later private watching; if there is a strong desire to see something then a second television is the preferred alternative. Conversely, what is remarkable here is the reported lack of conflict, a reluctance on the part of these women to admit to disagreement and tensions around the television, given, in most cases, their tendency to disapprove of this form of entertainment and use of time.

Male only

The way in which male only watching was reported was as much to do with mode and manner of watching as with content. Caroline described her attitude to television compared with her husband's:

I'm not, I don't think I am a natural watcher of television, whatever that is. James, by contrast, is one of those people who can fall into the sofa and switch off everything. He'll go into a protracted slump, you know, staring at the thing for the whole evening and that tends to make me cross, because then he is unavailable. It's a way of becoming unavailable. (Caroline)

Hilary reported on her husband's television watching:

> He watches more than me, he watches grotty trash purely to relax in the same sort of way Peter [son] does, but he always watches the news at ten o'clock, and if he misses the news he'll watch *Newsnight*. (Hilary)

It was noted earlier, in the 'Children only' context, that Hilary and Mary reported their sons' viewing behaviour as a relaxing diversion after intense school work, and women's accounts of masculine modes of viewing are often framed in terms of their need to switch off from 'external' pressures of work. This position is certainly shared by James Lull, who argues that men are also working while watching television, 'assuming an emotional and often physical involvement with their children, thinking about work, making plans, but also doing other "responsible" things like reading the newspaper or performing household tasks' (Lull 1990: 167). Whilst taking Lull's point that we cannot assume anything from mere observation, and indeed his is not a description of the 'masculine' mode of viewing outlined to me, it is important for my study to explore the impact that this mode of viewing has on their female partners. Caroline clearly believes that it is a way of switching off from the 'internal', domestic pressures also; he makes himself 'unavailable' to others.[3]

For Rene, who shared much of her television and video watching with her husband, it was what he chose to watch that created the male only context.

> But of course, he likes the factual side to it and he always watched *World at War*, and erm . . . he prefers factual things actually to fiction does Bill . . . whereas I like to be taken out of myself. I mean, I do agree with him that you should see these things to know what's gone on and to understand why they happen, but God, I was a kid growing up during that, I don't want . . . I feel as if . . . I don't want Nazis invading my sitting-room again . . . you know. I really don't. I get so depressed and I don't want Scargill shouting every five minutes either, I know it's happening, but, you see he will sit here and take that all day. Like for general elections, we're up 'til all

hours. We have . . . a list of constituencies from the *Telegraph*, we've probably got them for two years . . . and he bores me intensely with it all . . . because he goes overboard, he goes too far; I mean I'm interested, because I stay up and I like to see who's going to win the general election, but you know by about one o'clock who's going to get in. Well he stays up 'til five o'clock in the morning. No, I won't do that. (Rene)

There is a 'quality' versus 'trash' opposition in this group, but here we also have evidence of a 'fact' versus 'fiction' dichotomy which also emerges more significantly in the other groups. Whilst the quality-trash dichotomy brings the genders together, united against mass culture, the fact-fiction dichotomy, where it arises, divides along gender lines. The women in this group whose husbands and sons watch 'trash' acquiesce because they 'deserve' the relaxation and it is therefore justifiable.

Female only

In the previous chapter, it was noted that television and video watching was, in general, a low priority activity for the women who had some spare time at home to themselves. Also, it was seen that daytime viewing, a time when some of the women were at home alone or with small children, was extremely rare. However, there was some viewing within this context of both video tapes (hired and time-shift) and broadcast television, and in all cases this was brought about by the women wanting to watch something their male partners did not like. Apart from the women who watched children's television with their young children, Rene was the only woman who regularly watched recorded tapes and broadcast television, but never a hired tape, during the day. She had a regular date with the one o'clock news and *Sons and Daughters*, then showing at 3.30 p.m. But she would also sit down and watch recorded tapes, usually from the previous evening's broadcast. Did she do anything else whilst she was watching them?

Oh no . . . I settle down with my coffee and . . . I can't watch anything and not be relaxed, because I'm not watching it . . . I'm hearing it, but I'm not watching it, so it's something I'm not really interested in. That's what I mean by *Any Questions* [*sic*] – I don't mind it being on, but I don't want to sit here and avidly watch all these people rabbitting on. I can listen to them in the kitchen whilst I'm making coffee, or doing something. (Rene)

At the time of the interview, 2 p.m., she was watching a recorded episode of *Dallas*, a repeat of the previous series then being shown as a lead-in to a new series. I asked her if she had seen the *Dallas* episodes before.

No, I haven't, not this last series, no, I don't know what the devil I was watching when that was on. No, I didn't so I couldn't have had my recorder when they were showing that last *Dallas* series, I don't think . . . that was only last year . . . I might have gone off it, or there must have been something on the other side . . . why didn't I record it? . . . I think once you get out of the habit of watching this sort of thing sort of weekly, well then . . . it's not really important is it? . . . so maybe that's why I missed *Dallas*. (Rene)

Rene indicates the importance of viewing a series, like *Dallas*, routinely and regularly in order to become involved with it, and also the peculiarly unlocatable combination of circumstances which might lead to a lack of engagement. The repeat series had engaged her once more, but she was watching this on time-shift on her own during the day. Thus a pattern and rhythm of viewing was established which fitted into her daily routine. Establishing a viewing routine can be difficult for women, especially if there are a number of distractions and calls upon their time. Sheila's time was almost totally taken up with servicing and caring for her family and her mother, but she managed to mark out some solitary viewing.

I do like to see a good film, but I'm not too keen on . . . I like something based on fact . . . I like something that I know . . . I like a good story like, you know . . . *Woman of Substance*, and that type of thing . . . I like that type of thing.

Did you manage to watch that?

Yes, I watched all of that and I really did get absorbed in that because I'd read the book, you know . . . and erm . . . and I really enjoyed that, but then I had to come in here and watch it you see [laugh] . . . but I did enjoy it and I talked my daughter into watching and I think she watched most of it as well. (Sheila)

'In here' was the dining-room where the second, portable television was kept. She did not watch it on the main colour television in the sitting-room, nor did she record it to watch at another time on her own in more comfortable surroundings.

Sheila and Kay showed very little interest either in television (apart from Kay's devotion to *EastEnders, Dallas* and *Dynasty*) or in hiring videos, and neither was particularly motivated to create the space to watch something specific. However, Kay's partner was an avid television and video watcher, and was keen to involve her in choice, selection and eventual viewing. She told me that on one occasion he had hired a love story for her.

> *Slipper and the Rose* he got for me on video, but he didn't sit and watch it because it wasn't his cup of tea . . . he did something else while I watched that – got that one the other day, on the Saturday. (Kay)

Kay would always rather be doing something else, other than watching a video. She liked to be with her family and wished her husband would participate more in their general leisure time. It seems ironic, therefore, that on a Saturday evening she found herself sitting on her own watching a video hired for her by her husband, while he did something else.

GROUP 2: C1, C2

The typology outlined in Table 2 indicates a far heavier reported use of television and video than Group 1 and also a much clearer division of preferred programmes and films along gender lines.

Family together

In many of the households, and especially those with children, television is on all the time, even if no one is watching anything in particular. Children who were out at school had a tendency to switch the television on as soon as they came in and leave it on regardless. However, there were a number of women who made a point of watching specific programmes with their children. Early evening quiz shows were typical programmes which women could share with their children, with participation being an important part of the pleasure.

Table 2 Group 2: C1, C2

Context	Film	Television
Family together	*Star Wars;* James Bond; *Superman;* comedy; *Stir Crazy*; Animal House*; 10*; Chitty, Chitty, Bang Bang; Jaws; Blazing Saddles;* Walt Disney; *ET; Close Encounters*	*Countdown; Soap; Auf Wiedersehen Pet; Boys from the Blackstuff; Shogun; EastEnders**; Blockbusters**;* quiz shows; *Dallas**; Dynasty*
Children only	*Star Wars; Flash Gordon; Raiders of the Lost Ark; High Society*	children's TV; *Top of the Pops; EastEnders;* cartoons
Male and female together	*Trading Places; An Officer and a Gentleman; Deer Hunter;* Clint Eastwood; *Being There; Educating Rita; The Champ; Kramer v. Kramer;* comedy; adult comedy; *Lemon Popsicle; Blade Runner*	*Fawlty Towers; Open All Hours; Fresh Fields;* news; *Minder; Wogan; Duty Free; Face the Music; Call My Bluff; The Boat; Brookside; EastEnders; Butterflies; The Gentle Touch; 321; Magnum; Crossroads; Coronation Street; Crimewatch;* documentaries; *Dallas; Dynasty; Cagney and Lacey; Starsky and Hutch; The Brief; Travelling Man; The Bill*
Male only	action adventure; science fiction; war; boxing films; Stallone; *Rocky;* horror; space; Charles Bronson; cowboys; *Close Encounters*	*The Young Ones; Benny Hill; Monty Python; The Two Ronnies; Tomorrow's World;* space; astronomy; American football; sport; business programmes; news; *A Team;* boxing; documentaries
Female only	*Evergreen; The Jazz Singer; My Fair Lady; Ellis Island; Mistral's Daughter; Sarah Dane; Princess Daisy; Tootsie; Hollywood Wives;* romance; tear jerkers; *Who Will Love My Children?;* horror; *Reds; Tess*	*Mapp and Lucia; The Thornbirds; Far Pavilions; Dallas; Dynasty; Falcon Crest;* local news; chat shows; cookery; medical programmes; *Return to Eden; Butterflies; Lace; Master of the Game;* Al Jolson; *Sons and Daughters; Emmerdale Farm; Take the High Road; Gems; Coronation Street; Where There's Life; Quincy; General Hospital; A Woman of Substance*

* families with older children
** women watching with their children

I tend to watch *Blockbusters* with the children. We all sit there trying to answer them . . . my husband hates it, he's just so anti-television . . . he thinks there's far more things we could do than watch TV. (Jackie)

I used to like that kid's one that was on . . . *Blockbusters* . . . we used to watch that together, me and the kids . . . now I thought that was great, I really did like that . . . probably because I could answer some of the questions [laugh]. (Janet)

I like the one with the boxes . . . it's on early in the evening . . . *Countdown* . . . I like that . . . I like trying to do it faster than they can . . . I do it with my daughter sometimes. (Brenda)

These two programmes are broadcast at around 4.30 p.m. and the timing is important in that the women feel that they can sit down and watch something with their children before beginning food preparation for the evening meal. Also their male partners would not normally be at home, although Jackie's partner seems to have some knowledge of the programme. None of these women laid claim to any possible educative function of these programmes. Both quizzes are forms of word game, testing knowledge of vocabulary rather than general knowledge, and they stressed, rather, the participatory and social nature of the programmes. It was likened to playing a game with their children.

Jackie told me that one of her daughters had 'got this thing' about *EastEnders*, explaining that she liked the signature tune because they played it at school. I asked her if she ever watched the programme.

Sometimes. If I'm sat down, I must admit, I'm usually sat down by half past seven, sometimes we do, but sometimes I'm sitting here looking at it and not really seeing it, you know . . . I like to have at least an hour when I can just do nothing, and sometimes that happens from half past seven to half past eight . . . but I'm not really interested in the characters or the stories. (Jackie)

Television here provides a focus for 'doing nothing' even though there is no apparent interest in the actual programme. Jenny told me that the television would usually be on by 'news time'. I asked if that was the six o'clock news.

Yes . . . that's not particularly perhaps to watch the news because . . . well, that's right, that's why Jim [husband] puts the news on because we've got Teletext, so he'll actually dial up the news when he comes home, I don't, but did while he was away for that fortnight, so I must have missed somebody telling me the news, even if I hadn't read it myself . . . I'd pick up what was happening in the world then . . . and TV's on in the background and nobody will start watching it 'til half past seven, my elder daughter's got very much into soap operas, *EastEnders, Coronation Street*, and if I'm sitting around by that time I'll be half watching it and half reading, or . . . she always tells you what's going on at the same time . . . erm . . . then it'll probably stay on. (Jenny)

Jenny's attitude to *EastEnders* was rather different from Jackie's, expressing an element of fun and playfulness in their viewing.

We're hooked in a sort of comic way . . . like 'is he going to the wedding or not?' . . . you know, I couldn't care less [laugh]. I think it's very easy to join in with that . . . it's more like a joke than anything else the way we watch it . . . if Jim's been out he'll come in and say to Jane, 'Well? What happened in *EastEnders* then? . . . then Jane'll say '*Well* . . .' [laugh]. (Jenny)

In Janet's household, *Dallas* and *Dynasty* were watched with her daughter, although often the men were present.

Well, they stay up later at weekends, and my little girl loves it, *Dynasty* and *Dallas*, she loves it, and she is really involved in it, you know, with me . . . like, I'll go to her 'where did it end last week?' and she'll tell me . . . she's really . . . you know, she's really good company . . . it's nice having her against them three. They sit and think [sneer] . . .

Don't the boys watch it then?

They watch it, but they have the same attitude as my husband, you see, if you're sat crying, you know . . . you fill up . . . but my daughter's really . . . she loves it, she loves them programmes, she gets right involved in them. (Janet)

Like Kay, this household experiences a gender split when watching *Dallas* and *Dynasty*. The reproduction of female viewing pleasures is matched by the reproduction of male derision, but Janet seems to relish sharing the pleasure of *Dallas* and *Dynasty* with her daughter, again emphasizing the importance of the social nature of watching a programme of this kind. Again we see evidence of the different preferred modes of viewing by men and women. Here is how Janet described what happens when her husband rents a 'space' film, or wants to watch a documentary on television.

> Yes, I sit and watch them . . . I try to . . . you know . . . well, some I get interested in, you know, I mean, erm . . . but some, if I find boring I'll read, or if he knows I'm going to find it boring and he's at home, he gets them on a Wednesday when I'm out. And, like, if there's documentaries, he'll go 'I'm glad you're going out tonight because so and so's on – I can have that on without you moaning.' I don't really moan, but I'm bored, and I tend to talk to him when I'm bored, and he goes 'oh, are you not interested? Wait 'til *Dallas* is on', and stuff like that, you know . . . but I suppose that's the way that I show that I'm bored, I'll be talking through whatever he's trying to watch. (Janet)

Both seem to operate a sort of distraction strategy when their partner is watching a programme or film which is involving and pleasurable. The effect of this mode of watching is that the viewer, to use Caroline's term, becomes 'unavailable' to her or his partner – hence, the added pleasure of solidarity of viewing involvement which Janet gets from her daughter who, incidentally, is 7 years old.

Watching with children would often be a justification to sit down during the day, and watch a rented movie, as in Alison's case.

> Sometimes we watch during the day . . . I mean Mark was off last week with the strike* and his friend came up and I got them two, well he bought one himself and I bought one, and they sat and watched it and then the next day he was nattering me to watch it. It was *Superman*, so I did sit down, and I made the point. I got all my work done, I said, 'Let me get my work done first and then I'll sit and watch it with you' and I admit, I really enjoyed it [laugh]. (Alison)

*Teachers' action of the 1980s

We have seen from the discussion of the organization of spare time that Alison had strong guilt feelings about watching television during the day, and even here she made sure her work was done before she sat down. Again, the shared character of the viewing context permits self-indulgence; this woman would not dream of hiring and watching a video during the day on her own.

Susan, who had no guilt feelings about watching videos and television, enjoyed watching rented videos with her husband's children because it allowed her to indulge in fantasy.

> I love fantasy things, I love cartoons and Walt Disney things; total fantasy. Children's adventure stories, because, erm . . . John has two children from his first marriage and we used to get them films every Saturday when they came, and I was the first one to watch them. They got bored, and I would sit there watching all these knights in shining armour. Fantasy, I love it. (Susan)

Watching with children provides and justifies different kinds of pleasures. Those women who feel driven by guilt feel justified if they watch something with their children. Pleasure is derived from the social character of the event; these women would not indulge themselves by watching a hired movie alone and, in Susan's case especially, it provides a licence to watch children's and fantasy genres which she would have difficulty justifying watching by herself.

Some of the women in this group had adult children who were still living at home, hence the reported family viewing of 'adult' comedy. Edna thoroughly enjoyed watching films like *Animal House*, which she thought was a 'riot'. Jean, however, whose two youngest sons were still living at home, found explicit sexual scenes difficult to watch with them.

> You know, on movies when they're jumping into bed with each other . . . I sometimes get a bit hot under the collar, you know . . . if the lads are there. Sometimes, not all the time. Sometimes I grin and bear it and just sit and watch it . . . in silence, or I go in there and make a cup of coffee, and Jack [husband] will shout 'oh, Jean, we're getting to the exciting bit now' . . . you know . . . so he makes a joke of it, but I think he's trying to ease the situation, rather than ignoring it.

He's making a big play of it . . . making fun of it . . . I think he does it very well. I think the eldest, if he's at home, he's the one who is most embarrassed, I don't know why . . . the younger ones don't seem to mind. (Jean)

This woman's sons also hired 'blue' movies, which will be discussed in their specific viewing contexts, but occasionally she would insist on watching something on television. She gave as examples *The Thornbirds* and *Lace*, both of which she had read. She was asked if her husband watched either of these 'blockbuster' series.

Ahem . . . he watched them both, but only because I was watching them . . . it's so rare for me to say 'well this is what's on television and we are watching it' and they all said [groan], you know, the lads either disappear or sit and grin and bear it . . . Jack sat and watched all of them . . . I think his comments were that . . . well he wouldn't have chosen to watch those if I hadn't been insistent. (Jean)

Jean lived in a small house with only one living-room and, although there was a portable television in the kitchen, this was rarely used for evening viewing. The alternatives to viewing whatever was on were either to 'grin and bear it' or to 'disappear'. These options were taken up by her or by her sons, but her husband seemed to be a constant viewer and something of an arbitrator, watching both her choice of programme and her sons' choice of film or programme, and helping her through her embarrassment when necessary. The common ground upon which they were all able to meet was comedy and series such as *Boys from the Blackstuff* and *Auf Wiedersehen, Pet*, which provided suitable content for relaxed joint viewing. Another comedy programme that offered one household relaxed and pleasurable joint viewing was *Soap*:

One programme that we all watch together is that *Soap* . . . it's the only programme that we all three watch together. (Audrey)

This woman, in her early fifties, lived with her 27-year-old unemployed son and her husband and their viewing preferences were often incompatible. We talked about soap operas and the fact that *Soap* is a 'send-up' of the genre. She agreed:

Yes, it goes to the other end, to the ridiculous doesn't it . . . the situations that crop up [laugh], they pack everything in so well don't they? [laugh] . . . and yet it has a tenderness about it hasn't it? . . . you know, there are scenes in it that really brought tears to my eyes, it's so tender and so ridiculous. I don't honestly know anybody else that really likes it, and I say 'oh it's lovely' – they're lovely characters . . . and yet it's ridiculous, but so lovable at the same time. (Audrey)

Comedy did not always provide the common ground noted here and these differences, particularly across gender, will be dealt with in the appropriate context.

Children alone

The relatively few programmes and movies quoted by the women for this viewing context reflect the fact that television is constantly turned on in many of the households while children watch distractedly, but also that viewing is often collective because of the geography of the houses in this group. At the time of Betty's interview, in the afternoon, the television was on and her 4-year-old child was playing in front of it. Did she worry about what her children watched on television?

No because I pick the programmes I know he is going to watch. You know, they don't just watch anything that's on. I mean, I know it's on this afternoon, but it's only sport anyway and he's not really watching it. (Betty)

Julie, at home with her 2-year-old daughter always had the television on.

I mean, the television's on all the time, even if I'm in the kitchen although I bring my ironing in here and watch it. If I'm in the kitchen baking I'll have the telly on. You know, even for Jenny [daughter], Jenny likes it, 'cos I don't believe they can watch too much, unless they've something to do, say if she'd some homework, like when she gets older, I don't think it influences them that much, the television. I think they're better with something to occupy them rather than nothing at all. I mean she picks things up from the television. (Julie)

Hiring videos for the family and for the children only was much more common in this group than in Group 1 and did not need to have the justification of a birthday party. It was seen by many women as an alternative to going out for entertainment, especially during the school holidays, and in general they were much more relaxed in their attitudes towards their children's viewing than were the women in Group 1. For them television was an accepted part of the daily routine.

Male and female together

Comparing television choices for this context in Group 1, we can note the inclusion here (Table 2) of situation comedy, quiz shows and popular American programmes. Susan positively preferred American television to British, particularly the police and crime series. During our discussion I asked her if she watched *Hill Street Blues*.

> No, I don't watch that, it's weird. No, *Starsky and Hutch, Cagney and Lacey* and things like that, I like those. The British ones are very weak, the whole programmes are . . . erm, it's erm . . . very mundane, sort of getting up, good morning, going to work, and having their coffee, and pick up the 'phone and there's a terrible accident and they're all out . . . with the American ones it's all 'waahoo' [laugh] . . . a million things are going on at once. In the British ones there's one thing happening and it comes to the end and that's it. With the American ones there's so many things happening . . . you get a million stories on one programme. (Susan)

Energy and pace, plus what she saw as multiple story lines, were the formal elements that Susan enjoyed in American series and with which British products compared unfavourably. Megan gave a list of her favourite programmes, which were also predominantly American. Did she prefer the American ones?

> Yes I do really . . . [*Why?*] I don't know . . . I think it's more or less, the only way to put it is how the other half live, you know . . . if you can imagine that it's true that things like that do happen in places like America, I think . . . it's knowing what the other part of the world does, you know, things like *Coronation Street*, you can see things like that in the streets

round here, you know . . . it's just a matter of seeing how the other half live. (Megan)

However, one of the older women in this group did indicate her dislike for American programmes, such as *Dallas*.

They always seem to be unnatural somehow to me, their situations. Too glamorous, it's all too glamorous, the women . . . teethy . . . they've always got lovely teeth haven't they? . . . and, somehow, they all look alike to me, probably because of the teeth. They all seem so immaculate and so gorgeous . . . that's the plot you see, really, isn't it? It's the plots in these things, they're all about women with lots of money . . . to treat themselves . . . [tut, tut] (Audrey)

This woman thoroughly disapproved of the hedonistic and glamorous world of *Dallas* yet, paradoxically, this was often cited by devotees as one of the programme's major appeals. This will be explored more fully in the next chapter, but, in relation to Group 1, it is important to note that this woman does not use terms like 'rubbish' and 'trash' to describe *Dallas*, which would suggest that it was an inferior product of mass culture. Rather, she sees it as 'unnatural', and refuses to accept its particular form of realism and its ideological terrain. The fact that she took such pleasure in *Soap*, which for her had an emotional realism with which she readily engaged, indicates that she is not against American programmes *per se*.

Turning to comedy, Lynne said that there were certain comedy shows which she simply couldn't watch. Did her husband share her taste in television?

Erm . . . on the whole . . . er . . . his sense of humour is not the same as mine, like *The Young Ones*, he likes to watch that, I don't usually watch that, and a few other things as well that he watches.

He likes comedy? [Yes, yes] *And you tend not to?*

Er . . . I do, I mean, I like to laugh, everybody likes to laugh, but not the same things make me laugh that make him laugh.

Can you think of a comedy series that you have enjoyed?

Erm . . . I can't think of one that's running now, although we both like the one that's on last night . . . erm . . . that *Fresh*

Fields with Anton Rodgers, and whoever . . . we both like that, and I'm not sure why really . . . but erm . . . I erm . . . I quite like that. I don't think it's . . . I don't know really, I can watch that, without . . . and sort of when it's finished I feel as if I've been entertained . . . you watch some other things and you think . . . oh, thank God it's finished sort of thing, whereas . . . and Craig likes much more like your Benny Hill type thing, which I find not that funny. (Lynne)

Betty also reported incompatibility in comedy preference:

I like comedies, provided they're funny. I used to love to watch *Butterflies*. Derek used to sit there stony-faced, and I was rolling about laughing, that could be me so easily [giggle], that could be true to life. (Betty)

Hired movies in this context tend towards the male preference, but occasionally films would be chosen which were preferred by the women. Betty repeatedly claimed that her husband would 'watch anything', referring to him as a 'telly addict'. Would he watch 'weepies'?

He'll sit and laugh at me [laugh].

Would you say that you tend to avoid those films?

Well, if he went to pick one he definitely wouldn't pick one of those, but he would get one for me and sit through it laughing at me, you know. (Betty)

Alison described what happened when she and her partner watched *Kramer v. Kramer*:

We taped *Kramer v. Kramer* at Christmas and he watched it and I watched it when I'd just come out of hospital, and at the end I burst into tears – I was heartbroken, and he says 'bloomin' heck . . . just a film'. He pretends not to enjoy them and I think deep down inside he does. (Alison)

Many of the women in the sample would otherwise occupy themselves if their partners were watching something which they did not like. For Jean this was often the case. She was asked if she found herself watching a lot of things which she didn't particularly enjoy:

Yes, I would say so . . . which is the reason why I tend to sit in my chair and read . . . I've got this knack of being able to switch off and get lost in a book. (Jean)

Erm . . . well . . . my husband likes space and goodness knows what and things like that . . . he got an awful one, I don't know if it were . . . ooh, it were horrible, skeletons and stuff . . . erm . . . you see I don't like anything like that – horrors or anything. I just don't like horror films at all. I'm trying to think what the last one was that we got . . . I just can't remember.

What about if your husband hires his space ones, do you sit and watch them?

Yes I do . . . I try to . . . you know . . . well some I get interested in, you know, I mean, erm . . . but some if I find boring I'll read. (Janet)

I asked Betty what happened when her husband was watching a film she didn't like.

I could either sew, read, or do my painting – I can always find something to do rather than watching something for the sake of watching. I can switch off from the television. (Betty)

Jenny explained the difference between her and her husband's tastes in movies:

He's much more interested in the techniques, effects, the immediate . . . what I regard as surface cleverness of the film, rather than story. That's it isn't it? I like the story and he likes the way it's done . . . yes!

What kinds of films do you mean?

Thinking about what's on the video list, stuff we've recorded from the TV, that's the same kind of thing . . . when we come round to wiping things, you know, then it's who's fighting for what . . . erm . . . I suppose I tend to like, you know, *Tess* erm . . . *Reds* . . . *Dr Zhivago*, if you like the big . . . well, often romantic, but not . . . the big films I like. Jim's very much a special effects man, you know . . . we've still got *Jaws* when everybody else is bored to tears with it . . . and *Blade Runner*, *Alien* and all those, that's very much his thing . . . I might like them when I watch them, but when I'm on my own I wouldn't put one of them on.

When you're watching together, how is the decision made?

One goes down the list and suggests things that would be OK with them at that time, so you'll make a list of about ten things perhaps, and the other will say yea or nay . . . now if you're in a terribly different mood, I don't know . . . sometimes I might go down the list and there's some comedy stuff we've got on erm . . . perhaps Jim'll say no, let's watch a film . . . I suppose the comedy tends to be shorter . . . let's watch one particular thing rather than a few episodes . . . we sort of approach where we can agree generally, lots of list options for one another. (Jenny)

Three of the women reported that they had watched 'blue' movies with their partners. I asked Jean who hired them.

Well, the first we saw was the one my eldest son brought back from Saudi Arabia. I don't think he knows I've seen it though [laugh]. I wouldn't like to watch it when he was there . . . only just my husband and myself . . . I'm glad I've seen it but . . . I must be naïve you see, I mean kids today . . . they get blue movies as well and wait until I've gone to bed you see . . . now they'll sit and watch one when Jack's here, but not when I'm here, no . . . I don't know if it's out of respect to me or . . . embarrassment, I would certainly be embarrassed and I think they would be as well . . . so . . . you see they know a hell of a lot more at 19 or 20 than I did . . . it's taken me forty years to see some of it [laugh] . . . but it sets you off on a different track. I mean before videos came into this household there were 'girlie' magazines, it's just like that really. (Jean)

Michelle and Julie claimed it was curiosity which led to the choice:

Yes, yes, we've hired blue movies before, just to see what they were like, just out of curiosity. I wouldn't go in and hire them again, but we have been and hired one once. I don't think I actually watched it all the way through. Erm . . . we hired one once to watch with friends, for a laugh. (Michelle)

Yes, we've watched a few, just to say we've watched them.

But I wouldn't hire one a week, not to that extent. But sometimes we might have one on a Saturday night and I'd watch it, just out of curiosity. I think they're funny. (Julie)

Male only

In the previous contexts for this group, the women, although present when the television or video was on, would not necessarily be paying very much attention to the screen. This context, however, features those texts and genres which some of the women had very little interest in, or positively disliked; they would either go to bed or do something in the kitchen when their partners were watching them.

Descriptions of the movies in this context were necessarily vague, and respondents often resorted to the categories used by the video library to describe their partners' preferences. There were very few titles they could remember. This also applied to television programmes.

> but, as I say, he does like documentaries and things that are of 'interest' as he calls it, you know . . . so I go 'well of interest to you' [laugh]. (Janet)

What would he call Dallas *and* Dynasty *then?*

> Rubbish . . . he says it's stupid, you know, but he likes things that . . . well things that . . . oh! I'll tell you . . . like there was that thing on . . . what's it? *QE?* what's it . . . that bog man. Now that, he had to sit and watch . . . now I sat and watched that and was interested, you know, I can get interested in certain things, if it's something that really interests me I can sit and . . . but he likes anything like that . . . anything that you're learning from he'll watch. He loves *Tomorrow's World* and things like that, he wouldn't miss, you know, he likes to watch them . . . and astronomy, anything to do with astronomy he likes, Patrick Moore and that he likes, but I mean, I just don't understand things like that. (Janet)

This extract reiterates the 'fact'-'fiction' dichotomy noted in Rene's household, but also the value afforded to male preference for factual programmes compared with the fictional 'rubbish' preferred by the female. This distinction between what is 'serious' and 'silly' determines what is 'worth watching' and is a strong element in the justifiability of the male's programme selection. What is of 'interest' to him is definitionally good. Janet was encouraged to talk about her pleasures in *Dallas*, and this will be reported in the following chapter, but her conversation was peppered with comments like 'if my husband could hear me now' and 'it's a good job my husband can't hear this'. She was asked what programmes she liked to watch on television.

> My husband'd really laugh now . . . *Dallas* [laugh]. He thinks it's awful, and *Dynasty*; I like things like that, that's sort of, you know . . . you think . . . well do people live like that? Them type of programmes . . . you know, *Falcon Crest* and, you know, things like that. (Janet)

Throughout the discussion she was clearly suffering from mixed feelings of guilt and pleasure at being given licence to take *Dallas* seriously. Janet's husband spent a lot of his time at home working on his computer and she spoke of his dedication to this activity.

> you've got to be able to concentrate . . . I lose concentration, that's it with me . . . but I go to my husband, 'It must be really nice to be that involved in something . . . something to really get interested in that takes your mind off everything else' . . . he can do that, now I can't and I think, now why can't I do that?

But you can do that. You do it with Dallas *and* Dynasty.

I do don't I? But they're not important things are they?

Well, they're not considered to be important are they?

This is it . . . now, if I put that much effort, like, I go to my son 'if you put that much effort into your school work as you do into playing on the computer, you'd be brilliant' [laugh] . . . you know, but I suppose I'm the same myself . . . I want to have something that I'm really involved in, really, you know, like my neighbour on the estate, she's started to try and teach some Pakistani children and the mother English . . . she says to me 'why don't you . . .' and I say 'oh, they'd be all right, picking my slang up' [laugh]. But . . . you know, I've enough on my own without having that. But I'd like to have something that I'm interested in, to achieve something, just to say 'well, I've achieved that' . . . to

myself . . . it's myself I need to say it to, not everybody
else . . . you know, well, I've achieved it . . . so how on earth
do you go about that?

Now my husband . . . I don't know, he just seems to be
able to turn himself off, I wish I could, because I think that's
the way to keep yourself sane, I do honestly sometimes. You
see, men can sit down and do their thing and they don't feel
guilty. (Janet)

Her discussion of *Dallas* and *Dynasty*, which have low status
within the household, soon turns to an assessment of her own
self-worth and lack of achievement. She is laughed at by her
husband and sons for enjoying *Dallas* and *Dynasty*, but these are
the programmes which actually enable her to 'switch off'.

Other male preferences were indicated as follows:

I don't watch *A Team* or owt like that, that doesn't interest
me . . . Michael [husband] watches that . . . *Magnum* I'll
watch, I quite like that, but *A Team* I'm not interested in at
all . . . gangsters and guns I'm not interested at all, but all the
soap operas I'm interested in those . . . *Coronation Street* and
them . . . I watch quite a lot of telly, during the day, I've
always got telly on. I don't like documentaries or owt like
that, I don't like *World in Action*. (Cathy)

He hires a lot of erm . . . ooh . . . what would you call them.
Again, new films, but ones I wouldn't want to watch, like
erm . . . boxing films, Al Pacino, tough guy films, like that,
that's more his cup of tea. Violent films, action films, something happening all the time. (Susan)

Blood-thirsty [laugh]. You know, there's no way he'd record
Coronation Street or something like that. A film, yes. He tapes
a lot of things that he watches and I don't. You know, he
watches things when the children have gone to bed and I'm
at work. (Betty)

Jean described the kind of programme she preferred compared
with her husband and sons:

I like the romantic leading up to things, you know, the spoken
things between them. I like all of that kind of stuff . . . they
don't seem to . . . which you get in a book, you get more

talk between them, the leading up to it, whereas everything on television seems to be so . . . everything done for visual effects, of course . . . there's a difference between . . . something happening, with the interplay, when you can see something is going to happen . . . the interchange . . . it's nice when it is slow and you're saying . . . oh yes . . . I knew she'd say that, or I knew it would turn out like that, whereas men, I don't think they're bothered about that, they just sit and watch it and let it all happen. (Jean)

Her account of the difference between male and female preferences will be explored further in chapter 4, but there is evidence in all these women's accounts of genuine mystification about the appeal of those so-called male genres which are generally viewed in a male only context.

Female only

I have noted the feelings of guilt experienced by some women in this group about watching television and video during the day. For those women at home with young children this would be an obvious time for female-only viewing, and viewing with their children did indeed provide an excuse for daytime viewing. Some of the women used broadcast television actually to structure their day, framing it as a reward or indulgence towards which the completion of household tasks would lead. Janet regularly watched *Falcon Crest* and I asked if this helped her along with her work.

Erm . . . yes I think you do because you've something to look forward to, it's like a reward at the end of the day, you know . . . where you're sort of . . . well I'm doing this, but I can sit down for an hour . . . sort of thing . . . yes, I think it does . . . because some days you come home and you don't feel like starting anyway, and then you think, oh well, I've got that to look forward to, so therefore you get on with it. Yes, I think it probably does. (Janet)

Cathy, at home during the day with her small child, liked a lot of the daytime soap operas.

Yes . . . *Sons and Daughters, Take the High Road, Gems* . . . I've watched it before and I'm seeing it again . . . but it's

because I've nothing to do that I'll watch that telly this aft.
It's nice having the video because if I want to go out I can
tape things like that . . . I wouldn't be able to do before. I'd
have to stay in. (Cathy)

Sons and Daughters was her current favourite and she made sure
her domestic routine accommodated its viewing.

I get right involved in it, I talk to myself when he's at work.
I'm right into it . . . if I'm going shopping I like to think
ooh . . . mustn't miss *Sons and Daughters*, so I rush home for
that. (Cathy)

Janet and Megan are neighbours and, along with another neighbour, regularly rented video tapes which they would view
together during the afternoon, when spouses and children were
at work and school. Here is my discussion with Janet about this
viewing context:

Like sometimes, my neighbour over the road and Megan, if
there's anything, like we've just had one in three parts, I've
forgotten what they called it . . . *Evergreen* . . . that was it,
and we'll get things like that and now Megan's on about
another one that's in so many parts and, like she'll buy one,
I'll buy one and Rita'll buy one . . . and we'll do it like that
if it's anything we really want to watch, we do it like that and
sort of, you know, I'll get my work done, we'll have a cup
of coffee and watch it one afternoon.

Are you always agreed as to what kind of film to get?

Yes . . . we all like the same kind of film really.

Who gets the films?

Well I think it's usually Megan who takes time to go looking,
you know, she'd probably browse more than me, you
know . . . like if I didn't watch a film it wouldn't bother me
type of thing. It's nice, like once you get it, but I wouldn't
go probably looking for myself. I think . . . There again, it's
finding time to look for yourself . . . I think that guilt comes
into it again somewhere [laugh].

Do you feel guilty watching the films with your friends?

No, because I normally know when we're going to watch

them so, I sort of get things done so I can watch them . . .
so I can sit and think, well I deserve to watch this, type of
thing . . . you know, things are done, so, no I don't really,
in that way. (Janet)

I asked Megan how she went about deciding on the films to get
for those afternoon sessions.

It's me more often than not that . . . I'm the one that goes to
the video shop more than anybody. I mainly go to return the
films that Ian or Matthew's [husband and son] taken out
the day before, and I just tend to look round and ask if they've
got anything new, and she'll tell me about them. That's how
I got on to this *Evergreen*, and *Sarah Dane*, that was in two
parts, and another one . . . erm . . . *Mistral's Daughter*, things
like that. I like something with a story to it. (Megan)

I asked her if they watched the movie right through, uninterrupted.

Yes, we let it run all the way through . . . we usually, if it's
on an evening, we'll get a bottle of wine out then we don't
have to bother to get up and make tea [laugh]. (Megan)

This viewing context served several different functions for the
participants. It assuaged Janet's guilty feelings, it provided uninterrupted viewing time and allowed the women to select and
watch those genres of films which they were not normally able
to watch with their male partners. But there is also a qualitative
difference here in that the women feel able to take up the feminine
subject positions offered by these texts comfortably and pleasurably together, without fear of the male derision which they and
other women reported.

Another female-only viewing group was formed by Julie and
her mother. She was asked if she thought there were films made
specially for women.

Yes, definitely. Like *Who Will Love My Children?* I can't see
any man, well, not very many men, getting any pleasure out
of that. I mean . . . I watched that round at my Mum's and
she asked a few of us if we'd like to watch it and we all just
sat and cried. I can't see any man really being interested in
that. (Julie)

Susan enjoyed hiring horror movies, but she also hired other kinds of movies to watch on her own.

> Oh yes, love stories, sloppy things, anything I could cry over, erm . . . and a lot of the newer or later films that came out that I'd missed that weren't quite good enough for us to go to the cinema and see. Films like *Tootsie* . . . now I did see that at the cinema, but I had to see it again, John did not want to see it, he refused to watch it – he sounds a pain doesn't he? [laugh] – erm, *Arthur* . . . films that I couldn't be bothered to go and see, but I had to see. I'd watch them at home. (Susan)

Like many of the women, Jenny found it difficult to answer when I asked her what kinds of programmes and films she liked to watch.

> I find it easier to pick on things that he likes than isolate my own . . . I do like big stories, I suppose, like *Tess, Reds, Zhivago* . . . they cover a wide period of time and a wide range of characters, and I do like romantic stuff, if it's well done . . . erm . . . and then again, I like what you might describe as quite the opposite – little films about . . . *Gregory's Girl* and *Electric Horseman* . . . I mean that was really just Jane Fonda and Robert Redford, and I got that quite by accident one night and thought it was wonderful. I went on about it sufficiently so that Jim watched it and he also enjoyed it, and we overlapped there. But quite what it is about those sorts of films, I don't know . . . characters, good characters, a touch of romance, a touch of humour. (Jenny)

GROUP 3: D, E

The viewing choices of this relatively small group of women, five in total, compared with ten in Group 1 and fifteen in Group 2, are summarized in Table 3. Within this group, one of the households had young children, one woman lived with her husband and grown-up daughters, one divorced woman lived with her teenage daughters and occasionally with her boyfriend, and two young women lived with their parents. All were council tenants, except Brenda's family, who were council property purchasers.

The contexts which readily accommodated Groups 1 and 2

were not really flexible enough for this group, mainly because all but two of the households were made up of adults. However, Table 3 is broadly representative of different contexts as they arose in discussion with the women.

Table 3 Group 3: D, E

Context	Film	Television
Family together	*Kramer v. Kramer; The Champ; Porkys; Police Academy; Rocky; Dirty Harry;* Clint Eastwood; comedy; Walt Disney	*EastEnders; Coronation Street; Dallas; Dynasty*
Children only	musicals; children's films; Walt Disney	*EastEnders; Coronation Street; Dallas; Auf Wiedersehen Pet; Top of the Pops; The Young Ones*
Male and female together	*Aliens; Who Will Love my Children?; The Champ;* horror	Best-sellers; *Sherlock Holmes; Travelling Man;* snooker; Olympics; World Cup; cricket; boxing; *Fawlty Towers*
Male only	cowboys; war; *Rocky;* boxing films	*Cannon and Ball;* motor cycle racing; car racing; snooker; football
Female only	weepies; Richard Gere; romance; horror	*Falcon Crest; Sons and Daughters; Dallas;* best-sellers; *Coronation Street;* local news; medical programmes; *Lace*

Family together

In the majority of these households the television was on all the time. Brenda, in the only household with small children, operated the nine o'clock children's curfew which is assumed by the broadcasting organizations.

> Later on at night our kiddies are in bed and you can sit and watch, because, I mean, they're at it all the time, they're either wanting something or trying to talk to you, so after nine o'clock type of thing, I try to get them out of the way by then [laugh]. (Brenda)

Barbara and her daughters regularly watched the then thrice-weekly soap, *Crossroads*.

> Yes, it starts with *Crossroads*. Everything . . . tea's got to be ready, or it's got to be ready for when *Crossroads* has finished. Everybody watches *Crossroads*, unless, like Mary [daughter], she works Friday night, so we tape it for her. We like it . . . I don't think it's because it's so good, I think it's sort of, you can't believe what's going to happen next. (Barbara)

Regularity in watching a favourite soap opera, as well as the pleasure of speculation and discussing plots and characters with members of the family, is an important and recognized element of viewing practice. Family viewing of films also often triggered talk and sometimes tears.

> We all watched *Kramer v. Kramer* together when it was on at Christmas, on television. We didn't say much, but I found I got more reaction from my eldest daughter, because when we went to bed she says . . . and I said 'are you thinking that's going to happen to me and your Dad, what's happened on that film?' and she said 'Yes, and I don't want it to happen to you' . . . I came down and told my husband, he said 'Oh she's a softy' . . . She's not a child to show her feelings, but sometimes the odd thing comes out. I said to her 'Oh, we argue, like everybody else, but we're friends soon'. She does notice things like that, whereas, if she sees murder, or anything like that in a film she wouldn't think . . . but if she hears it on the news, then she does. You know, these children who'd been killed, Jasmin [Beckford] and that, she was asking about that, asking why . . . an 8-year-old. (Brenda)

> There was a video we got and we all watched it, called *The Champ*, and it's about a boxer who's on his own with a little boy . . . and he returns to fight for some money for this little boy, and he's in this fight and he gets knocked out and he dies on the table. And then . . . it was really funny, because we were sat there on the settee and her little boy were on the floor, and he's playing, you know, and he just looked up, and this little boy ran up to his dad, and tears were running . . . we burst out crying, but we were laughing as well . . . I like that kind of thing. (Sandra)

Barbara was a horror fan and she described one rare occasion when she had watched a horror film with her daughters and their boyfriends.

> There was a film we watched last year and the girls were here and the boys were here, and we sat watching this film and I was sat at that end, and the lads were here and, right at the very end he propelled himself out of bed, he jumped out of bed. He was supposed to be dead, and all of a sudden, the girl was tidying the covers up, and that, and all of a sudden he was out of bed. Now I knew something was going to happen at the end, it just couldn't possibly end like that. I mean, it was too peaceful an ending, something was obviously going to happen, and I sat there and everybody jumped, they didn't expect that. I killed myself laughing, I thought it was hilarious, but it made them jump – our Mary was frightened to death. (Barbara)

Apart from demonstrating her knowledge of the horror genre, this anecdote indicates the social aspect of watching movies at home and the cross-generational contexts which such occasions provide. This is not always the case. Barbara reported that her daughters often dominated television and the VCR.

> Karen [daughter] tapes *Top of the Pops* and Spandau Ballet and she tapes all things like that, so we don't clash with them, I try and keep out of the way when she's playing that, I mean she plays hers over and over and over again, but I'm never in to tape anything like that for me. Country and Western – I'm never in and they never think. (Barbara)

Doreen also found difficulty in watching her choice of television programme.

> Well, it's my eldest girl, she watches it more . . . she puts the TV on when she comes in from work and she watches it all night if she can [laugh] . . . we often have a barney over the programmes because if you're not careful you miss them . . . you know . . . she says 'I want to watch this' and I usually give in, anyway, I think oh . . . [shrug]. (Doreen)

Children alone

In view of the fact that two of the women were young and living with their parents, generational differences emerged more strongly than in the previous groups, focusing mainly on comedy and music. The VCR was used to alleviate this conflict. There were also problems with sexually explicit material, as noted in Jean's case when her sons rented blue movies. In the case of Christine, 21 years old and living with her parents, it was her father who disapproved of 'rude things'.

> If my mum wants a video I'll get it for her and we'll sometimes watch it. My Dad's had a few but he didn't like them . . . he generally has war films and I don't mind them so I'll watch them but he says. 'If there's any rude things I want to know . . .' I mean, I'm not bothered with things like that, but I think he is with us all being lasses [laugh] . . . he gets a bit embarrassed, but I don't blame him, and he told me he'd let me have my video on that condition. (Christine)

Male and female together

Sport was a major category here. Boxing, the World Cup, the Olympic Games, and snooker were all favoured by women in this group, programmes which, in previous groups, only figured in the male alone context.

> He likes the nature ones and sport. I like them as well. My husband isn't keen on football, but we both like rugby and boxing. (Brenda)

> He likes nature, you know, the nature ones, erm . . . I don't think there are any on just now, but there was one on the other week on one of the sides for about an hour . . . he watched those, well we both did, we enjoyed them. (Doreen)

Situation comedy was not very significant, compared to group 2, although Doreen enjoyed *Auf Wiedersehen, Pet*. I asked if her husband liked to follow serials.

> No I don't think there is much, really, in fact, he goes to sleep actually in the chair [laugh] . . . he'll be sitting watching it then he just drops off to sleep . . . although, I like those *Auf*

Wiedersehen . . . I don't class that really, but it is a serial isn't
it? I've been watching that, I enjoy that, first and second time,
but he thinks it's horrible. I think it's funny, so I watch that.
(Doreen)

The films quoted by the group for joint viewing crossed the
gender boundaries. Doreen again:

Yes, yes, we've had one or two . . . I can't remember the
names of them . . . we watch sort of . . . what, was it
now . . . er . . . one of them was Rocky Stallone, and he'd
been to Vietnam – that was pretty good . . . and erm, forget
the name of it now . . . Harry, *Dirty Harry*, Clint Eastwood.
I liked them, you know, they were quite good. (Doreen)

Brenda and her husband had watched *Who Will Love My Children?*
together.

He thought it was good, he was sniffing . . . he was sort of
taking the mickey out of me crying to stop himself crying.
(Brenda)

Sandra, who lived with her parents, found it more comfortable
to watch movies with her married sister and brother-in-law.

Sometimes, yes . . . what we usually do, we [laugh] we don't
get blue movies, but they tend to be a bit rude, you know. I
mean my Dad wouldn't watch them . . . so at Pamela's, we'll
get a tape and we'll have something like that instead of going
out, and I stay there for the night and we watch a couple of
films, you know, and we sometimes get blue ones then . . .
if Phillip's in the pub his friends will say, oh we got a good
film last night . . . right, we'll get it. We get a few, but there's
some that even Pamela won't watch, so I don't watch them.
I don't really like that kind of thing, but, you know, some of
them are a bit rude, really humorous, you kind of laugh at it,
Lemon Popsicle, that kind of thing. (Sandra)

Male only

Because of the constitution of households in this group, reported
viewing for this context is necessarily thin.

Although the women said that there were differences in preferred programmes and movies, most of them were happy to

watch with either their male partners or their fathers. There were times, however, when the married women in this group would go and do something else, or sit and read when they weren't interested in what was being watched.

> If there was something on that, you know, I was interested in I would watch. Then if they had a film I didn't care for, I'd go sit in there and read, you know, I go out of the room and read. (Doreen)

Female only

Generally this required the women to be alone in the house, either during the day or in the evening. Brenda regularly watched *Falcon Crest* and *Sons and Daughters*. She was asked what her husband thought of the programmes she liked watching.

> Well, the ones I watch in the afternoon, he, you know, thinks they're daft. But when he was unemployed he was sat watching *Sons and Daughters* himself and the odd times he's got home early he's said 'Well, who's that and what's she doing' . . . and I say 'Oh, you don't like it' [laugh].

> *So he wouldn't get interested in it?*

> Yes, but I don't think he'd get like me. But, there again, that's my half hour, like, I bring Laura [daughter] home at about twenty past three, so I have that time 'til four o'clock before I start on the tea, and I try to make that my time. The kids'll go get changed or play out . . . my eldest daughter, before she went into junior school, she used to like watching *Sons and Daughters* with me, so she tends to tell the others to pack it in . . . she'll say 'Oh, be quiet, we're watching this' . . . you know. (Brenda)

Television is used by this woman to mark out time for herself during the day, two of the daytime soap operas fitting into her daily schedule of child care.

The kinds of films, television programmes and books that women like watching and reading will be explored in the following chapter.

SUMMARY

Identifying different viewing contexts and related texts for the three main groups in the sample reveals differences in viewing preference between groups and within the groups as contexts change. By breaking up the notion of a monolithic domestic viewing context, we can also see which members of the household unit have priority at specific times and, by listening to how the women account for this, get an idea of the negotiations involved in establishing viewing choices. An important dimension of this would appear to be the ways in which women from different groups justify the claims to the screen of other members of the household.

As far as children's viewing is concerned there is a more consciously expressed effort at control from Group 1 than the other groups. For these women television did not constitute a problem if it was used by their children selectively or as a means of relaxation after hard work. For Group 2, television was, in the main, a much more dominant feature of the household and was more or less accepted as a part of life. Although we have noted that the women in Group 1 claimed to share their partner's tastes in films and television, we can also see that some negotiation takes place. Often there is a partner who is somehow in 'credit', and so has earned the choice. This applies to those households throughout where one partner is the dominant viewer. If a preference is expressed by the non-viewing partner, then it is likely that she or he will get her or his way. In Groups 1 and 2, many of the women consider their husband's employment as being the only justification necessary for him to take priority over the screen. Many would also put their children's choice before their own; in this way, the women themselves accept a place at the bottom of the viewing hierarchy. While the male only viewing context can and does exist when their female partners are at home, for the female only context to exist it is usually necessary for the male partner to be absent, either at work or leisure. This means that the women have to select their viewing time carefully, often during the day. However, as we have seen, this is not unproblematic as many feel guilty whilst watching television or video during the day. Janet's complicated work and reward patterns, which she uses to justify watching a video during the day with her friends, serve to remind us of the ideological constraints

under which some women live. This means, of course, that very
often women are watching television programmes or movies
which they do not enjoy and would not choose to watch themselves.

If we address our attention to the texts associated with Group
1 contexts as seen in Table 1, we can see that there is a preference
for 'classics' and prestigious series on television. Also, the idea
of Britishness as a sign of quality is important in this group.
There is resistance to the products of mass culture and a desire
on the part of some of the women to distance themselves from
those products. There were, however, two women in this group
who liked American serials and series, particularly *Dallas* and
Dynasty, but faced the derision of their partners and children
when they watched these programmes. These two women can
be seen as systematic exceptions in this group, systematic in that
they both left school at 15, neither of them pursuing higher
education nor a career. Their partners, on the other hand, had
developed successful careers within their fields.

In Tables 2 and 3 we see much stronger divisions across gender
and related texts. Documentaries and current affairs were cited as
being enjoyed by male partners and not by women. However,
'factual' programming has a much higher prestige in these households and is automatically taken more seriously. In Table 2 sport
was almost always viewed in a male only context, whereas Table
3 shows less of a gender division for this category of programme.
The ways in which women in Groups 2 and 3 spoke of their
partner's preferences is revealing in that they tend to reinforce
the gender differences and keep the divisions in their place. Partners are mystifyingly involved in politics, space, science, science
fiction, action adventure, and so on, just because they are men.
The statement 'I don't know what he sees in them' indicates
how inscrutable these men can seem in relation to their viewing
pleasures. However, this inscrutability extends to their relationship to 'female' genres. The emotional responses which these
films and programmes elicit from the men would seem to present
difficulties. Various masking strategies are employed; pretending
not to be affected and laughing at their partner's tears being two
reported in this group. There is a reluctance by men to view such
genres and as a result they rarely appear in the male and female
together viewing contexts.

VIEWING MODES

In the light of this analysis of the different viewing contexts and their associated texts, I will now briefly discuss the 'modality' of viewing associated with the hiring of tapes compared with, on the one hand, broadcast television, and on the other, the cinema.

John Ellis refers to broadcast television as 'intimate and every-day, a part of home life rather than any kind of special event' (Ellis 1982: 113). He also argues that broadcast television, in order to address the domestic (and distracted) audience, has developed its own particular form. This, Ellis argues, is a segmental form, made up of very short units which constantly claim the audience's attention in its endless 'flow'. In its domestic setting television's regime of viewing is very different from, say, the cinema:

> TV does not encourage the same degree of spectator concen-tration. There is no surrounding darkness, no anonymity of the fellow viewers, no large image, no lack of movement amongst the spectators, no rapt attention . . . TV is treated casually rather than concentratedly. It is something of a last resort . . . rather than a special event.
>
> (Ellis 1982: 128)

If we accept Ellis's claims about the nature of broadcast television and its audience, we can see that the use of a VCR for time-shifting and the hiring of pre-recorded tapes has the potential to disrupt this endless 'flow'. The user can subvert the schedules imposed by the broadcasting organizations and also potentially alter the regime of viewing. In other words, the user can make television into a special event. Rene, for example, reported that recording off-air and renting a tape made a difference to her mode of viewing.

> Mmm . . . it's completely different, yes, to television yes . . . I don't say it's different to watching a recording that you've bothered to record from your timer, it's no different to that, but it is different to the television being on and you being . . . well, I mean, if you've gone to the trouble to record some-thing, then you do it because you want to watch it. Now that is exactly the same as hiring a film. My television can be used, yes, as the radio, just as background, but recording, and hiring, that is different. (Rene)

stment of time and money and the exercise of
ut, for Rene, her viewing of tapes as something
npared with the background 'flow' of broadcast
ly of the women told me that the investment of
ng a tape and the exercise of choice had, in the
their hiring, made a significant difference to their
wing.

> Yes, we all watched it then, you know, it was 'C'mon, first film's going on the video' and we all downed tools and watched. (Edna)

> We tend to sit and watch together if he's hired a video, we start off like that anyway, and if it doesn't catch our interest, slowly but surely we'll drift off. (Kay)

Most of the women did say that their modes of viewing had altered as the 'novelty' of hiring tapes had worn off, or that the films selected did not appeal to them.

> At first, we prepared coffees and sandwiches and biscuits and sat there watching from beginning to end.

> *And that's changed?*

> Oh yes, absolutely. Well, because you can choose what you want. I love horror films, but John won't watch them and he loves those boring war films which I won't watch, so we have our own individual films to buy, which is pleasing in one way, but difficult in another. (Susan)

> Well, I would say Melanie's [daughter] the only one who doesn't sit down and watch them all, there's an odd one or two, the horror ones he brings home that . . . if I'm not doing anything I'll sit and watch it but I don't make a point of . . . ooh . . . we must watch that, you know, but he does bring a variety home really. (Megan)

As we saw in chapter 2, these women are describing the kinds of viewing modality that many of them adopt for television even though they are watching (a) a film, which would not generally conform to Ellis's definition of televisual form, and (b) one that has been selected and paid for. In both cases the films belong to genres that do not engage their full attention. However, as Susan indicated, if it is a film they really want to see then their attitude to viewing is very different, particularly if they are alone in the house.

> A few weeks ago Ian got *Educating Rita*, he got it one night when I was going out, and he'd forgotten I was going out, and I came home from work and watched it in the afternoon. It didn't bother me that I was sat here on my own watching it. Janet had seen it so there was no point in asking anybody else to come . . . it didn't upset me, just sitting here watching it. I find it quite peaceful actually; I usually put the answering machine on so the 'phone doesn't distract me or anything like that, if there's something I know I really want to watch and get interested in, because I tend to not stop it or pause it when I'm on the phone, then I'm re-winding it, it upsets me. (Megan)

This woman hired tapes to watch with friends in the neighbourhood – a viewing context which was explored earlier in this chapter.

Alison indicated her own difficulty in ignoring distractions. She said that she didn't like television very much. Did she enjoy watching a hired film?

> Yes, yes I do . . . if I can sit down and relax and watch it . . . I find it difficult to do that, I don't know why.

Do you find you're distracted when you're watching it?

> Well, it's 'will you get up and make me a cup of tea? I'll stop the video' [laugh] . . . erm . . . I do like, I don't mind sitting and watching a film but I've got to be in that frame of mind. I've got to be able to know that I can sit down and watch it without being disturbed. (Alison)

This woman found it very difficult to eliminate the distractions.

> Like, if he comes in and he's rented a video, straight after tea he wants to put it on. I say 'well, let me finish the washing-up first'. I mean, I just wouldn't enjoy it if I knew it was all to do. (Alison)

The women were asked how watching a video at home compared with going to the cinema:

Well I do prefer going to the cinema because you get a better projection of what you're supposed to be seeing. A film at home, you can turn it off when you want to, and if you're bored you can just turn it off and go make some tea, or whatever, and come back to it. If you're at the pictures you're there and you sit and watch and sit still for an hour and a half. When you're at home you tend to move around a lot and think, this bit's boring, I'll go out, you know . . . at the cinema it's full attention. (Susan)

I think you . . . when you're in the cinema you're not in control of the film, you can't stop it to go to the loo or anything like that, so you're not going to maybe spoil the entertainment value of it by doing things like that, and you're not going to stop for a coffee or anything like that, or if the 'phone rings . . . so sometimes I think you lose by watching it at home in that respect . . . but then I don't think there's that many films that it's going to make that much difference to the film anyway . . . I don't know. (Lynne)

For one household, Maureen's, the video offered a welcome control over hired movies.

If there's a lot of sex on films, we . . . or if we've hired some we've fast forwarded it, you know . . . I don't see the point of it – everyone knows what goes on, so there's no need to put it on the screen. (Maureen)

Two of the women who enjoyed horror movies would create conditions which were very similar to the cinema in order to maximize their pleasure.

I mean, if I know I'm going to watch a really good film that I'd heard about and read about, I'd make sure that John was out in any case – he can't even bear to hear a scream on television because he knows I'll come running in. So I do try to pick a good horror movie when I'm by myself. For some strange reason I turn the lights off, I close the curtains and I scare myself silly [laugh], stupid isn't it? But, when you're at home and something really frightening happens, it is frightening, more frightening. You tend to look at the doors, opening and things like that. I watch them when he's away at night.

Mad . . . then I can't sleep [laugh] I turn on all the lights.
(Susan)

Barbara also liked horror movies and she watched them late at
night.

I prefer to watch them on my own, all the lights out, nice
and quiet and that's it. (Barbara)

However, going to the cinema is not simply about watching a
movie, but is a social 'event' and as such was important to Janet.

If there's something going around that they would like to see,
and it's one of their birthdays, then that's what we do. OK,
you can wait and see it on video, but it's not quite the same;
you're taking them out, it's different to having a video at
home, isn't it, you're taking them out – it's different . . . so,
if there's been something mentioned they'd like to see, yes,
we will take them to the cinema and then take them somewhere for a meal, and do it that way. It's nice, and I think
it's a novelty for the children. For myself, if I could go to the
pictures or watch on video, I would prefer to stop at home
and watch it, myself, but I think it's just the novelty of going
out, and you know, going out as a family . . . you know.
(Janet)

SUMMARY

It is clear that any discussion of viewing modalities must take
account of the distinction between use of the VCR as against
broadcast television, but also divisions of gender in relation to
modes of viewing. It would seem that women are more likely
to be distracted viewers, certainly of broadcast television, but also
of hired movies. In many cases this distracted mode is the result
of their partners watching genres in which they have little or no
interest, but there is evidence to suggest that some women find
it difficult to devote themselves to the screen at all when
surrounded by domesticity. As we saw in chapter 2, there are
exceptions to this, especially when women are able to view alone,
mostly during the day. This viewing was seen as 'my time', and
was motivated by the desire to 'switch off' domestic demands.
This is much less likely if other members of the family are
present. In addition, the choice of evening viewing is rarely the

woman's, priority being given to partners and children. Women will therefore find something else to do whilst watching a programme or film which does not really interest them.

David Morley's research confirms this 'female' mode of viewing, and, as Morley also talked to men, it is interesting that, according to him, 'Essentially the men state a clear preference for viewing attentively, in silence, without interruption' (Morley 1986: 150). Many of them spoke with dismay of their partner's tendency to be doing other things whilst the television was on, talking to other members of the family or interrupting them. This would seem to suggest that there is a masculine mode of viewing which is concentrated and single-minded and a feminine mode of viewing which is distracted and lacking in concentration. Unless we situate these viewing modes within the domestic context and the social relations of power which appear to prevail, there is a tendency to fall into an essentialist explanation of male and female behaviour. But in the light of previous discussion in chapters 2 and 3, with regard to female domestic obligations and the apparent male right to spare time, what is evident here is the difference in position that men and women occupy within these familial arrangements and the relationships of power and authority which exist across gender. Charlotte Brunsdon suggests that this empirical evidence

> offers us an image of male viewers trying to masculinize the domestic sphere. This way of watching television, however, seems not so much a masculine mode, but a mode of power. Current arrangements between men and women make it likely that it is men who will occupy this position in the home.
>
> (Brunsdon, quoted in Morley 1986: 148)

We can see from evidence reported here that women do take pleasure in adopting the concentrated gaze. This can be seen in the examples of Susan and Barbara with their horror movies and other accounts of individual viewing and, as we have seen, joint female viewing. We cannot therefore speak of a 'masculine' mode of viewing which is only practised by men. Rather, we must see particular modes of behaviour as being contingent upon the specific social dynamics which are in operation at the time.

Chapter 4

Viewing and reading preferences

Ena Sharples's still in Blackpool isn't she?

(Rene)

It is clear from Tables 1–3 in chapter 3 that male- and female-reported preferences for films and television programmes are often aligned with those popular genres associated with the masculine and feminine within our culture and therefore with men and women in our society. This chapter will look at the ways in which the women expressed their enjoyment in and relationship to the various films and television programmes which have been discussed in the previous chapter. As we saw in chapter 2, reading was an important activity for many women and their discussions of different genres of text provide a counterpoint to accounts of their engagement with visual media. In this context, albeit to a lesser extent, radio also figures.

It was noted that some of the Group 1 women shared their partner's tastes in films and television programmes and, in some cases, reading and viewing preferences extended beyond 'popular' texts. However, the main focus of this section is on that collection of genres which appear to have particular appeal to the women in the sample. These are often referred to under the umbrella term 'women's genres', and include, for example, romance, family saga and soap opera. However, it is important to select categories with which to order and analyse women's viewing and reading experiences, enabling differences to emerge as well as the more obvious similarities. For this reason I have chosen to explore the women's expressed preferences across a range of texts and media, under the ordering categories of 'reading', 'television programmes' and 'films', rather than under categories of genre. As

I indicated in the previous chapter, with reference to Kay and Rene and their expressed pleasures in viewing *Dallas* and *Dynasty*, educational factors often outweigh other 'class' determinants in terms of preference and choice of genre. Kay and Rene's viewing of these American products set them apart from other women in Group 1 and I have therefore found it more useful to re-group the women for this chapter according to their educational background. Thus, Group A is made up of those women who left school between the ages of 14 and 16, and Group B of those women who have been involved in higher education at some time in their lives.

GROUP A: EARLY SCHOOL LEAVERS

Reading

Many of the women in this group reported that they read books for pleasure. The frequency of reading varied from 'chain reading' of Mills and Boon to the occasional reading of a recommended book. Cathy's reading of Mills and Boon began in the family home because they were read by her mother and grandmother.

> I've allus had them, because my mum's allus had them you see, they were always at home . . . I used to pick them up. Like, my Mum or my Gran have always passed them on. (Cathy)

As we saw in chapter 2, she is able to fit her reading into the interstices of her daily routine of domestic work and child care; Mills and Boon offer a manageable commodity for this purpose.

> I don't really get the thickish ones, I normally go for the quick ones. (Cathy)

Other women found that the very familiarity of the Mills and Boon narratives meant these books could be easily accommodated, especially if the women had very little mental energy left in the evening.

> If it's the sort of evening where I know I'm a little bit tired and likely to go to sleep fairly quickly I'll take one of those in with me with my coffee because I know I'm not going to be . . . very rarely anyway . . . just occasionally you get one

that's quite good, but it's very rare. You can pick some books up and within the first half dozen pages you know exactly what's going to happen, you could even write the dialogue yourself. (Edna)

I read those a lot in bed; sometimes if you're tired and when I was poorly I read things like that, because it's easier just to, you don't have to take them in to understand them, if you miss a page . . . well you more or less know what's going to happen. You know what the ending's going to be before you start, you know. With Mills and Boon you know she's going to end up with the man she hated in the beginning. (Julie)

Kay told me that her preferences for fiction had been established in childhood, through popular texts.

I have a brother, and he used to read *The Eagle, The Victor*, and I used to read *Judy, Schoolfriend*. And then I can remember being hooked on the romances when I got to sort of 13, oh, I used to read, oh, such rubbish, really when I look back, but, oh, I did enjoy them. Magazines – *True Love* – [sigh] and I used to get really involved with those. I used to cry over some of the stories in them. My daughter has just been going through a phase of reading some of those books, she's absolutely devoured all of those.

Do you think they taught you anything about relationships . . . about what to expect?

More about what you expected than what you got . . . I mean, the boys weren't reading those, were they? They didn't know how to behave, did they? [laugh] (Kay)

Barbara and Kay read romantic fiction regularly and both told me how they felt when they had finished a book.

I always hate to come to the end, when it gets to the last couple of pages, and you know very well how it's going to work out. You always know the end, you know how it's going to work out and I hate it coming to the end . . . I hate coming to the end and I hate starting a new one . . . I think because you've got into the characters and you feel you know them. (Barbara)

I always . . . I feel bereft when I've finished a book. Oh, I think, oh . . . I'll have to start another one and I might not like it . . . I do . . . mm. (Kay)

We can see a continuity of fictional genres preferred by Kay, and one which would seem to be carrying through into the next generation via her daughter. Also, there is a continuity in the almost passionate engagement which this woman has with her reading, 'devouring' romances as a teenager and feeling 'bereft' at the end of a Cookson historical romance as an adult. Rene shared Kay's pleasure in Cookson, but not wholeheartedly.

I love Catherine Cookson, and she's not a particularly good writer, as it were, but she tells a damned good tale. (Rene)

The importance of a good story was a crucial element in Rene's enjoyment of a book and many of the women spoke of their preference for well-developed stories and characters.

I like the family saga type of thing, you know. *A Woman of Substance*, it's those kind of books I love, you know . . . the good story, a good tale sort of thing. (Rene)

A very popular book and television adaptation, which several of the women talked to me about, was *The Thorn Birds* by Colleen McCullough.

Well, I thought that was a good book you see. I thought it was well written; that was a woman who knew Australia. God, when she described when she went down to live with Luke in . . . when she gets married, I mean, I could feel the flies, I mean the way she described the area. (Rene)

For Rene, what constitutes 'good writing' is that which constructs a totally believable setting within which the characters and plot are developed. Janice Radway makes a similar point about how women in her study of romance reading required this mimesis: 'The fact that the story is fantastic, however, does not compromise the accuracy of the portrayal of the physical environment within which the idealized characters move' (Radway 1984: 109). *The Thorn Birds* was one of the relatively small nucleus of texts which emerged throughout my interviews with Group A, commonly known, and certainly marketed as best-sellers. Such texts were often consumed by the women across the three different media in which they appear: reading the book, hiring the pre-transmission video tape and viewing on television. Over half the group had read at least one of these best-sellers and would always make a point of viewing the adaptation. (This will be discussed in the 'Television' section.) Edna, an avid reader, described her preferences and buying patterns, which were based on knowledge of the author.

> I like Judith Kranz books . . . I wait for her books coming out and I wait for Danielle Steel's as well and I'm always too eager to read them, so as soon as they come on the bookshelves I grab them. I always buy paperbacks, well, I've got *Master of the Game* in hardback but I can't really afford them. It's a shame because you can't fill a bookcase with paperbacks like you can with hardbacks can you? (Edna)

It is worth bearing in mind that these best-sellers have a very wide distribution and are available in outlets such as supermarkets and local newsagent shops, as well as chain stores such as W. H. Smith and Boots. These are the typical retail outlets through which the women purchased their books, rather than specialist book shops. However, in many cases women did not buy books but borrowed them from family or friends and some frequented second-hand bookstalls on local markets. About a quarter of the sample used the public library, but out of this only one woman went alone, the rest taking their children and occasionally borrowing a book for themselves.

Although Lynne, Susan and Megan were not regular readers, on the occasions when they did read a book they found they couldn't put it down.

> The last book I read from cover to cover was a [laugh] romantic novel that somebody lent me who said it was good . . . I was carrying it around with me whilst I was doing everything else, you know, go to the loo, take the book with you, sat in the bath with it . . . as soon as I got up on a morning, you're sat there reading . . . eating your breakfast. I'm like that if I get into a book, I cannot put it down. (Lynne)

> Occasionally I read, you know, you cannot read a book for six months and all of a sudden, pick up this book and it's . . .

well, under the desk at work, it's by the 'phone, it's in the bath, it's everywhere you go, this particular book, yes. (Susan)

Sometimes . . . if I'm reading a book and it's really got me really bound to it, yes I can pick it up and read two or three pages, and sit there two hours, and think 'my God, I've not done anything else' . . . but it's to really get me like that has a book. (Megan)

I asked Lynne why she couldn't put the book down.

I think it was because I wanted to find out what happened.

Do you think you knew what was going to happen?

Well, I suppose you always knew that the heroine was going to have a happy ending, but, *how* she was going to reach it, it was a different sort of . . . that was what kept you going through every page. (Lynne)

The romance guarantees the happy ending, but how the heroine gets to that point is sufficient to keep these readers reading. Edna perhaps expresses most accurately what the majority of women got out of their reading.

It's a form of day-dreaming I suppose, isn't it, being lifted out of yourself, as I like to be when I watch a film. (Edna)

What their preferred books seemed to offer was a fairly undemanding entry into a fictional world with a familiar narrative structure. But, on the other hand, as we have seen, these books are capable of demanding attention as well as providing legitimate space for day-dreaming and resistance to the immediate demands of the domestic world. To use Megan's phrase again, a woman can get 'really bound to it' to the exclusion of everything else. We will consider the potential for such involvement with reference to this group's television viewing.

Television

We have seen in the previous section that so called best-sellers were very popular with this group of women, and in particular *The Thorn Birds*. The television adaptation of this novel was transmitted by the BBC in the UK in January 1984. Although it

was not being shown at the time of the interviews, it was relatively recent and memorable for those who had watched it. It is
worth sketching in the background to the critical debates which
were taking place at the time and the way in which this highly
popular mini-series became an emblem for 'bad' television. It was
derided in the press and even in Parliament as imported commercial trash, and was seen as evidence that the BBC was reneging
on its public service responsibilities. It happened to coincide with
Granada's prestigious adaptation of Paul Scott's novels about the
decline of the British Raj, *The Jewel in the Crown*, which was
praised in the press as an example of 'quality' television in the
British public service tradition. Rene, who, as we have seen, had
enjoyed reading the McCullough novel, was aware of the criticism surrounding it.

Oh yes, everybody thought it was awful . . . Wogan had a go
at it and everybody.

What did you think about that when you enjoyed it so much?

I just tend to ignore them frankly. I mean, the daily paper that
we get, the *Daily Telegraph*, I mean, I don't know who their
critic is but if he says something is rubbish, you can guarantee
I'm going to enjoy it. Or, if he says it was absolutely fantastic,
and it will be something that to me is a complete bore. The
bad crits. don't bother me at all, in fact, sometimes they tend
to spur me on to watching . . . absolutely.

Did you watch The Jewel in the Crown?

Oh yes, we watched that.

Did you enjoy that?

Well, while I was watching it, yes, I enjoyed it, and at the
end of it I thought, 'well, my God, nothing's happened' . . .
I thought it was very, very drawn out. Beautifully acted, now
my husband thought that was magic. He really did enjoy it, he
thought it was very authentic and . . . I did. I watched it, I
watched every episode . . . erm, it was a bit slow moving for
me. (Rene)

The adaptation of *The Jewel in the Crown* did not have an obvious
resolution, leaving the central character with an undecided future,
a state of affairs which Rene found unsatisfactory. The lack of

resolution of some books, programmes and films was also commented upon by Audrey and Edna.

> I think really they should have a proper ending, for me anyway. I feel that they should either make you realize it's going to turn good or turn bad, but some are just left, where they ought to have a tail end leading towards one bit or another . . . not particularly all the bows all knotted as though they had been tied up nice, but just so that you could see some way out of it, some just stop so abruptly. I like a programme and a film a little bit tidier [laugh] I think it's because women have little tidy minds and want to know [laugh]. (Audrey)

> Erm . . . I'm one of those terribly uneducated people that can't do with sad endings, or endings left in mid-air . . . I want everything nicely tied up in little pink bows, all at the end with everything sweet and happy. (Edna)

What is interesting about these remarkably similar responses from older women to the question of endings are the different reasons given – one based on gender and the other on education.

Many of the women in this group had a very high level of involvement in and commitment to one or more long-running serials (*Dallas, Dynasty, Falcon Crest*) and soap operas (*Emmerdale Farm, Coronation Street, Brookside, Sons and Daughters*), to the extent that they would not miss an episode, most recording it on the VCR if necessary. For these women viewing these serials was an inescapable part of their daily and weekly routine. Like reading habits and preferences, their liking for specific soap operas had been established in early life.

> I've been watching *Coronation Street* for 20 years. I've grown up with the characters, I mean, I was a little girl when I started watching it, and I've grown up with these particular people who are part of me. I don't sit and think about them all day long, but they are part of my life. (Susan)

> I've always kept up to *Emmerdale Farm* . . . and I'm right happy for Pat because she's pregnant . . . I love stuff like that . . . 'ooh, she's pregnant' . . . and Michael thinks I'm silly, but I get right into it like that, you know . . . it's as if . . . it's like a mate. (Cathy)

Susan and Cathy had a very strong commitment to *Coronation Street* and *Emmerdale Farm* respectively, feeling as if they actually lived with the characters. This echoes the nature of Rene's involvement with *Coronation Street*.

> *Coronation Street*, I mean, I sit down and watch that . . . after or before we've eaten . . . we work our way round it.

What did you think about Ken and Deirdre?[1]

> Oh no. I didn't agree with the outcome of that. I think they should have split up because it's turning out now as the story line's going along, he's fancying his secretary . . . it's not coming to anything . . . but he's a bloody liar. Yes, I was very cross with him . . . he should have said . . . yes, he did fancy her, let's face it, there are two of us . . . he's not being completely honest with her. I haven't liked that particularly. But even at the time, even when she married Ken Barlow, I thought, well, they're not alike. This marriage . . . you know, if it were somebody living on our street that we'd known for a long time we'd think, oh God, no, I don't give them long. (Rene)

Rene first of all indicates her pleasure in regularly sitting down and watching *Coronation Street*. Her response to the question about Ken and Deirdre has interesting 'slippages' between her recognition of 'the story line' and her exasperation with the character, as if he was someone she knew or who was 'living in our street'. This is less evidence of a confusion between fiction and reality than of her very close involvement with the plots and characters.

Susan talked nostalgically about the setting of *Coronation Street*:

> It reminds me of where I used to live when I was a child in that type of area, it was all like that, back to back little houses, it's very real. (Susan)

I asked her if she thought *Coronation Street* still represented reality.

> Oh yes, it is very real still. Because that's how most people's lives are – very boring, drudgery and dull, it's a bit depressing to watch because it's the truth. (Susan)

For Susan the 'realism' is more to do with the familiarity and predictability of the problems and worries of the characters, aided by the continuity and open-endedness of the genre, rather than the setting. 'Realism' was often invoked as an important criterion for enjoyment of the serials.

There was a marked difference in the responses to the American long-running serials, and often direct comparisons were made.

> I mean, *EastEnders* and *Coronation Street* are really down to earth, aren't they? You can imagine yourself living that type of life, but you couldn't ever imagine yourself living the *Dallas* and the *Dynasty* . . . [laugh] I'm ashamed to say, I like the soaps, I like the fantasy really. (Kay)

Susan suggested that the characters in *Dallas*, which she watched faithfully, didn't behave like 'real people'.

> They're not real. People couldn't put up with the rubbish they put up with . . . erm . . . I mean, it's very difficult to say, because everybody's an individual . . . I mean, take that Pamela and Bobby, they both love each other so much, but nobody opens their mouths about it. I mean, if I was there, I mean, you know, 'listen here . . . I'm here, and I still love you and I want you as my husband . . . and that's it' . . . and, well, you've got to do that. But I suppose if people did come out and say things straight away how one would say it, there'd be no series . . . I suppose, otherwise *Coronation Street* wouldn't have carried on for hundreds of years. (Susan)

Sandra gave a more complex reading of *Dallas*, identifying what Ien Ang refers to as 'emotional realism' in the text (Ang 1985).

> I think *Dallas* is a bit more realistic in a glamorous way . . . I mean *Dallas* is a bit far-fetched because the women just stand around with fancy ball gowns on, but they are realistic in the way they sort of shout and scream at each other, and let their human emotions out. In *Emmerdale* he says he's off to see his fancy woman and she's there combing her hair in the mirror . . . like on *Dallas*, Sue Ellen would have tried to shoot him . . . *Dallas* is more real in emotional ways. (Sandra)

How characters behave in certain situations, measured by what the women themselves thought they would do in similar circum-stances, is crucial to the credibility of the soap operas, but not necessarily to their enjoyment. I asked Janet if she thought that the American serials she watched were like real life.

Oh definitely not, no . . . oh no, definitely . . . unless it's like that in America . . . I've no idea, but it's definitely not like it is here is it? . . . well my life . . . I don't know about yours, but mine isn't, oh no, it's too silly, really, same with them all, but I suppose it's like that if you're rich, I don't know.

Do you ever get cross with it because it's too far-fetched?

No. I don't think I do, you know. Sometimes I laugh at her in, what's its name, *Falcon Crest* . . . the daughter . . . you know, I find her amusing sometimes, but no . . . I don't think so, because I think you get really into it and you don't care do you? Like all this swopping about with bringing Miss Ellie back, you know . . . I think, do they think we're stupid? . . . I think that is absolutely ridiculous, but you sort of ignore it all, it takes you away for an hour doesn't it? You get that involved . . . for all you think it's far-fetched, like I'm sat there, you know, crying when they're burying Fallon, and I know that she's not dead . . . because you've read it in the papers. (Janet)

Here the powerful elements of story in which she becomes involved are strong enough to maintain suspension of disbelief, even to the extent of being able to cope with changes of actor playing the same character. However, she does express her feelings about the producers in making these changes, and what they think about her and other members of the audience. She compared soap operas with other forms of television programme:

There's no star really in soap operas, they're all there for the same amount of time, there's no one person that holds it up whereas, a lot of the serials, there's a star and it's all about that one person. But in soap operas, well I don't sort of follow one person more than anybody else really. (Janet)

Involvement would seem to be a combination of story-involvement and character identification. The large number of characters in soap opera, in contrast to other forms of popular television drama, discourages identification with a single character and, together with its multiple story-lines results in what Robert Allen has referred to as a 'diffusion of interest and identification' (Allen 1985: 94). However, it would seem that knowledge of the characters themselves and their personalities was a crucial part of involvement in the serials. Janet told me that she liked the characters:

> Yes, I think that's what it is with me . . . for all I think you're supposed not to like JR, I think you're forced to like him in a lot of ways. I think you get involved with the characters.

What about Alexis?

> I think she's great. I think you're supposed to hate her aren't you, but she puts the part over so well . . . really she does . . . she puts it over so well that you're forced to like her . . . yes, I like her. I think she's something that I think . . . oh, I'd like to be . . . she's so strong-willed and I'm not, and I think . . . it must be nice to be so sure of yourself . . . you know, to be like her, she sort of, you know, takes over, doesn't she? And she's so confident, it must be nice to be like that. (Janet)

Other strong female characters were seen as worthy of emulation; Brenda watched *Sons and Daughters* regularly and told me which characters she liked in the programme.

> I like Beryl, she's a home-loving person . . . I like Barbara too, she's a strong, dominating person . . . not too dominating, but she's not the sort of person to be put on. I tend to think I'd like to be a bit more like that. I like her because compared with some of the others, they've always got that 'softy' talk, you know, some of the women on telly, haven't they? (Brenda)

In their study of soap opera viewers, Seiter *et al.*[2] note that many of their female respondents expressed admiration and affection for the 'villainess' or strong female characters in soap operas. Likewise, Janet admires Alexis and desires to have some of her character traits. She spoke further about the female characters in *Dynasty*.

> I know Crystal's very placid isn't she? . . . but she's strong in her own way . . . and, there again, if you said who do you like best in her and Alexis, I would say Crystal, but yet again, there's that admiration for her . . . I think some of the things she does are horrible, but, I don't know, you can't help but admire her because she's so strong-willed. But, say Crystal and her were having an argument, I'd want Crystal to win . . .

that type of thing . . . if my husband heard me now he'd think I'm crackers [laugh]. (Janet)

Janet expresses her pleasurable, almost illicit, involvement in the 'world' of the serial and the range of female identities she can take up when watching the serial. This enjoyment extends to reports in the press about future developments of the serial, her own knowledge of the characters, built up over years of watching, and the way in which Crystal and Alexis interact in the narrative.

Rene, however, compares *Dynasty* with *Dallas*:

Dynasty just reminds me of a comic strip, as if they've taken characters, you know, like *Superman*, out of a comic strip and they've put them as human beings on the screen, to me it's no credibility at all. Now I'm willing to believe that there is some credibility in *Dallas*. I've never been to Texas but I think skulduggery business-wise between the oil tycoons . . . I'm tempted to think that could well go on and that's why I watched it for so long. (Rene)

Although she begins with a discussion of the formal properties of *Dynasty*, what makes *Dallas* more credible for her is the fact that it relates more to a possible 'real life', not because it draws on slightly different modes of representation. However, Rene did express a liking for elements of the setting of *Dynasty*, as did Kay.

I don't really watch it for the story line . . . I just love to see the beautiful clothes and the beautiful houses, not really for the story at all. (Kay)

Dynasty I've never liked. The plots are very thin. I like the dresses, that's a silly thing to watch for . . . some of the dresses that Crystal wears I think are absolutely beautiful . . . that's why I like *Hart to Hart*, because of the gowns and the outfits that Stephanie Powers wears . . . they're gorgeous aren't they? (Rene)

Many of Ien Ang's respondents spoke of their pleasure in the clothes and the settings of *Dallas* interiors, and she suggests that their awareness of glamorous *mise-en-scène* indicates that her viewers are well aware that they are watching a fictional world and are not accepting the illusion of reality directly as constructed in the text (Ang 1985: 47). This is undoubtedly the case for Kay.

> I think I watch *Dallas* and *Dynasty* because they are so over the top and I probably find them very amusing. I've got a tremendous sense of humour and always want to laugh . . . you know . . . this can't be so . . . you've got to be joking . . . never a hair out of place, you know. (Kay)

The women who were most committed to American long-running serials, described them as presenting a world of fantasy.

> *Dallas* is more 'high-falutin', I mean, *Coronation Street*, you can imagine it happening in your own life, but you can't on *Dallas*. (Julie)

> Money's no object, they don't think 'Oh God, the gas bill's coming next week' or anything like that . . . I suppose it's a fantasy world really, you'd like to think you'll one day not have to worry about the next bill that's coming in . . . you know. (Megan)

> I think it's because it's just . . . you look at these big houses and everything and . . . going around in these flash cars, I mean, it just takes you away from everyday life . . . you're in sort of make-believe. (Janet)

This element of the American product did not appeal to all as fantasy.

> No, I don't like them at all, they make me . . . I can't describe how it makes me feel. All that money and really nice clothes, and they're all beautiful . . . it doesn't make me angry . . . I suppose it makes me sick. They've just got it all . . . and nobody works. It makes me sick. (Christine)

Susan believed that soap operas were produced for and appealed to women. She was asked why she thought that.

> Well, it's because, as much as women know it's a fantasy world, men know it's a total load of rubbish. I mean, it is, but men know it. They know that people just don't live the way these particular people are portrayed, it's impossible. It's rubbish for men, fantasy for women, all the soap operas.

Why do you think fantasy is important for women?

Erm . . . it takes . . . it takes away all the bills and the every-day living away, I mean, everyday living is wonderful by half, but occasionally, you do just want to get away from it all. You can't jump on a jet and go on holiday, so you'll go to another country and watch how they're supposed to live.

Do you think men need fantasy?

They need fantasy in a different way, erm, detectives and wars, that's their fantasy world, a tough, strong world . . . not the sloppy, who's fallen in love with whom, who's killed JR and . . . it's rubbish. That's their escape, science fiction is their fantasy. (Susan)

Did Janet think that men needed make-believe?

Well, if my husband's anything to go by, space, yes . . . but they don't . . . I don't think men are as impressed by things like that . . . my husband isn't, you know, impressed by money and things . . . no . . . he likes his space and things like that. (Janet)

She felt that it was the substance of *Dallas* and *Dynasty* which would not appeal to her husband; the substance was, as far as she was concerned, 'family life'.

I don't think I'm interested in their oil wells, I think it's the families that I like it for . . . to think . . . oh, you know, his daughter's dead, you know and oh . . . Crystal's having . . . yes, I think it's the families, for all it's big and splendid, you can still see family life in it . . . you get really . . . you feel for . . . I think it is the family life that draws you to it, it's not . . . I'm not interested in them having oil wells and good-ness knows what, it is family life. (Janet)

For Janet, like Sandra above, *Dallas* and *Dynasty* have what Ien Ang has identified as 'emotional realism', which overrides the 'external unrealism' (Ang 1985: 47) which she herself described. Julie also felt that soap operas were for women.

I think a lot of story lines in soap operas are very very weak and I think a man needs something to keep his interest more than a woman. That makes a man sound more intelligent, but that's not what I mean. Well, my husband, it's got to be something worth watching before he'll sit down and actually watch it. He won't just watch anything – I'll watch anything. Not with interest, not sit down and really watch it, but I'd watch anything. Andrew wouldn't, he'd rather get up and do something. If it's on, if *Coronation Street*'s on he'll watch it, he hates *Crossroads*, he hates *Brookside*, I don't know why because that's the best on. He says he doesn't like them, but then if he misses them he'll say 'What happened to so and so' . . . but even then I think, he thinks it's unmanly to watch them, I think so anyway. (Julie)

Janet had similar suspicions.

Well, men just aren't interested in that sort of thing are they, and I think that's probably why, you know . . . I think . . . and then I think, 'Well would my husband admit it if he did like it?' (Janet)

Julie's point that typical story lines were weak and therefore insufficient to hold a man's interest relates to the narrative organization of much soap opera: very little 'action', no high drama, and multiple plot lines. As she observed,

You can watch a soap opera for six weeks and you think, well, nothing's happened, and then it suddenly gets interesting. (Julie)

The willingness of soap opera followers to bear with their favourite, even when nothing seems to be happening, is an important feature of soap viewing (Brunsdon 1984: 86).

Whether their partners would actually admit to enjoying soap operas is another and quite separate point. David Morley notes in his study, *Family Television*, that the men he spoke to were reluctant to 'admit' that they enjoyed fiction, claiming rather that they preferred factual television programmes (Morley 1986: 162). Clearly many men do watch and enjoy fiction in different forms, but the fact that they feel they cannot admit to taking pleasure in what is obviously a women's genre is significant in itself. Interestingly, many of these women do not really know what their partners feel about the soaps.

The women took great pleasure in soap operas and the American long-running serials, but spoke about them in negative terms, such as 'rubbish', 'soppy', 'fantasy' and 'make-believe', comparing them unfavourably in some cases with their husband's fantasy genres. A hard, tough and real world is what men disappear into, rather than into the world of emotion and glamour.

Emotion and glamour were an important attraction of the mini-series which many of the women in this group watched. Those who watched had usually read the book and so were quite often very critical of the adaptation. These criticisms were usually about the selective nature of the adaptation, although this was recognized as inevitable.

> They miss a lot of the story out . . . on TV they're jumping all over the place from year to year . . . in a book you do get a full picture of it all. I mean, they have to do it otherwise it would go on for months. (Susan)

Many of these mini-series are family sagas with a strong female central character whose fortunes are followed throughout the book and, in some cases, become part of a series with a generational development of female characters.[3] The combination of a strong female central character, a powerful story focusing on the vicissitudes of family life, as well as setting and costumes combined to form a glamorous *mise-en-scène*, produces a text with very strong appeal to the women in this group.

In this group there is a distinct preference for fiction over nonfiction. Susan's comment about documentary programmes was typical:

> They're telling the truth, and the truth to anybody is really pretty depressing . . . it's like, I don't want to know most of the time, I don't want to know. I mean I do know, but I don't like it to be shoved at me every five seconds. I need the relief of these stupid things, absolutely. (Susan)

There was also a consensus about the news. Many of the women watched the national news, usually with their male partners, but several said they preferred watching and listening to local news on television and radio.

> I listen to Radio Aire, I like that. And I do like *Calendar* [local ITV news], because, there again, you recognize places, and things like that, I do tend to watch that. (Janet)

The liking for local news was related to familiarity with the places and events reported, events which are, in national terms, incidental.

Film

The importance of films with a 'good story' featuring distinctive characters came through very strongly in this group, whatever the genre. Lynne compared her preferences with those of her family.

> I'm in the minority as to what I like. Because Laura, the eldest girl, she's more into '*Star Wars*-type' films and my husband is as well – he's a big kid at heart when it comes to things like that – and I sort of, I suppose, typical woman, you know . . . love story thing, or something with a bit of 'go' in it . . . I like more of a story than a visual impact, but they don't, they like James Bond and everything . . . erm . . . whereas I'd rather have a story. (Lynne)

Her husband's preferences she saw in terms of action.

> Oh, the science fiction . . . action adventure . . . he's a real . . . you know, sort of into the Errol Flynn, swashbuckling, out with the swords, you know, he's not exactly our era is he? But you know, there's nobody . . . he's more in that field. He'd rather see action than story. He likes to see somebody physically acting, like *Rocky* films, he thought they were good and things like that . . . I didn't think they were bad, but, you know, he likes things with action and to see people moving, whereas . . . I can watch a film where people, if it was a good film about two people just sitting talking, I could watch it, where Craig wouldn't, you know. (Lynne)

For Lynne the slow and gradual unfolding of a story was an essential part of the pleasure, whereas her husband would sacrifice this for visual impact and action. I had a discussion with Kay about the difference between her and her partner's preferences.

> I don't think there are many men that really like love stories . . . too sloppy for men on the whole.

> *Mmm . . . why don't women like things like spy films and those sorts of things?*

Basically, I think it's because we're not interested in the first place to find out what it's all about . . . you've got to listen to the dialogue constantly to find out who's doing what and why . . . I think really women are more for visual . . . for entertainment, you know . . . not all women, but I know a lot of women are like that . . . most women like *Dallas* and *Dynasty*, don't they? Men don't . . . the glamour side, dialogue is secondary really.

Except when it's a love story; the dialogue then becomes quite important doesn't it?

Yes, it does, yes, it's softer though, somehow, isn't it? It probably pulls on your heart strings a bit, I don't know . . . I think you can associate with that . . . I've never been a spy – do you know any spies?

No. But most men don't know any spies either.

Yes, but underneath . . . there's a spy trying to get out . . . [laugh]. I don't know . . . it's like the cowboy, or the war film. I mean every man wants to be a hero . . . would love to be a hero.

And women don't want to be heroes, or heroines?

No, I think most women want to be . . . they don't want to *be* a hero, they want to *know* the hero [laugh]. (Kay)

I have quoted our discussion at some length because Kay suggests that men and women engage with particular kinds of fiction, and have distinct desires which certain fictions gratify. Women, she implies, are able to associate with the emotional and the world of human relationships, whereas men can associate with a world of which they have no direct knowledge. Underlying Kay's talk is the opposition private and female versus public and male. The limit of female desire in terms of the public, non-domestic world, is to 'know the hero', not to engage fully in this world as hero.

The women who watched movies together in the afternoon, noted in Table 2 of the previous chapter, typically selected romance, melodrama and the family saga for these viewing sessions, which could be freely enjoyed without male disapproval. Having a good cry was an indulgence which some of the women sought, but preferably on their own or with other women. Julie watched love stories and 'weepy' ones with her mother and some friends. They had recently watched *Who Will Love My Children?* and I asked her what the film was about.

> It's about a lady, she's got ten children, she's got cancer and she knows she's dying and she gets a home for all her children, and she lets them go to this home while she's still living and she gets them all in a family. Well, not many men'd want to sit through that. Same as that *Last Snows of Spring*, you know, with the children. It's morbid really to watch. (Julie)

They had all sat and cried whilst watching this movie. Julie and Betty, both mothers of small children, said that these were the kinds of films which most affected them emotionally. Crucial to their narrative is the fact that the female protagonists invariably have ineffective spouses, usually alcoholics or womanizers. The films present a world of mothers and children, telling stories about the loss of children or the loss of a mother. Julie felt that this 'reflected' what would happen in real life.

> I think if anything like that happens the woman has to cope with it . . . so I think a woman can relate to that situation more than a man. (Julie)

Specially recommended by *Woman's Own* magazine, *Who Will Love My Children?* was a very popular film with this group, especially for joint female viewing, and was considered to be of no potential interest to their male partners. Cathy was an avid reader of romantic fiction and this was also her preferred genre of movies. She could identify her kind of film very quickly from the 'blurb' on the back of the video package.

> Well, when you get a video you can read what it's all about on the back, but I don't know, I can tell right easily. I can pick one up and just read a couple of lines . . . I really know what I'm going for. (Cathy)

She explained to me why she 'wasn't interested' in her husband's preferred genres (war, horror, action adventure):

> I don't know, I just can't get into it, you know, guns and that . . . I don't know what it is, I don't know why I don't like 'em . . . but I don't. I can't get into the story as much as I can get into the other things . . . probably because I'm not

interested . . . I really like a romance . . . and I think I'm
going to like it, so I'll sit and watch it and I'm more interested
in it, but not other stuff. (Cathy)

Like Kay, Cathy explains that she is not interested in the substance
of the male genres and has no expectation of enjoyment, therefore
she does not become involved in the narrative. Her anticipation
of pleasure in romance and her ability to recognize 'her' genres
from the briefest outline, is symptomatic of her selective story
competence.

War films were enjoyed by many of the men but this was not
always the case, particularly if the movie did not conform to
traditional genre conventions. On a rare occasion, Audrey had
selected *The Deer Hunter* from the video library for Sunday evening viewing with her son and her husband, a lover of war films.
She told me that her husband had not enjoyed it and I asked her
if she knew why.

Well [pause] I think he, possibly because, he said, they were
all nutters. My husband's the type that if people are different
from him – he's a bit dogmatic – if they're different from him,
they don't exist, sort of thing . . . but people are different
[laugh] . . . and I'm sure there must have been loads of
instances similar to that, they do exist and they are people and
everybody's different aren't they? And probably the film itself
upset him because it was slow to start with, and then it was
on a cause that he doesn't identify with at all.

What did you think of it?

Well, I enjoyed it. They were all so lost weren't they? I mean,
he didn't enjoy it. It wasn't straightforward enough, you
know . . . I think he was cross at the beginning. It floundered
a bit at the beginning and he wanted to be getting on with it
[laugh]. (Audrey)

For Audrey's husband, *The Deer Hunter* did not conform to expectations of the genre. For Audrey, however, although she too
found the film difficult to 'get into', she did become emotionally
involved in the story and the characters, finding both more 'true
to life' than other war films.

In general the women in this group expressed their dislike of
horror movies, often in contrast to their male partners. However,

Susan, as we saw in the previous chapter, took great pleasure in watching this genre, examples of which she hired from the video library and watched when alone, as her partner positively disliked them. I asked her if she liked all horror movies.

Most of them, yes. I mean, I don't like disgusting bloodthirsty ones. I do like 'ghosty' spooky things. I really frighten myself to death, I do [laugh]. (Susan)

Betty's husband would often hire horror movies and sometimes she would sit and watch them with him.

I think when it's a horror film I prefer something like *The Exorcist* rather than someone chopping people's heads off with an axe – I'm not into that sort of thing, but the more spooky ones – you know, I think 'I'm not going to watch this' and you're there, peeping through your hands. I prefer to go for something more like that. (Betty)

Julie's baby-sitters often hired gory horror movies and she had watched one or two 'out of curiosity'. Did they frighten her?

No. Rather than horror, I'd rather watch one of these suspense films. Not gory, you know, the other sort of horror. Not horror, *Frankenstein* horror – it could happen. (Julie)

The horror films the women preferred had somehow to convince them that this sort of thing 'could happen', as Susan explained in her comments on *The Evil Dead*, a then recent and notorious 'splatter' movie.[4]

I didn't like that at all. Now John [husband] chose that for me . . . I watched it and I actually turned that off. I didn't like that at all, it was all that horrible gore. Now I don't like that sort of film. I think that's rubbish. I like to be frightened not sickened. And it's not possible, not possible. People coming back from below and starting hammering on . . . oh, a joke. (Susan)

She then went on to give an example of the kind of horror film she really enjoyed.

Now, *Amityville Horror*, the first one was a bit boring, but *Amityville Horror II* is excellent. Well I think it is because it's spiritual and supernatural . . . that's the horror bit I like, the supernatural. When you're not quite too sure . . . when they smell a smell you think [sniff], yes, that's possible because . . . I believe in things like that. (Susan)

Horror movies must be rooted in what are 'believable' situations for the women and all three show a preference for a coherent story, with situational suspense preferred to the special effects of the 'splatter' movies. Susan was asked if she knew more or less how the films were going to end.

Oh yes [laugh], oh yes, exactly [laughter] and how . . . that's part of the excitement of it all. (Susan)

As we have seen previously, two of the older women were quite clear about the importance of neatly resolved endings. For those who read romantic fiction, a happy ending was expected. But Julie had reservations about this.

I think a romantic book has got to have a happy ending really, hasn't it? A love story's a love story. I mean, usually it just ends with them getting married. I mean, if they went on for five years it might not be so happy, but that's how love stories end, with them getting together. So really a love story ends at the beginning, doesn't it?

Do you expect happy endings from other things?

Not always. I mean with Mills and Boon you know she's going to end up with the man she hated in the beginning, it's laid on . . . but, no if they're being realistic they don't always end happily. But a lot of the series on TV, anyway, well, they finish at such a pitch that they know they can come back. (Julie)

The open-ended nature of many series on television had been recognized by Julie; Susan and Cathy told me about soap opera narrative:

When you're watching it on Monday, erm, the things they say and the actions we know what's going to really . . . or think we know what's going to happen on Wednesday, and it does [laugh] . . . and from Wednesday we know what's going to happen the following Monday. But you have to watch it, just to make sure you're right. There's not a lot of surprises in there. (Susan)

Wednesday's tries to keep you in the lurch for something to happen on Monday . . . it's usually the big . . . (Cathy)

Cathy spoke about her knowledge of story and action, rather than narrative structure, but she recognized the 'cliff-hanger' ending which kept her wanting to watch.[5]

Oh yes, I'm always saying I know how it's going to turn out . . . I'll cheat though, I look in *TV Times* and see what's happening for each . . . but there again, when it's on like, Lynne last week were going with that Andy, and I said, 'oh, she'll end up going with him' and she did . . . I think . . . I've watched it for that long I can tell what's going to happen, I can tell what they're going to do . . . I mean sometimes I don't know, because sometimes they put it in the paper, and that spoils it, you know, you know what's going to happen, but I still watch it, like . . . and they always end so good one day that you've got to watch it next day to see what happens. (Cathy)

Cathy said that what she liked about *Emmerdale Farm* was the fact that it never stopped, it just goes on and on.

One story ends, but there's always another one, there's probably about three stories going on at once, so as one sort of . . . as the peak of one story's waning away, another one's coming up. (Cathy)

We can see here that knowledge of narrative structure is there for preferred genres and that this competence brings with it expectations and pleasures, particularly in the soap opera and romance.

GROUP B: LATER SCHOOL LEAVERS AND GRADUATES

Reading

Caroline, and to a lesser extent Hilary, were both resistant to television, claiming not to like it very much, but they both said that they read 'extensively'.

Oh, I read very extensively, I've been reading a lot of contemporary novels this year, I've been reading some literary criticism, various essays erm . . . I read quite a lot of poetry, erm . . . those are the main areas at the moment. (Caroline)

Oh, well, I read the newspapers for book reviews, I tend to follow things like the Booker Prize. I also, I'm in with a group of women who exchange books that they buy, so we tend to cross-recommend books; the sort of thing like *Hotel du Lac*, that sort of thing. It's a sort of social activity in a way, although I've always read. Occasionally I read classics again as well. I very, very rarely read poetry. I always read novels, or occasionally things to do with work, journals. (Hilary)

They both spoke of their reading pleasures in relation to their own lives:

It is relaxing because it takes you outside . . . I'm not going to use the word 'escapist' . . . it takes you outside of the environment in which you live, and of necessity, well not of necessity, just the way it's worked out . . . my environment as a child and even my environment now as an adult running a family is very restricting . . . it's like the armchair traveller, reading, it's the next best thing to doing it yourself . . . I have very limited contact with people that I can talk to on an intellectual basis, I'm also quite tired so it's hard work to read a philosophical treatise, or a Shakespeare play, or a poem, you don't sit down and relax with something like that, it's a bit too mind bending. I can't read absolute trash of the Georgette Heyer, or whatever the modern equivalent would be. There's this middle market which does make you think, but it isn't so exhausting that when you're tired you can't get through more than two and a half pages without falling asleep . . . it pushes you forward, it's well written, because, after all, I was trained. (Hilary)

I asked her if the fictional worlds she entered were quite similar to her own.

Well, I wouldn't say, the sort of characters, for instance, in Anita Brookner . . . I suppose it's a middle-class world, her world. I didn't like *The Bone People*, that was ghastly . . . it was so appalling and very slow, I couldn't get into that. I think they are aimed at a specific, when I come to think about it, they are a little bit aimed at . . . I've never really thought about it . . . aren't they? . . . sort of . . . when you come to think about it, like Margaret Drabble . . . I mean she's writing for a specific sort of graduate. (Hilary)

In spite of her comment about the books she read having to be 'well written', it would seem that setting and story are crucial to her enjoyment and offered her compensation for what she felt was a very 'circumscribed' environment.

so you're meeting people through the book that are rather like-minded people, who you would be talking to if your environment wasn't circumscribed . . . that may be what it is . . . I think all my books are aimed at the glossy middle-class graduate market [laugh]. (Hilary)

Caroline's response indicated the compensatory aspect of reading pleasure, but in terms of formalistic qualities, not those of setting and story. She introduced this topic in the context of an account of the dissatisfactions in her life.

I have a desire for some kind of *order*, or some kind of harmony in things at all kinds of levels. And I see that in all sorts of ways in my own life. I feel that at a gross domestic level, I'm always battling for some kind of order, some sort of resolution of Lego with Lego, rather than Lego with marbles. Ironing ironed and garden relatively free from weeds . . . and at a higher level than that there is something about the need as a family for our potential conflicts of interest to be harmoniously arranged, instead of janglingly at odds, and then, in – yes, I can see that kind of progression going right up through my thinking about things, wishing that the children, for instance, in the evening were not watching 'He-man' which is a jangling product of a culture which is in many respects extremely alien to them . . . but there is somewhere a current running through all this that is not actually about a better age, a previous age that is better, but it is about some sort of search for some sort of harmony, and wishing there were more . . . you know . . . and seeing that there isn't.

Where does your reading fit into this?

Well it does. I think that is maybe why I like essays because there is a resolution. I mean, they are not trying to impose a harmony, but there you see a kind of intellectual order, you see clear thinking and some kind of resolution, and it is compact and contained. Also I like reading poems because, although poems are descriptive of any number of emotions and so on, they are complete in themselves and the parts work harmoniously to say whatever it is going to say. (Caroline)

She found her life was full enough of conflict and discord without watching different forms of conflict and violence on television or at the cinema. These two women used their reading as a form of resistance. For Hilary it was to compensate for the limitations of her traditionally feminine role. For Caroline, it provided a brief respite from day-to-day life, which is spent

trying endlessly to find a balance between domestic and maternal responsibilities and the demands of work which feels from time to time to be very considerable . . . and, you know, also dealing with James [partner] and his problems with the practice . . . all around us we're in some kind of minefield all the time. (Caroline)

Other women in this group used different kinds of books depending on their energy level. Beth would pick up an Agatha Christie novel if she was tired, but said she also read Angela Carter, Timothy Mo, J. G. Farrell, and that she read Jane Austen once a year. Much of her reading was associated with her work, which occupied most of her time and thought. Jenny, who had recently given up an Open University degree course, was enjoying her relative freedom to read.

I've been reading some trashy who-dunnits . . . I'll more or less go and pick out authors, or go by the reviews on the back cover, pick them up . . . devour them, about ten a week . . . they've got to be pretty bad for me to put them down . . . if I'm into a good book, I'll be reading while I'm cooking, erm . . . gaps in between anything, while they're eating, before I wash up, erm . . . constant, and then curl up and carry on with it when I think I've finished for the evening. (Jenny)

Clare often felt exhausted in the evening and was reading Barbara Taylor Bradford's *Hold the Dream* at the time of the interview.

It's quite a long novel but it's not taxing . . . I can read quite a lot of it before I fall asleep. I read *A Woman of Substance*. I certainly read it before it was on television . . . I think possibly

I saw it in a bookshop, erm . . . and I thought, you know, it's a sort of family saga. I thought I would find it interesting. (Clare)

Like Hilary, her reading could not be 'taxing' as she was usually very tired when free to read, but also she was keen to point out that her choice had not been motivated by the television adaptation of the novel. Shirley told me about her reading, which had changed drastically since she had children.

I suppose I might get hold of the Booker McConnel prize . . . I don't want to be seen as a person who reads four or five fiction books a year and therefore buys the most obvious ones, but that's often the way it is at the moment. (Shirley)

All the women I have discussed so far in this group expressed their wish to read more for pleasure and all were university educated. However, the books that they did read tended to be those contemporary novels associated with literary prizes and which received wide coverage in the press, radio and television. As Shirley said, they appeared to be the most 'obvious' books to choose to read.

Television

Just as reading was important to many of the women in this group, so television's literary adaptations acquired a status not afforded to many other forms of programming. I asked Maureen if she watched serials.

It all depends really, if it's based on a good book, we would watch it, like D. H. Lawrence, or something like that. (Maureen)

Hilary spoke about the formal elements of one of her current favourite programmes, *Paradise Postponed*, a series adapted from the novel by John Mortimer, in a positive way.

Yes, we like the dialogue. It is also . . . the music is very nice and it's visually very attractive. Yes, I think I would say that, the music is much better than you normally get. (Hilary)

This woman and her family had become, to use her term, 'hooked' on both *Paradise Postponed* and *First Among Equals*, but

she pointed out that she had read both the books before watching
the serials. This could account for the fact that she and other
members of her family took pleasure in how the adaptation had
been done.

> What we actually like is some of the wit and the cleverness in
> the exchanges and some of the speeches that the old man has.
> And also, there's anticipation because three of us have read the
> book, so we're watching what's going to come next and we've
> got involved with the characters as it's gone on. I think it was
> quite slow starting, but my husband likes that as well. (Hilary)

She compares *First Among Equals* with *Paradise Postponed*, but
again refers to the structure of its verbal form:

> I suspect storywise *First Among Equals* is more compelling. I
> felt with *First Among Equals*, when I read the book, it's very
> piecemeal. It's as if he wrote it on the back of envelopes, lots
> of exciting little incidents, that somehow hang together as a
> story, so dramatically it's probably more effective. It has all
> these high drama bits. (Hilary)

First Among Equals and *Paradise Postponed* could not be described
as 'literary' – indeed, Hilary was quick to point out that she
found *First Among Equals* when stranded in a Scottish hotel with
nothing to read; but the fact that they were television adaptations
from novels seemed to justify her interest in them. She referred
to *Paradise Postponed* as 'quite clever', claiming that she didn't like
historical serials or soap operas.

> Although *Paradise Postponed* is slightly like a soap opera, it's a
> rather classy soap opera. (Hilary)

She did not go into any detail about other television programmes
that she herself watched, speaking about her taste more generally
for 'quality' plays and films.

Mary was the only woman in this group who regularly
watched a soap opera with her family. Some of the women
were rather antagonistic towards this genre. Caroline spoke of
television programmes like *Dallas* which, whilst having 'powerful
elements of story', were lacking in certain significant qualities.

> A lot of my argument about the television is to do with the
> paucity of human motive which is shown in a lot of the stuff

that my daughter will watch . . . I sometimes think, these
people are shown as motivated by greed, lust, envy and the
finer kind of gradations of why people behave as they do are
hardly ever touched on . . . and as a kind of image, you know,
of how life is, this is very thin indeed, but presented with a
kind of wham, bam . . . there's not so much attention to other
kinds of detail (Caroline)

Clare told me that she didn't watch soap operas. I asked her if
she positively resisted watching them.

Er . . . [long pause] . . . it's hard to say, I think . . . I think
it possibly is a resisting. I feel they might take over, because
most of them are on a couple of times a week and always
having to watch that. I know I do it with *The Archers*, but it
is on twice, and I'm always doing other things and it fits in
with, you know, things that I'm doing at that particular time.
(Clare)

The other young woman at home with children in this group
also regularly listened to *The Archers*, a daily radio soap, again,
because it fitted into her daily schedule, but she did not watch
any of the television soap operas. Clare had earlier told me that
she was very interested in human relationships and people and I
pointed out to her that this was the substance of the genre.

Yes. I've just seen the illogicality of that . . . I think it's the
constant thing. Every week, Tuesday and Thursday, Monday
and Wednesday, or whatever. I feel that you become enmeshed
in them . . . having said that I do watch *Howards Way*, which
is perhaps classed as a soap, but that's only for thirteen weeks
or whatever, you see, that's more of a serial, and I know
there'll be an end to it. I think the thing with the soap opera
is the escapism, going along with what I was saying about it
taking over. Some people seem to get so involved, they're
almost living the lives of the characters and it's so important
waiting for Tuesday night to see what's going to happen next,
and I'd rather be living my own life. I don't want to spend
all my time just living for half an hour in the evening. (Clare)

Becoming 'enmeshed' in a long-running serial and its alleged
escapism is what Clare is resisting here, with attendant fears of
addiction. These fears, also expressed by others in the group, are

responses to the very conditions which give pleasure to the
women in Group A. Maureen was highly critical of the American
soaps.

> I don't like American soap operas at all . . . they just feel like
> they're so false, not that I've been to America . . . all beautiful
> women never a hair out of place, you know, straight teeth,
> pearly white, just totally unrealistic to what I think it would
> be in America. I like things which are more down to earth
> and what appear to be more truthful. (Maureen)

As we have seen earlier, the phrase 'down to earth' is often used
to describe the social realism of British soap operas compared
with the kind of realism constructed in *Dallas* or *Dynasty*, which
is rooted in film melodrama. In Maureen's response there is some
suggestion of a belief that *Dallas* and *Dynasty* set out to represent
a 'reality' which she sees as 'America' and which she considers
is a false representation; her response is largely based on the
improbability of the characters. One of Taylor and Mullan's
respondents had, on visiting America, confirmed Maureen's
opinion: 'I was expecting to see all these beautiful women walking
round with really outrageous clothes wherever I went. But they
weren't. They were all fat' (Taylor and Mullan 1986: 24). All
these accounts assume a direct relationship between 'the world
out there', whether the East End of London or Dallas, and the
world of the fiction.

Films

Although there was a certain amount of shared preference claimed
between male and female, certain differences did emerge in this
group. Maureen, who claimed that she and her husband generally
agreed on what was a good film because of their shared standard
of education, said that they liked 'good films' which had 'good
producers and good directors'. I asked her what kind of films she
liked best.

> Love stories, but mainly the old ones, I prefer the old black
> and white ones when I can have a good cry . . . if they've got
> a nice story to them, I watch them.

Would you say that love stories are good films?

I wouldn't say they were good, well-produced films no. I think it's basically the theme of what's running through. I can't really say I've seen a very well produced weepy love story . . . as in something like more of your epic films, something like that. It's totally different, but I think it's a totally different audience. (Maureen)

Here she claims that 'women's films' do not qualify for the label 'good' because they are not well produced, but also there is some elision of production value and 'theme'. According to Maureen, the actual content of the romantic love story itself automatically excludes the film from being seen as a 'quality' product. For this woman the differences between what men and women like were obvious.

Obviously a man's not going to like a soppy love story, really . . . er . . . and not all women are going to like films with a lot of violence. (Maureen)

Mary described how she identified with the films she enjoyed:

I can identify with the emotions in films, emotions that I've come across, or certain situations perhaps. I actually go through the emotions and what is happening. Things you know about. (Mary)

The emotional world and the world of human relationships was an important source of enjoyment, particularly of films.

I watched the Sunday première last night, *The Love Match*, I enjoyed that, that is the sort of thing that I tend to like, you know, human relationships.

Does your husband like those as well?

[hesitation] . . . yes, he likes those as well, but there are also lots more things that he likes that I don't like . . . the horror things and science fiction that just doesn't . . . I'm interested in people . . . I think that's why I don't like horror films and science fiction, because I can't relate to it at all. (Clare)

A story must involve character development and exploration of human relationships, and its setting must be 'believable', unlike, according to Clare, science fiction.

and Colin says, well it's his form of escapism . . . you don't have to believe it can happen. But I like to believe that it could, I suppose, I like historical things as well, because that happened, it's interesting to see how people lived. (Clare)

Jenny and her partner watched movies together regularly, either from the video library, or from their own archive. As we saw in chapter 2, their tastes were similar in many respects, but there were certain differences. Jenny was asked what elements of a film she valued more than her husband.

I do like big stories, I suppose, like *Tess, Reds, Dr Zhivago* . . . they cover a wide period of time and a wide range of characters. And I do like romantic stuff if it's well done . . . I don't know . . . characters, good characters, a touch of romance, a touch of humour.

What are his reactions to your favourites?

Well . . . *Tess* drives him mad, but I'm sure Hardy drives a lot of people mad [laugh] . . . this self-destruction that goes on all the time . . . erm . . . I don't know. He doesn't make comments particularly, perhaps they are quite romantic films I like, aren't they? quite slushy . . . (Jenny)

I asked if the kinds of films her husband liked had a lot of characters, extended time-span, etc.

No . . . If it's caught you up sufficiently, I will get very involved with the story and very involved with the characters, in a way that Jim won't. We're exactly the same in our fiction as well, er . . . I can't . . . he's always been very much into science fiction, and the thing I can't get into when I read science fiction is that they've got peculiar names, that they aren't characters, that the world they're set in is of primary importance, and they're secondary. I like it the other way round, and I think probably the same is true of films. (Jenny)

We see here the gender differences in this household in terms of the valuing of the story and the characters as against techniques, effects or 'surface cleverness' of the film. Jenny's comparison with fiction is also interesting in that it reveals her need for involvement with identifiable characters and their motives, whereas this is not of primary importance for her husband.

SUMMARY

As if speaking for many of the women in the study, Barbara told me about one of her favourite films:

> Love Story . . . I've seen that about half a dozen times, I think it's just as good, no matter how many times you watch it – it can still make you cry. Men find them soppy, don't they? I think probably because they're frightened that they might actually feel some little bit of sympathy or feeling . . . men don't like to show their emotions very much do they? (Barbara)

Women from both groups suggested that not only did their partners keep their emotions close to their chests, but that they positively disliked films and programmes which foregrounded emotional life. Their ways of dealing with such texts when they did encounter them ranged from laughter and derision at their partner's emotional responses, to denial and suppression of their own emotions and feelings. The kinds of films and programmes which they liked were more likely to involve physical action than emotional interaction. In Group A we can see the strongest example of this gender division, although it is present right across the study, and while this might be confirmation of fairly predictable male and female genre preferences, what is more significant is the way in which the women themselves spoke about the different genres. Time and again they used derogatory terms to describe 'female' genres, terms not used in their descriptions of their partner's preferences. Using the women's own observations, we can see an emerging set of opposing descriptions of male and female genres respectively.

'Male' genres	'Female' genres
hard	soft
tough	soppy
real	fantasy
serious	silly
factual	fictional

We noted that women who had attained higher education tended to have similar tastes to their partners. Their descriptions threw up another set of oppositions which are not apportioned to specific genres but are expressions of a more general stress on 'culture'.

Positive evaluation	Negative evaluation
classics	popular
quality	trash
important	trivial
British	American

The women with most formal education tended to associate themselves and their partners with cultural products of positive value, distancing themselves from what they saw as 'low culture'. However, in households where tastes were not shared, positive descriptions were more likely to be used by women in relation to their male partner's preferences, and negative ones in relation to their own. Women with higher education tend to take up a position in relation to popular texts which is shared by their male partners, but not by the other women in the group. The example of soap opera preferences shows this most clearly. With only a few exceptions, the majority of men seemed to dislike or expressed their dislike for soap operas, particularly the American products. Almost all the 'educated' women shared this dislike, many making a point of distancing themselves from these programmes. Within the different household cultures, therefore, we can see dominant cultural values reflected in definitions of cultural products, and also a clustering of positive evaluations around male-preferred texts.

Education was a major factor in the different preferences expressed by the women. However, what all the women in the sample took pleasure in was a text which foregrounded personal relationships, believable characters and a strong story. These elements which constituted an enjoyable text featured throughout the sample, regardless of education, with women often comparing this taste with their partner's preference for action and 'effects'. It is useful to summarize these responses in terms of theme:

Male	Female
heroic	romantic
public	domestic
societal	familial
physical	emotional

Obviously the above divisions relate to traditional male and female genres, but it is important to bear in mind that these preferences cross traditional boundaries. Thus, if a war film dealt with the emotions of its characters a woman might become engaged in its fictional world, as we saw in the case of Audrey and *The Deer Hunter*. Similarly with the horror genre. Science fiction perhaps epitomizes a male genre where special effects dominate the product and where, in books, setting was more important than character. Rene said, speaking for several other women, 'It leaves me cold.' Being able to relate to characters and identify with the emotions and situations in which they found themselves was crucial to enjoyment. This need to identify with a text was common to all the women, but differed in degree. It can range from a matter of simple recognition of character-types or familiarity with their predicaments to a feeling of actually being one of the characters, as we saw in some accounts of the pleasures of soap opera.

It is worth examining this relationship to the text more closely as, once again, education becomes a strong determining factor. Those women in the sample who had a higher standard of education tended to distance themselves from texts, or certainly expressed a desire to do so. This emerged most clearly in discussions about soap operas and serials in general; these women feared 'addiction' and didn't like the idea of becoming 'hooked' on serials, especially on television. They also considered the term 'escape' to be pejorative when applied to reading or viewing and would not use it to describe their use of texts. It is this same group of women who hired movies from the video library and read the books on the Booker Prize short-list from a position founded on externally validated knowledge, in effect, from a position of control. This control of reader over text was enabled by a 'space' which had been created by public critical discourse, allowing the reader to distance herself from the text. It was essential to maintain this distance and not become, in Clare's words, 'enmeshed in it'. For most of the remaining women it was the power of the text to involve and 'enmesh' them which marked it out as pleasurable. As Janet said of *Dynasty*, 'it takes you away for an hour, doesn't it, you get that involved'; Susan used the expression 'you give yourself to the screen'. Soap operas were enjoyed because you *had* to watch them, because you had become part of them and because they went on forever. There was an apparent need to relate directly to the fictional world, and texts that encouraged and permitted this direct access were pleasurable.

Chapter 5

Technology in the domestic environment

> Once I learned how to put a plug on, now there's nobody else puts a plug on in this house but me.
>
> (Edna)

It was obvious from the interview material that these women had an incomplete knowledge of the workings of the video recorder. The similarity of the women's reported experience in relation to technology was striking and I have therefore chosen to discuss this aspect of the VCR generally across the sample, aiming to provide an account of the range of attitudes and approaches they have in relation to entertainment technology. It is important to point out that technologies such as the VCR have a life even before they enter the household, for example, in discussions about the appropriateness, or otherwise, of its purchase, and also that technologies have a developing biography within households after they have been acquired. The contours of the biography are determined by, amongst other things, different and changing patterns of use and their relation to other forms of technology. Therefore, these aspects of the VCR will be explored throughout this section. I will begin by exploring the processes whereby the women actually gained the knowledge and skill required to use the recorders. Very few of the women learnt how to operate the video recorders on their own; this generally means that whatever knowledge they have has been mediated mainly through their male partners. This in many cases relates back to decisions about the purchase or rental of the VCR.

> We got an instruction book but he had a rough idea anyway; he was probably more familiar with it anyway because until

we'd started looking he'd been the one who was up on them, as it were. (Lynne)

The decision-making process is referred to later in this chapter, but it is important to note here that the five women who were most at ease with the operation of the video recorder were either instigators of the acquisition or, in one case, already familiar with the machine before the current domestic arrangement began.

When new pieces of domestic technology are acquired there are, under current consumer supply practices, two main channels through which user information is gained. The first is that the person who delivers the machine will set up the VCR, tune it to the existing television set and, perhaps, run through the operating procedure. The second is the manual or instruction booklet provided with all machines. The former is usually a quick 'run down' given at speed and not sufficient in itself for the user to become totally competent. The latter, of course, is a permanent source which can be referred to when necessary, as the user develops her or his competence.

The majority of women interviewed said that their partners had initially studied the instruction manual and learnt how to operate the video recorder.

Well when we got it my husband read the instructions and, you know, he told me. (Janet)

Michael used to work it at first, he got the knack of it great, he knows how to do it. (Cathy)

He learnt, then showed me . . . I mean because he bought it. (Beth)

This in turn led to the men operating the recorder more often and on a regular basis, thereby becoming familiar with the various modes of operation and gradually reducing the necessity for consulting the manual. The women, on the other hand, did not use the machine regularly enough to become familiar with it and had to consult the manual if they were to use the recorder, particularly for setting the timer switch for pre-recording.

I can programme the video – I need the handbook because I don't do it very often. (Beth)

I can put the tape in, switch it on and find the bit without having to consult the manual, but it is the pre-programming to make it come on at certain times, on which channel and so forth, I don't have the facility to do that, I haven't done it frequently enough to know how to do it without consulting the manual. (Caroline)

Jim can set the timer, but I have to look it up in the book . . . and whereas I can do it I always have to check back in the book . . . so I suppose most of the time he does that. When he's away I cope with it perfectly well. (Jenny)

Many of the women felt inadequate because of their lack of knowledge and some explained this in terms of not being technically minded.

I don't even know how to work the thing properly . . . I mean I'll try if I'm desperate, I'll press every button and I'll eventually get on what I want, but I'm certainly not . . . I'm not machine minded really. (Kay)

I do feel it's passed me by, this technological revolution. (Shirley)

He does the recording for me. The first video we had I could do it myself, it was just very basic, but as we progressed it got very complicated and I still to this day can't work out the timer, it's just a joke; I'm not very good at that sort of thing. (Susan)

Some insisted in a self-deprecating way that it was their own fault through sheer laziness, or not having bothered to learn.

Well I still have to think about the video. Mainly my own fault because I haven't bothered to do it often enough and bothered to look in the instruction book . . . the timing bit I haven't bothered with, because, then again I don't say that I couldn't do it because there aren't many things I can't do if I put my mind to it . . . I just haven't bothered, you know, there's always somebody here to do it and, then again, it's just pure laziness and apathy because, you know there'll come a time when I probably may want to use it then I'll have to learn how to do it. (Sheila)

I operate it to record when I'm there. I'm not very good at programming it, in fact I tend not to. But it's never really arisen much. I suppose it's laziness, I ought to learn how to programme it but I never need to do it; I suppose if I did I'd sit down and learn to do it, but I've never actually needed to.
(Hilary)

It must be noted that a stated lack of enthusiasm for television and video in many cases accounted for a disinclination to become more familiar with the technicalities of the machine. Those women who were keen television viewers made it their business to get to know how to operate the machine, even though the knowledge was mediated by their male partners.

> He was the one who read the book and found out how it worked. (Rene)

But Rene soon familiarized herself with the operation of all aspects, including the timer, so that she could record programmes of interest when her husband was away.

For one woman there was more at stake. Her male partner assumed not just knowledge, but control over the video so that her son (not his child) had to ask him to record things on his behalf. She and her son took steps to alter this situation.

> I've just learnt. Me and Mark [son] did it last week together, we got the book out, but right from us having it we've never sat down and done it. We fathomed it out between us. Because sometimes Mark feels he wants to record something and Brian'll [partner] say you can't do it . . . and he wants to tape things for himself. (Alison)

Other reasons given for not having gained the knowledge were more complex and were much more to do with the division of labour in the home and appropriate 'territories' mapped out across gender. Two of the older women had been quite calculating in their maintenance of ignorance, a tactic based on years of practical experience.

What about setting the timer?

Oh no, I haven't got a clue, no. If there's anything I want recording I ask one of the boys to do it for me. This is sheer laziness I must admit because I don't read the instructions. When I'm reading the instructions it will not go through, it's like a knitting pattern or a sewing pattern, I just cannot get it through into my thick skull, but the minute I start and work with it, then I carry on quite happily just looking at the directions as I go on . . . but to sit and read it, you know, you've to do this and do that, and hold this button when you're pressing that [shaking head].

So you're not . . .

No, I'm not going to try. No. Once I learned how to put a plug on, now there's nobody else puts a plug on in this house but me . . . so [laugh] there's method in my madness, oh yes. (Edna)

The second woman, in her fifties, living with her husband and grown-up son, could use the video to put a tape in, play it back and rewind it. But, when it came to the timer switch:

I have been explained to very quickly, and I've looked at the instructions [giggle]. I am what I am, I'm termed as being a bit thick . . . it took me a long time to learn to drive [laugh] and it takes a long time for things to sink in. But on top of that I really don't want to be taught how to do it, really deep down, I know that, because if so it will be my job to deal with it . . . that's the truth. (Audrey)

Some of the younger women also had their reasons for not operating certain parts of the video and one, referring to it as her husband's 'preserve', said,

Roger uses it more than I do, in fact I'd probably be hard pressed to actually work it myself, I've always left it I must admit to him.

Have you ever set the timer?

No, I don't think I have, no.

Has there not been an occasion when you've needed it?

No, because I would say to him, I'm going to be out tomorrow night, could you set it up . . . a weak and feeble woman [laugh] . . . I have put it on for the children sometimes, not the timer, but I can put a disc [*sic*] in and turn it on.

Did you make a conscious decision not to learn?

I don't know, really, I mean I'm sure I could if I read it up and did it but, erm . . . I suppose I have consciously decided in effect.

You said earlier that it was Roger's preserve, is that why you don't . . .

Erm . . . no, I didn't mean, you know, that he would be cross or anything if I did, I just meant, you know, traditionally it has been his affair, the technicalities of it. (Shirley)

Tradition, custom and practice, already established as family routines before the arrival of the video recorder, obviously play an important part in the division of labour, especially where there are children in the household.

Who decides normally whether you're going to record something?

I would say Craig because he's usually the one that gets around to doing the actual setting it up, if it's going to be a setting the timer up job and what have you. Although I must admit that I often say tape that, tape this, so I suppose really, it seems that he does it more because he actually gets the job of doing the setting up.

Is that because you can't do it?

No, I can do it, but I usually find that it's one of those jobs that he's capable of doing and he can be getting on with that whilst I'm doing something else that he's not capable of doing . . . usually if we're going out I'm usually brushing hair and putting bobbles in and saying 'Set that up' and we're sort of rushing out and I say, 'Oh, I want to watch that, set that up' and, erm . . . (Lynne)

It would seem that there are decisions made by the women, either consciously or subconsciously, to remain in ignorance of the workings of the VCR, so that it is their husband or partner's job to set up the timer. This, of course, has the function of a 'service' for the household unit, that of timing an off-air recording for joint watching; the more calculatedly ignorant women had perhaps recognized this latent servicing element and resisted it in view of their already heavily committed domestic servicing roles. One woman had learnt her lesson with the plug (as we have seen) but the other, interestingly, had learnt hers through knowing how to erect the screen for the showing of home movies, which was her job every Christmas and some Sundays.

> All this time and I'm just learning. I had to set it all up, I had to put the screen up [laugh] we'd say on a Sunday night 'we haven't seen any films for a long time' and he'd say 'get it all set up' [laugh] you see my reluctance [pointing to the video]. (Audrey)

For those women who have not made a conscious decision to remain in ignorance, but for whom it simply 'just happened' or 'there's always someone there to do it for me', this has negative repercussions. It means that they never get to use the recorder, or not often enough to become familiar with it, relying on their partners or their children to set it for them. The same effect is produced by both strategies: the women remain ignorant. What is important, though, is that they feel stupid because of their lack of knowledge in this area. What can be accounted for in terms of material restriction – having particular domestic duties to perform rather than being able to sit down and study an instruction manual and its application – is then turned back on the women, often in their own consciousness, as a presumed basic inability to understand technical things. For three of the women I talked to, the same was true of the home computer.

> When we first got the computer and we were all learning to play with it and fiddling, I had much less time and everybody got computer literate, they were all much more adept at it much more quickly than me and I got really left behind and I felt really pissed off with it. They had all this time and they can now play the games and Jim's got into the first stages of programming. They left me way behind so that I couldn't really appreciate it and enjoy it and I was very much aware at the time that I resented that and that it was purely a time thing. (Jenny)

She has recognized that whilst her family were free to devote themselves to playing with the computer, she had other calls on her time which placed her on the margins of the learning process. She goes on:

> I keep thinking I'll set it up again now I've got some more time when this work finishes, but I probably won't because

the initial impetus has gone . . . the novelty has worn off for everybody else . . . it would be a very deliberate thing for me to settle down to do it and anyway nobody else would be interested now [laugh] so I'd just be doing it for myself . . . And I think that happens perhaps in other areas because I feel I've got less time or I'm doing something else or I've got other responsibilities . . . I'll get left behind, or I'll simply 'agree' rather than 'suggest' sort of thing. (Jenny)

It is also interesting to note her prediction about her future use of the computer when she may have more time. The likelihood is that she will not learn how to use it because it would, in her words, be 'doing it for myself'. This relates to the discussion in chapter 2 about reluctance to indulge in activities which are motivated by self-interest. Another woman was very keen to learn how to operate the computer; her husband used it a lot 'as a computer, not just for games'. I asked her if she had tried to learn.

When we first got it and that yes . . . but I find that if things don't go in straight away I lose interest, there seems to be such a lot to take in, like I sat reading some of the books, he has a lot of books on it, some very basic ones, but I think . . . I'm all right so far, then you get . . . mind you, you've always got other things on your mind, what we're going to have for tea and things like that . . . you've got to able to concentrate . . . (Janet)

These two men were 'hobbyists' and were envied by their wives for their ability to switch off from the daily routine and concentrate on their chosen pastime. Although the first speaker is quite aware that it is lack of time which prevents her from engaging fully with the computer, the latter fails to make the connection between the many and frequent demands made upon her time and her inability to concentrate, simply believing that her husband is much cleverer than she is. What is important to note in both cases is the significance given to those particular activities chosen by their male partners. This is not a simple matter of available time, but of the right to time which is claimed by the men, as if what they are doing is significant by virtue of the fact that they are doing it. This has been explored in chapter 2 because it obviously has far-reaching implications for the organization of domestic life, but here we can see that this claim to time and how it is spent gives the male of the household the opportunity to become techno-literate much more quickly and effectively than his female partner.

The third woman in a home-computer-owning household had managed to familiarize herself with the computer. She did not have children; the computer was used in her husband's work, and they had decided to learn together about it; but in order to do so she had to overcome certain barriers.

> Well I hated it at first, I didn't even want to turn it on. I thought, no, this is far too advanced for me, I don't know what it does and I don't want it to do anything. I was frightened of the computer because everybody was saying women can't pick up computers as easily as men and children. (Susan)

She had overcome these prejudices and found that she 'had a brain' after all, although her husband had enabled her to 'find' it.

> He's a very clever person and he educates me in silly little things. I mean, I left school at 15 and I didn't have a full education because my parents weren't interested in me having one, they wanted me to get married and that was it. But John's educated me, and I have got a brain . . . it sounds terrible doesn't it? People say, oh, women haven't got brains, well they have, they're just not allowed to put them to use properly, and I have got one. (Susan)

This 'mastering' of the computer had given her confidence to find out how to work the video, but again she blames her lack of knowledge on 'laziness'.

> It was just laziness, like the computer, you know, there were too many knobs and too many . . . it's one of these complicated ones and I couldn't be bothered learning how to do it, I was depending on him to do it, like at first I was depending on him to play with the computer. That's his. But now I can do it . . . so if I can do a computer I can certainly do a video, my God. (Susan)

This woman performs complex ideological work in order to explain her relationship to technology. She recognizes the social constraints which agencies like the family and education place on

women, but ultimately the blame rests upon her own personal
'laziness'. Her husband, although he had a very similar education
to her, is seen by her as naturally more intelligent and inhabiting
a world of knowledge which he is able to offer her through an
educative process. Janet had a very similar attitude towards her
own background and her male partner, although he did not perform the same educative role.

> I left school and went to work in Boots . . . and I was only
> young when I met my husband . . . and I just wanted to get
> married and have children, that was my only aim in life . . .
> I mean it didn't seem important if I did anything. But then
> when you've got them you think oh, I wish I could do
> something . . . just to say, I've done that. Like, I keep telling
> my husband that I'm going to write a book, so buy me a
> typewriter. He says, just get a word processor and goodness
> knows what, and a printer . . . but whether or not I will
> do . . . I might do.

> *And what about the computer, would you think about learning how
> to use that?*

> I would like to really I think, just to say, well yes I can do
> it . . . I don't mean just for playing games . . . I mean as a
> computer . . . yes because there again I can say well, I can do
> that . . . I think I get riled at it because I can't . . . I think ooh
> I wish I could and then I could speak more on a level with
> my husband . . . you know I could, you know, converse
> with him and be on his level type of thing . . . mind you, I
> suppose I haven't sat and read like he has, he reads hours,
> you know, about goodness knows what. (Janet)

This woman, a self-defined full-time housewife, implicitly suggests the ways in which women are ideologically placed by the
notion of the 'feminine career', and its limitations; her ambitions
to write a children's book were not to seek external recognition
necessarily, but to show her family that she could do something
too. Her aspirations in this respect have been deflected on to the
necessity for her to learn how to operate a word processor, but
furthermore, to break into the masculine world of the computer
and the 'knowledge' which she sees her husband as possessing.
This woman goes into the library with her children and sees
children's books and thinks to herself, 'I could write something

better than that', but at home the possibility of her writing a book is, paradoxically, undermined by her ignorance of computer technology. This particular kind of technology therefore is used in these two homes as a symbol of technological and intellectual ability, of indisputably male territory to which a woman can only gain entry via her husband.

One of the 'calculated ignorance' strategists, referring to the more mundane example of changing a plug, claimed that this kind of technical knowledge 'makes the men feel superior' and she, for one, was willing to be complicit in this state of affairs. Although less explicit, neither Susan nor Janet in any way seriously challenged that male superiority.

Although, as reported earlier, the majority of the women did not operate the timer functions on the video, the reasons they gave for this and their implications are complex and far-reaching. I have discussed the right to time, but it is also clear that the 'cleverness' or 'superior knowledge' which the males are able to accrue enables them to maintain their position of authority and superiority in the eyes of many of the women.

Most VCRs and many television receivers are supplied with a remote control unit which facilitates the changing of channels and the operation of record and playback of the VCR from 'the comfort of your own armchair' (Sony VCR manual). Indeed, compact disc players and other video or sound systems are now also supplied with this facility. The remote control unit itself assumes a single viewer or controller, but very often, of course, several members of the household will be watching television or video at the same time. The majority of the women reported that, if they were in the television room, then the male members of the household, either father or son, would invariably hold the remote control.

Oh, he has that – I never know what I'm watching half the time, we'll be watching one thing, then he flicks over to something else, it drives me mad. (Susan)

Yes, now this is interesting; when we sit down to watch the video with some specific programme in mind that we know is on the video, James tends to have the remote control, and I spit with rage at his flicking from thing to thing instead of locating on what it was we wanted to watch. (Caroline)

Well, it tends to be Peter [son] who grabs it; I never do that, it usually tends to be Peter or Phillip [husband], not me who operates it. But, I mean, there's a wail of protest if someone's watching something [laugh]. (Hilary)

Tony [husband] likes to play with it, he likes to sit and play flicking around from channel to channel. (Michelle)

This male domination of the remote control unit has also been noted by Dave Morley in his study of families in London's East End and observed by Peter Collett when he video-taped households watching television.[1] This obviously has ramifications for the question of control over the material to be viewed, a topic already discussed in chapter 3.

What of the women who did regularly operate the video recorder? One of these, a young woman teacher married to an often out-of-work actor, had already owned a video recorder when living alone. She therefore was quite at ease with all functions of the recorder, and often used VCRs in connection with her work. However, even her case is not straightforward.

Who sets the pre-recorder?

Well, whoever's in. [*If you're both in?*] I'd probably let Tony do it. I mean if he was upstairs, I'd do it, but if he was in the same room as me I'd probably say 'do that'. I can do it, but I'd rather sit and watch him do it, in the same way that I would always sit in the passenger seat of the car, because I'd much rather be driven, and I would sit in a chair and say, 'Would you get me a drink'. I like to have things done for me. (Michelle)

This partnership was unusual in the sample in that she was the main regular earner. Michelle and her husband 'shared' most household tasks – shopping, cooking and washing – but in fact, because of his irregular employment he did most of the domestic work. However, she shows her desire to maintain some distinction, or to return to more traditional male and female roles, where he does things for her. But this could well be the effects of a rather complicated 'barter' system within which she was usually in credit because her full-time work enabled him to pursue his rather uncertain career.

Of the four other video-competent women, two were

unmarried women living with their parents – Christine and Sandra; they had been the instigators of the video rental, and here age is an important factor.

> My Dad won't touch it at all, he gets me to set the timer for him . . . I think he's scared of blowing himself up, he goes mad if I ask him to touch it. (Sandra)

Another was a divorcée living with her grown-up daughters and occasionally her boyfriend. She did, however, admit to not using the timer switch very often, although she did know how to operate it.

> I'm good at fiddling, I didn't look at the book, I just worked it out as it came, I'm quite good at fiddling like that. (Barbara)

The young full-time mother, Julie, was totally in command of the video recorder. In fact, before beginning our discussions she set the timer to record a programme she would be missing because I was there. Her husband never used the video.

> Occasionally he'll say 'will you record something?' if he knows it's on, but that is sort of my department [pointing to the video], is the television and the video.

> *How did you learn how to do it?*

> Well the man who brought it showed me, but it didn't really sink in I don't suppose, and then I learnt from the book. Andrew still can't operate the timer and everything, but it's just because he hasn't sat down and worked it out, he just leaves it to me, it's easy. (Julie)

Here we have a male partner who makes no claims to technical knowledge of the VCR and his partner experienced no difficulty in studying and applying the manual to the operating procedures.

Very few women experienced any kind of 'block' with, say, the hi-fi or cassette players, and many of them used these machines quite often. Those women who used them very regularly expressed a keen enjoyment in listening to music, some taping off the radio, others playing records or tapes during the day or if they were on their own in the house in the evening. The pleasure that these women gained from listening to music seems to have been a motivating factor in learning how to operate the equipment, but in general they considered hi-fis and cassette players to be much easier to use than the VCR.

> Well we've always had one [cassette player] at home . . . it's just the video. (Cathy)

> I make up a tape for myself with the songs that I like. Usually on a Sunday when the Top Twenty's on, I record the songs that I like. (Kay)

We have already noted that Kay does not work the video and is 'not that interested really' in recording off television, but will regularly record music on to a sound tape. She often sits in the same room as the family whilst they are watching television.

> No, I never sit anywhere else. I always sit where the television is . . . I can read, or I put a record or tape on and sit with the headphones on and totally ignore the lot of them [laugh]. I sit and listen to music. (Kay)

However, some of the women experienced difficulties with the more technologically advanced pieces of entertainment equipment in their houses, often referring to these as 'gadgets'.

> We've got so many gadgets in this house you see . . . so many radios, computer radios where you punch a thing in and it goes to the station, but I live with it and, well, I feel as if it's nothing to do with me. Not that I'm frightened of it, I think being in an all-male household it's rubbed off. I carry a screwdriver, I can fix plugs and if anything's broken I can do it. But I don't know whether it's easier not to do things yourself, or whether I see men doing it so much, messing about with the electrical things, soldering irons and that. And I think I could do it just as good as they can . . . I think I could work all these radios and things, and do the timer on the video. (Jean)

This woman is a teacher in a large inner-city middle school where she regularly operates a VCR and tape cassettes as part of her job. At home, living with her two grown-up sons and husband she feels as if 'it's nothing to do with me' and, indeed, doesn't work the timer on the video recorder. She realizes, of course, that she can, or could do it, but within the household there seems to be an assumption about what men do which is carried over into practice. This is confirmed by Cynthia Cockburn's research, in which she notes that some women who work with technology or 'tools' in paid work outside the home relinquish this expertise to their male partners in the home (Cockburn 1985: 219).

Many of the households had more than one television set. The main colour television and VCR were mostly in the sitting-room, with portables in either the kitchen or bedroom. Some of these second televisions were complicated and also presented problems in their operation.

> The TV in our bedroom is one of these really complicated things which is TV, radio, cassette player and an alarm thing in it . . . I don't know how to switch the TV on, it's got so many knobs and things on it, and it's also got a peculiar switch whereby it'll switch off after an hour and I'm forever in the middle of watching something and it goes off . . . you've to get out of bed and work out how to switch it back on again . . . it's probably because I've never bothered to say, look just show me how to do this . . . erm . . . Then on the occasions that you have to do it, I'll fiddle around and not remember what I've done the next time . . . I'm the same with the alarm clock, setting it or changing the setting . . . you see I haven't done it that number of times that I can remember . . . I think it is the number of times you do it. (Jenny)

It appears that older pieces of equipment and perhaps those with which the women were familiar before their current domestic circumstances, present no problem in terms of operation. Added to this are motivational factors, such as, wanting to record music, or, in some specific circumstances, wanting to record television programmes off air, which will be sufficient reason for the women to become familiar with the machines, and to use them regularly enough to achieve ease of operation. On the other hand, the newer and, almost by definition, more 'complicated' or technologically advanced pieces of entertainment equipment tend to be off-putting for women and they are largely the preserve of the adult male or children of the household. In some of the households there is a reproduction of 'appropriate' tasks with the children.

What about your children, how do they use the video recorder?

Erm . . . my son, erm . . . well if his dad is out on business and can't get back for a certain programme, I mean, he knows it all, he's been primed . . . so when father's not there my son takes over.

What about the girls?

My youngest daughter definitely not, but my eldest daughter, yes, she knows how to work it, yes, but there again if she wants anything recording she'll ask her brother, you know, she won't be bothered. If he's not here she'll do it, but she'll say to him, 'Will you record so and so?' if he's in. (Kay)

These women, of course, routinely operate quite sophisticated pieces of technology in the course of their domestic work: washing machines, cookers, microwave ovens, food mixers, sewing machines, etc. Almost all the women were perfectly at ease with these machines and most registered surprise when they were referred to as technology. The one exception to this was Caroline who had adopted a 'Luddite' attitude towards technology in general and resisted what she saw as the pressure to technologize the home. She believed this to be 'technology for its own sake' and that rather than simplifying households tasks it had the effect of making them much more complicated. However, the rest of the women did not appear to share this view and when new kitchen equipment had been purchased they had read through manuals and instruction books and had quickly become familiar users. In the majority of cases, their male partners had not staked their claim to this knowledge, leaving the women to work things out for themselves. This is important for two main reasons. First, it is an indication of assumptions about appropriate 'female' technology and second, when knowledge or expertise is not rendered 'masculine' then the women appear to have a less problematic relationship with technology.

We noted that the video recorder timer switch seemed to present the biggest difficulties for the women, although many of their cookers also had a time-setting function. The women used this facility without difficulty, but very few of the men could operate the cooker timer; for example:

Does your husband operate the cooker timer?

Only the minute timer, not the pre-set timer . . . he uses it so he doesn't forget something that's on, but if we were going out and I was putting something in the oven to cook for when we got back, that would be my job. (Shirley)

He can't set the timer on the cooker [laugh]; it's disgusting. (Jenny)

When I went away we discovered that my husband didn't know how to operate the timer on the oven. (Hilary)

These are glaring examples of the gendered division of labour which have nothing to do with technological competence but everything to do with social use. However, it goes further than this in that the fact that the men cannot work the cooker timer is not seen by the women as evidence of masculine technological incompetence, in the way that their own inability to operate the video timer might demonstrate – in their own eyes – such inadequacy in themselves. It seems that women's technical competences are rendered invisible, along with the invisibility of their domestic work. Hilary, for example, argues that it is her husband's lack of time which leads to his lack of expertise in the kitchen, whereas she felt that her own lack of expertise with the video recorder was due to her laziness, or 'natural' lack of technical competence.

DECISIONS TO HAVE A VCR

I said 'well, if you're having your Teletext, I'm having a video.' (Rene)

As already indicated in this chapter, the decision-making processes which led to the rental or purchase of a VCR are of interest, partly, as we have seen, because it is the instigator who is more likely to have a knowledge of the workings of the VCR, but also because he or she also has a vested interest in demonstrating the value and usefulness of the machine, thereby justifying the decision. To look at the kinds of negotiations which preceded the acquisition of the VCR, and the positions taken by the various actors involved, is to place the women's uses of and attitudes to the VCR within a particular context.

'Daft money'

For Hilary and Caroline the decision to buy the VCR was their husbands' but, in both cases, this was because there was, as Caroline put it, some 'daft money' available. Here is Hilary's account of the background to the purchase:

> We don't make decisions in a very organized way, we tend to make spontaneous decisions. My husband earned a bit of extra money and we decided that we'd spend it on that for Christmas. So it was really like most of our decisions are, fairly spontaneous.

> *You got it at Christmas-time?*

> Yes, we got it just before Christmas . . . but we've just bought a CD player and we did that spontaneously, nothing to do with Christmas. I suppose it's a privileged thing to be able to do in this world. But we do tend to do it spontaneously rather than sort of plan things. We have a sort of feeling that grows up . . . we'd like this thing . . . and when there seems to be enough . . . we tend to buy it, but it's not rigorously planned. (Hilary)

Whilst Hilary implied that the decision to buy the VCR at Christmas was coincidental, as we shall see this is a popular time for VCR acquisition. However, Hilary distances herself from the Christmas factor and reveals her rationalization of the purchase of entertainment hardware. She implies freedom of individual choice; in her words, a spontaneous purchase, rather than something thought through and planned. In this way the desire for consumer durables is made to seem a natural phenomenon, one which is in their control and does not appear to be imposed from outside, for example, by advertising or friends.

More specifically, her husband bought the machine.

> Well, my husband tends to mostly operate it anyway, still. I don't know why, but it just tends to be he does. (Hilary)

Caroline reported a similar pattern of events, from decision to purchase, to use.

> James was working in the university and he was the university's 1 per cent cut and he was paid off; in effect, he got redundancy pay, and this resulted in everybody getting

redundancy presents, including the second house in the country and including this new television and the video . . . it was . . . you know . . . there was suddenly some daft money and, you know . . . it was his choice to buy it, it wouldn't have entered into my scheme of things. (Caroline)

Winning consent

The purchase of the VCR was often the subject of negotiation, largely, but not always, instigated by men, with a variety of 'carrots' offered. Beth's husband, for example, had a work-related reason for the purchase of the VCR, but, as she pointed out, her house is full of 'gadgets'.

> We've got several tape recorders, we've got an early Sinclair computer and a later Sinclair computer, certainly a wireless for each room . . . it's just that we've always had video recorders before anybody else had video recorders . . . the only thing we haven't got is a compact disc player . . . but that's just because we'd just bought a whole new stereo system. But we bought a video recorder. We were working for the Open University at the time and he made this great case that we really needed a video recorder so we could watch our pro- grammes, and we didn't watch many OU programmes. (Beth)

At another point in the interview I asked her why they had got the video, and she replied,

> Because George loves gadgets. He bought it, I wouldn't have bought it, but then he buys all those things. I buy silly things. (Beth)

For three of the women, the reasons for the decision to purchase the VCR had resulted in the women being marginal to its use. Sheila and Kay were 'not interested' in getting a video, although their husbands and family were very keen. Kay felt that her husband and family were already watching too much television.

Were you in favour of getting the video?

> No. I was dead against it until the Royal Wedding. That's where I slipped up you see. I said I would love that, you know, for posterity, to have . . . and he said, right . . . I'll go

and get a video recorder and you shall have it [laugh] and that's what he did. (Kay)

Kay hardly ever recorded things – 'I don't even know how to work the thing properly' – and whilst her husband's case for getting the video was that he would be able to record things and therefore go out more with her, this hadn't actually happened. In effect, he had ended up watching more.

> Well, because he records . . . there's always something on the other side he wants to watch, so he'll watch one channel, record the other side, and then he has a backlog of things that he's got to sit and watch, so even when . . . like Monday night is very bad on television, there's nothing really on, but he's got a backlog of stuff that he wants to watch, so . . . (Kay)

Similarly, Sheila, whose teenage children were the main instigators of the purchase, rarely used the video recorder and was not interested in its use.

The prime motivation in Shirley's household for the purchase of a video recorder was the desire for a video camera to record their children.

> Roger had been toying with the idea of getting a camera for some while and eventually we bought it to coincide with the second daughter . . . so . . . that was the incidental reason for it, although I suppose we do use the video for recording. (Shirley)

Whilst they did use the video, as we have seen in the previous chapter, Shirley did not feel it was 'her territory'; her husband operated the camera and tended to dominate the use of the video recorder.

Rene was very keen to get a video and its purchase was part of a bargain.

> We needed a new television and my husband said, right, we'll have one with Teletext. I said, well, if you're having your Teletext, I'm having a video.

Why did you want a video?

> Well, because of the things he used to watch. Say, for instance, *Match of the Day* on a Saturday night, well, there could be, as

I recall, *Tales of the Unexpected* on the other side which I
enjoyed, but because I got my own way so much during the
week, I thought, well it's only fair to let him watch *Match of
the Day* in colour. Now, I would either take the television up
to bed in the winter, or I'd go in the kitchen and watch . . .
and it's damned uncomfortable in the kitchen and I don't
always particularly want to be in bed. You now, watching
television, particularly because I fall asleep, you know, if I take
the television to bed I've really . . . it's got to be really something special that keeps me awake to watch it, so that's the
reason I wanted a video. (Rene)

Rene is a keen video user and so is her husband, although he
was not in favour of having a VCR; his reaction to her wanting
a video was 'you watch enough rubbish already', associating the
VCR with entertainment as against 'his' Teletext, the provider of
information.

Another important bargaining position was the argument that
the video was 'for the children' and this often came into play
at Christmas. A number of working-class women reported that
the VCR was rented at Christmas 'for the children' because of the
good films on then, which they could record.

It was my husband really wanted it in the first place. I honestly
didn't think we'd watch it. I mean we do. But all the time I
thought, oh we don't really need one. Then it got to Christmas
time and he said it would be nice for the kiddies . . . so . . .
(Betty)

For those households on low incomes with young children, it is
not surprising that economic factors and lack of freedom to go
out were motivating elements.

He bought a video because we couldn't afford to go to the
pictures. It was expensive when there's five of us going.
(Alison)

The other factor for two of the women was the fact that they
worked in the evening and it meant that they didn't miss their
favourite programmes (soap opera).

He decided he wanted a video, he's wanted one since a couple
of years ago and I said no . . . I'm not interested. But then
when I started on in the evenings . . . he says 'Well, we can

get one now because then I can tape *Coronation Street* for when
I'm at work' . . . so I wouldn't be without it now. (Cathy)

There is no doubt here whose decision it was to have a video
and here is a very clear example of this kind of negotiation.
Brenda reported that they wanted a VCR mainly for recording.

The Olympics were coming on and I was working in the
evening, and my husband would tape things we could watch
together when I came home.

Can you remember whose idea it was to get the video?

Well, my husband had seen one and we talked about it and
said . . . when they first came out we said, no . . . because
what was the point if you wanted to watch something, if you
were out you'd stop in and watch it, if you really wanted to
watch it . . . but then I started working evenings and he found
out what it was like looking after three kids [laugh]; that
clinched it. (Brenda)

Everybody's got one

The acquisition of VCRs by friends and colleagues was an important additional factor behind the decisions for lower-income
groups. VCR-related talk becomes a feature at work, in the neighbourhood and at social gatherings and in this way information
about the advantages of the VCR is shared and non-owners can
rapidly be persuaded to become owners.

Well, they were all getting them where he works, and he
thought it would be a good idea. (Alison)

I think Megan was the first to get one round here and, you
know . . . well that persuaded us really. Most people have got
'em now. (Janet)

Two of the women declared that it had been a joint decision to
purchase the machine. These were Susan and Michelle – full-time
workers, married but with no children.

There's nothing else to do

Two of the women were under 21 and living with their parents. Although one had a job, working in a supermarket, and the other was unemployed, they both had a very limited amount of money to spend on going out and lived in an area which, as far as they were concerned, offered very little in the way of entertainment. Christine, the one in employment, said,

> There's nothing to do . . . I think it's with not many of us having much money and it costing so much to go out, I think that's the reason. I don't go out during the week, unless it's a special occasion, I mean there's not much going off, except pubs that are open . . . it's a shame though because we're only 21 and we've no life, really. (Christine)

Sandra, unemployed, was also short of cash and both these women went to the cinema very infrequently.

> I think I've been once so far this year. I went about twice last year. It's only if there's a film that I really want to watch and usually my sister goes with me because we both like the same kind of films, but normally we can get a video and watch it at home, all the family can watch it together. (Sandra)

> Sometimes, on Monday nights we'll go 'cos it's only a pound in for any age, and if there's a decent film on we'll go, but there haven't been many films. We go see cartoons and weepies, that's all we do. I sometimes take my sister, or sometimes go with people from work if they want to go see it as well. (Christine)

The main reason given by Christine for renting a VCR was that there was nothing good on television during the week when she had to stay in.

> My life's more or less come home, have my tea, watch television and go to bed about nine o'clock and I was just getting fed up and all my friends, well some of my friends at work, have got videos and they were saying, 'Oh I watched so and so video this week, and it was really good' and I thought, well, if they're watching all them films and there's nothing on television, I might get one. (Christine)

Again this is evidence, as seen earlier, of peer group pressure to acquire a VCR. However, she found hiring films from the video library often beyond her means.

> I haven't watched one for a while, it's just a matter of going down and getting one, I'm a bit skint you see . . . they cost a pound to one pound fifty; it isn't much, but with me going out on Saturday and Sunday and spending more money than what I intended . . . I haven't been able to afford one and my dinners at work has cost me a bit more, and I've got some new things, new clothes; there are a few new films, but not many that interest me, so I think that's the reason. (Christine)

Unlike Christine, Sandra found that there were lots of programmes on television that interested her and that she wanted to record. Her married sister and brother both had a VCR and she found she was constantly asking them to record things for her. She therefore managed to persuade her father to rent a machine.

> Well, my brother had his video for about a year and a half, and my sister had had hers for nearly a year and I had some tapes at her house, you see, and I used to ring her up and say . . . oh quick, you know, put the tape in, I want this taping and . . . I don't know, I think my Dad got fed up with the 'phone bill and I kept saying, you know, it's wonderful, you'll be able to sit here with all your cowboy films on a Saturday . . . so I kind of persuaded my Dad to get it. (Sandra)

Both these women were the dominant users in the household and both claimed to use it more for hiring films than recording off air.

SUMMARY

It would seem that class and education are not significant variables in attitudes towards technology in the home. Gender is the key determinant in the use of and expertise in specific pieces of domestic equipment. This in turn can be seen to relate to the gendered division of labour within the home and its associated technology. Recent research into the acquisition of radio and television has identified very similar patterns of use and decision-making across gender (Moores 1988; O'Sullivan 1991). In the light of the women's attitudes to older forms of entertainment technology such as radio and cassette recorders, we can perhaps see their resistance to video technology as a passing phase. This would certainly find support in Sherry Turkle's arguments in relation to 'computerphobia', which she argues is transitional. However, we can see from this study that there is more at stake for many of the women. One point to make is that it seems that the women will always be 'lagging behind' in mastery of entertainment and information technology. However, the crucial point to be drawn from this analysis is that the domestic context and the social relations within it have quite powerful consequences in relation to women and new technology.

Jonathan Gershuny has created an index showing the extent to which different pieces of domestic technology are used by women and men (Gershuny 1982). Using time-budget survey data he found that the men in his study mainly used equipment like electric drills and electric saws to perform one-off jobs with a highly visible end product. The women used technology for the execution of day-to-day chores, the end products of which are usually immediately consumed, technology such as the cooker, the washing machine, the iron, and so on. Also, Gershuny notes that the more 'hi-tech' a device is, the more likely it is to be male-dominated in its use. His study indicates that entertainment technology falls within a neutral cluster, being neither female nor male specific. Unfortunately, he does not include the VCR amongst this equipment, but we can see that most of the women in the study do not feel proficient in the operation of the VCR, and in particular with the time switch for pre-setting recordings.

Advertisements for domestic and entertainment technology often imply a male or female operative through both visual and textual codes. Early advertisements for the VCR stressed its 'hi-tech' nature, were very rarely seen in a domestic setting, and emphasized technical complexity in its use and operation. In an interview during August 1987 with Mastercare Ltd., a follow-up service agency for VCRs, I discovered that a very high percentage of call-outs for engineers resulted from malfunctions of timer mechanisms, largely owing to user error. This led to design changes and a number of campaigns stressing the simplicity rather than the complexity of time-switch mechanisms and, significantly, women were often represented as operatives in these advertisements. Conversely, micro-wave cookers have been

marketed on their simplicity, but here the operatives are male:
'so simple even men can use it!' (Hitachi advertisment, 1987).

The ways in which consumers are addressed through advertisements on television, in the press, and in magazines would seem
to have an effect in terms of the assumed knowledge and use of
specific pieces of equipment in the home. This places women at
a disadvantage with regard to use of the VCR, and those members
of the household who have time to become VCR-competent tend
to dominate its use.

The majority of the women were persuaded into the purchase
or rental of the VCR by their partners. This makes sense given
gender specific concepts of 'spare time' in the home and the
targeting of advertising campaigns. The men were looking
towards further home entertainment and leisure provision for
which the women themselves could see no need. Their spare time
is limited, and the VCR is conceived as needing time for its use.
It is interesting, however, that some of the men managed to
persuade their reluctant partners by convincing them that they
did have a need for the VCR. Consent was also often won by
virtue of an 'event'. Christmas was the most common, but public
events such as a royal wedding and the Olympics were also cited
as key factors in the eventual decision.

There is also evidence, particularly in the lower-income groups,
of access to a VCR becoming the norm in social and work groups
and an important part of conversational currency. In the higher-
income group this dimension was not explicitly stated. However,
the fact that available disposable income is spent on the VCR,
rather than on any other product or service, indicates their awareness of the product. Simon Frith has plotted the middle-class
consumer's gradual approach to this moment of acquisition:

> We read of new devices that cost huge amounts of money and
> seem to have no immediate purpose; we follow reports of the
> prices coming down and domestic value going up; we see or
> hear the machines at work for richer or more foolish friends;
> we find ourselves thinking one day 'if only *I* could do that',
> and then the price or rental costs suddenly seem right, we get
> the equipment for ourselves and soon can't live without it.
>
> (Frith 1988: 91)

It is the case, however, that for some of the households the VCR
was seen as a necessity, mainly because of lack of disposable

income for trips to the cinema, or because of the presence of children. There is thus a marked distinction between households: between those where the VCR was thought of as an indulgence or impulse buy, the purchase of which was made possible by available extra cash, and those where the purchase or rent of a VCR was a major expense to be carefully considered and planned.

Chapter 6

The VCR: time-shift

> I think when we did attempt to watch Laurence Olivier's *King Lear* we watched that at a fairly fast pace [laugh] edited highlights [laugh]. (Caroline)

All the households in the sample had access to a VCR. About two-thirds had purchased a machine, the rest paid a monthly rental. Although there were rented machines in each of the categories, they tended, predictably, to cluster in the lower-income group, where only one machine had been purchased. Over half the households had owned or rented a VCR for more than two years at the time of the interviews. With the exception of two women all my respondents were interviewed at home and in all those cases the VCR was installed in the main living-room of the house along with the colour television. Similarly, over half the sample had a second television, usually a portable black and white set kept in the kitchen or the bedroom.

There are two major uses to which a VCR can be put: recording from broadcast or narrowcast television for viewing at a different time, commonly known as time-shifting, and playing pre-recorded tapes. This chapter deals with time-shifting and the organization of off-air recordings. As we shall see, time-shifting is not a simple matter but takes different forms and is the result of a range of motivations. The discussion is therefore structured around the different forms of use of time-shift tapes and the apparent motivations behind the recordings. Sean Cubitt has addressed some of the implications of time-shift, in relation to the disruption of the 'immediacy' of broadcast television, as he says 'the aura of live television, the uniqueness, the here-and-now-ness of the broadcast event, is demolished by the use of the

VCR' (Cubitt 1991: 35). The concept of live television as an ideology is discussed by Jane Feuer and, indeed, cited by Cubitt in relation to the VCR. However, Feuer's ontological discussion is not related to the domestic VCR at all, but rather to the apparatus of the television production; recording and editing on video tape results in the majority of television programmes being already recorded. Yet, as she notes, the idea of television as a live medium persists. Cubitt's argument is based on the assumption that the existence of a technological facility in the home will automatically lead to its use. There are, however, as we shall see, particular kinds of television product which 'insist' on being viewed in 'real time', that is when they are broadcast, just as the schedules often provide the required complicity in daytime viewing decisions. We cannot therefore assume that broadcast television, its schedules and its sense of 'immediacy' are automatically demolished because of the significant presence of the domestic VCR; what we must explore is the relationship between the two and the kinds of choices and investments which are made in time-shifting.

In the following extract from my conversation with Hilary, she describes two distinct functions of time-shifting:

> We got quite committed to *Blott on the Landscape*, but I think what happens is, that if you're out and you miss an episode . . . you see *Blott on the Landscape* was on on a Wednesday, and I'm out that night . . . so he recorded it and we watched it together at half past eleven. But if we didn't do that, it then becomes difficult to fit that episode in, if you don't instantly watch it, then you often lose the serial.
>
> Other things I record . . . I'm still . . . it was on about a month since, a play called *Death is Part of the Process*, I'm still waiting to watch the second half of that which I'll watch on my own because my husband won't be interested. So I'm waiting for an evening when he's not in to watch that . . . I'll probably watch that on Friday evening. (Hilary)

These different functions are distinguished by the perceived pressure to view. The short-term function reflects the viewer's desire to keep up with a serial or series, and thus viewing is necessary before the next episode otherwise, as Hilary reports 'you often lose the serial'. Her example of recording a one-off play is a medium-term operation, where pressure to view is less acute and the replay can be fitted in when she has some spare time *and* when her husband is out of the house. This medium-term function tends to create its own pressure, made manifest in the unwatched tapes which pile up as evidence of intentions not achieved.

Caroline told me that they mainly recorded films from broadcast television and I asked her if she had recorded anything other than films.

> Mmm . . . we have recorded . . . we gather up . . . things that I like watching are *Minder* and *Hill Street Blues* and stuff, we'll generally record those and watch them later . . . erm . . . odd bits of documentaries, erm . . . sporting things sometimes . . . less so this year, but in previous years we've recorded the cricket highlights, you know . . . they tend to be on late in the evening, and watch them the following day . . . erm . . . erm . . . I can't think of precise instances.

Have you recorded serials?

> We did . . . record *The Jewel in the Crown* I think and watched that later, but I haven't watched any series. Jane, my daughter, records . . . what is it she watches? . . . *EastEnders*, I think, and watches that, but we haven't gathered up a whole series, we're not systematic really. (Caroline)

Shirley reported that they did use it for some off-air recording, mainly for short-term viewing.

> If I'm out on a Wednesday at choir rehearsal, then he'll record *MASH* so that when I come in we'll sit down and see it . . . that's a short-term thing. (Shirley)

For Caroline and her partner the original motive for purchasing a VCR was medium-term use.

> The aim is, and it's been reasonably well achieved, the aim is to use the video to assemble some stuff that you want to watch, and then watch it, set aside an evening and watch it and in the winter particularly we got quite close to doing that. (Caroline)

But she went on to say,

> How it was used originally . . . the view was that a vast library of pirated films was going to be built up from TV and

watched, that was planned at the outset, but it became rather random very rapidly thereafter. (Caroline)

This indicates the novelty dimension of VCR use which is undoubtedly an important aspect of the life of the VCR in different households, but Caroline then identified another major problem:

> I think there comes a point where there is more to be watched than time to watch it and there doesn't seem to be much point in going on recording them. (Caroline)

The whole concept of time-shift is premissed on the assumption that there is a potentially unlimited amount of time available for viewing. Again, busy domestic life and routines intervene in this picture as unwatched videos stack up on the shelves. This point was made by Shirley:

> We try, if we do record things, we do try to see them very soon, otherwise it gets silly and you haven't got the time to watch the programme . . . I mean if you haven't got time to watch them in the first place you probably haven't got time to watch the recording. (Shirley)

Beth stated that the short-term function was hardly ever used, not even for her beloved *Star Trek*.

> I mean, if we go out, well we miss it, and very rarely do we record something, certainly I wouldn't record *Star Trek* if I was going out. I might record a film I particularly wanted to watch. (Beth)

She did, though, record *Star Trek* if she was in, because at that time she would be putting the children to bed; she would then watch it later the same evening. However, major use was as a medium-term source of films and some work-related documentary programmes, recorded via the timer if they were out.

As we can see, this group of mainly middle-class women intended to use the VCR for medium-term viewing, but this is actually not often achieved. There was also a distinct bias towards what were often described as 'quality' programmes and films as well as educational material recorded for their children. I will return to this topic in the section dealing with long-term archiving of tapes.

Organized shifters

Susan and her partner were avid users of the VCR for time-shift and she used it as a fail-safe device whilst watching her favourite soap opera.

> I sit and watch it [*Coronation Street*] and record it in case there were any interruptions. So I have a tape in just in case. Somebody always phones up, guaranteed. I used to take the phone off the hook. (Susan)

When they were both watching television in the evening, they would automatically put a tape in.

> Well, the funny thing about our video, we tend to watch it as . . . we tend to watch something on television and record it as we're watching it. Whatever it is. We put a tape in, just in case . . . erm . . . if there's some film on and they don't describe them correctly in the papers, it can be fantastic and they'll say it's rubbish, we will turn on that film and record it and start watching it, and watch it all the way through. If it's rubbish, we just go over it again, otherwise we keep it. (Susan)

When they went out for the evening, which was quite often, they would plan what they were going to record.

> Yes. If we're going out we work out what to record. If it's a *Dynasty* night or a *Dallas* night or *Coronation Street* night, it will be recorded for me and anything on that side before and after, for three hours, it will be recorded round there. If that's not on he can watch whatever he wants and record whatever he wants. It sounds very selfish, but as long as I watch my *Dynasty, Dallas* and *Coronation Street*, I'm a happy person. They're my three main things to watch, mustn't miss them. (Susan)

Like Susan and other television enthusiasts, Julie planned her recording.

> I see what's on telly in a morning on the Teletext and I record if I'm out in the day. I think afternoon programmes are as good as evening ones and, like I'm out tonight and I know *Dallas* is on because it's on every Wednesday, so I shall ask him to record it, I don't really sit down and say what I want, I know what I want recording.

I record films, a lot of the TV serials. I don't record as much now *Dallas* and *Coronation Street* when I'm in, but I have to record *Brookside* because he won't let me watch it when he's here [laugh]. Anything like that, anything after nine o'clock we record that. We use it . . . I bet we use it every day just about.

I recorded *Master of the Game*, it was on a Sunday wasn't it, and it was a Bond film on the other side, so we watched the Bond film and recorded it, and then I watched it on a Monday when Andrew was working. (Julie)

Is there anything that your husband likes that you don't want to watch?

Sport . . . I record racing for him, or if there was a documentary about a sportsman, you know, sometimes they have these interviews . . . racing people and all those sort of things. Andrew'd like anything like that, so I'd record that for him.

I asked Rene, another self-defined television enthusiast, if she decided what she wanted to record.

You mean in *Radio and TV Times*? . . . oh yes, absolutely. Yes, we both go through the motions, you know, every night, looking. This is why we buy them. (Rene)

They often recorded late films for viewing on a Sunday afternoon as well as keeping up with their favourite series and serials. She was asked if having the video had changed their viewing patterns.

Oh it has, absolutely, I mean we spend a lot more time actually viewing. (Rene)

She was one of the few women in the entire sample who felt very easy about watching a tape during the afternoon; in fact, she was watching a recording of *Dallas* when I arrived for the interview. She would quite often settle down with her coffee and watch something she had recorded the previous evening.

I think that's one good thing about the machine, if you do want an early night and yet there's something on television that you feel you don't want to miss, well you can record it. (Rene)

What is notable about these women, compared to the others in the group, is that they have little or no guilty feelings about television watching, although Susan did express a little fear about her viewing.

> I can't possibly say, right it's two o'clock, turn the television on, I've got too many things to do during the daytime, I couldn't, couldn't do it to myself, that would be a total addict [laugh]; I'm about three quarters of the way there [laugh]. (Susan)

But she, like Rene, would watch a pre-recorded soap opera that she had missed the night before. Megan also used the time-shift regularly.

> Well, I usually find that most programmes . . . you always get a set of good programmes on each side so you have to tape one side and watch the other one and then either save up for weekends or afternoons if there's nothing on, and then watch what I've taped. Every Saturday we tape BBC more or less six o'clock until . . . depending on what's on, but we tend to watch ITV. We do tape an awful lot, I mean if we go out we set the video, if we go on holiday we tape programmes, well, we usually move the video, but we have a thing with the neighbours going and, like, if Janet is away I tape for her and if I'm away she tapes for me. (Megan)

Many of the households owned a small number of tapes, an important factor differentiating between short-, medium- and long-term usage. Cathy and Megan made short- and medium-term use of the VCR, although Megan only had three tapes.

> We tape of lot of soaps, like *Dynasty* and *Dallas*. And if there's any films come on, I tend to tape a lot of films . . . more for rainy days when the kids are off school and that, films, like *Blazing Saddles*, that's just been on; I taped that for the kids to watch when they're off school. (Megan)

It was very rare that tapes went unwatched in these households. I asked Julie if they had recorded programmes that they never got around to watching.

> Occasionally, yes. Like, we've recorded *The Travelling Man*, there've been two episodes and we still haven't watched them and there's another one on tonight. I mean, I've had time to

watch it but, as you can see, the state of the house at the moment, Andrew hasn't . . . so if it ever got that I needed the tape, I'd say 'oh well, you're just not going to have time now to watch' and then I'd wipe it off, but if it were something . . . but if it was the third one and we'd watched two, if we'd got into it, I wouldn't have done, but you see we haven't seen it at all. I mean, we might not, we might catch up and get round to watching it. (Julie)

TIMER

These four women were quite methodical about their taping and viewing and knew what was on each of the tapes. They were enthusiastic about television and about the time-shift facility which the VCR provided and they had a commitment to off-air recording which was not shared to the same extent by the other women. Julie used the time-shift function herself but Cathy relied on her husband to record things for her; Megan, who found herself in the house more than the rest of her family, tended to use the manual record function.

'Real' time

I indicated earlier in this chapter that there are problems experienced in recording certain forms of live television. Rene, although an avid user of time-shift, was very clear about what she did not want to record.

The only thing I don't like on the machine is if anything's happened. I like to come down. Now, I'm not an early riser, but when the Brighton bomb . . . Bill watches breakfast TV whilst he's having his breakfast and he said, 'come on for God's sake get up' . . . so things like that I wouldn't have liked him to have recorded it for me to watch two hours later, I do like to watch that whilst it's actually happening.

Anything else like that?

Well certainly elections, by-elections, this kind of thing . . . I like it as it's happening. It wouldn't be the same if I know about it and watching it three hours later, no. (Rene)

Here even short-term recording will not do, and real-time viewing is preferred.

Time-shifting *Dallas* presented some problems of a different nature for Janet. It meant that, until she had seen it, she couldn't talk about it to her neighbours who had watched it.

> Well, like, we'll go out on a morning and we'll say . . . like if I haven't managed to watch it, it's 'don't tell me . . . don't tell me what's happened . . . I haven't watched it' . . . or we might go 'oh, what do you think? Oh . . .', yes we do. (Janet)

A very important part of the pleasure of television serials is the gossip about them the following day. Whilst VCR time-shifting allows more convenient and sometimes more pleasurable private viewing of these serials, it means sacrificing the shared experience of viewing at a regular time of day.

Kicking off the shoes: time out

For some women the VCR was used to allow them to watch a favoured programme 'in peace' at some quiet time. Janet often taped *Falcon Crest* if she couldn't watch it during the day. When did she actually watch it?

> Erm . . . well I can't watch it when I come home because I'm busy with kiddies, plus, you can't relax if they're in and out, do you know what I mean? I feel as if I've been cheated of that hour if they're in and out . . . can I have this . . . so, I'd probably watch it when I come back from swimming at about eleven o'clock, because, as I say, we go for a drink and I'd just sit and watch it then. I like to tape *Dallas* because I go out about quarter past eight, so I tape that you see.

So when do you watch Dallas *then?*

> Well, there again, well I wouldn't have time to . . . I'd either watch, say, I'd been to Leeds, I'd watch one at night when I come home, and one the next morning. I'd wash up, and, you know, just sort of tidy round and I'd watch it then, for the simple reason if you don't they tape over it [laugh] . . . you know, if you leave the tapes there you end up with kiddies' programmes or something on and they tape over them, so I do try and watch them as soon as possible, for that reason, otherwise they just go. (Janet)

The VCR can be used to resolve or avoid potential conflict. Audrey's husband dominated the television during the evening, effectively preventing her and her son from watching the kinds of programmes they liked, and she observed,

> He'll move it from programme to programme and that's where we find the use of the video because, erm, if there's something I don't like and he does – he gets his way unfortunately with the television you know [pause] – and Geoffrey [son] or myself will set the video up to record, mostly travel things, we like travel and documentary type programmes you see. (Audrey)

Similarly, some women used the VCR to tape programmes which they knew their partners, and sometimes their children, would not want to watch. For example:

> I tape, sort of the medical things, you know, the women's things that have been on, operations and things like that, and the AIDS programme and things like that, I will watch when he isn't in because he won't want to watch them. (Michelle)

She also recorded films off air.

> I like the old black and white ones. I watched last weekend, *The Bursten Rebellion*, the one about the schoolteacher. I like them about true stories; I would tape something, a film that was basically true, and then I would watch it during the day, whilst I was ironing or something like that. (Michelle)

Several of the women in the study worked part time, some in the evenings and they found time-shift enabled them to watch after work. Rene, who was 50, had been a keen cinema-goer in the past ('I've queued for hours at cinemas') and this had left her with an affection for the films of that period. Her husband recorded them for her when they were on television and she was out at work.

> Well, you see, weekends I work on Saturday lunch time and my husband takes the dogs on a Saturday and, erm, if there's been a good film on, because my favourite era for films were obviously the thirties and forties, I mean rather forties and early fifties, and the Bette Davis films I can see them over and over again, and they do quite good ones on Channel 4 and BBC 2 on a Saturday afternoon. If there's anything worth watching he'll have recorded it and whilst he's out in the

garden I'll sit here with my feet up and a coffee and watch what's been recorded in the afternoon. (Rene)

Cathy and Brenda used the VCR to record programmes when they were at work. Cathy worked in the evenings and her husband recorded *Coronation Street* and *Emmerdale Farm* for her.

Like, he taped me *Coronation Street* the other night, I watched it this morning and that'll be it, he'll rub it off tonight and tape me *Emmerdale Farm* . . . that's what we use it for . . . it's great . . . something to look forward to when you get home. (Cathy)

Brenda had just been made redundant from her evening job as a packer, but she used to watch recorded tapes when she got home after her shift.

Yes . . . when I got home . . . you sort of, when you're at work you feel tired then you come home about ten at night you seem to need an hour to unwind . . . it's usually twelve o'clock before we went to bed. (Brenda)

The VCR offers the opportunity for certain members of the household to view late at night. Sheila told me that her 18-year-old daughter often watched 'her' programmes late at night.

It's usually late, and to everybody's annoyance, she manages to watch what she's recorded, yes. (Sheila)

Similarly, Sandra, the youngest woman in my study, found the VCR gave her the opportunity to enjoy her own programmes without parental distractions.

I tape comedy . . . I like *Auf Wiedersehen, Pet* and *The Young Ones*, erm . . . my mum and dad can't stand them . . . they don't see how it can be funny, they don't see how *The Young Ones* can be funny at all . . . you try to watch it and my dad'll fall asleep and start snoring, you know, and my mum's sat there knitting away and [sigh]; I think, 'Forget it – I'll tape it and watch it when I'm on my own.' (Sandra)

Barbara liked to stay up late at night and, again, the VCR was a source of entertainment for the small hours.

I'm not one for going to bed at night; now if there's two films on, I'll tape one, that means when the television goes off I can sit up and watch another one. It can be two or three o'clock in the morning before I go to bed. So I can sit up instead of having to go to bed. (Barbara)

Bad timing

Kay, Sheila and Shirley seemed to be on the margins of the household's television and video decision-making processes. For Kay this appeared to be a positive choice. She was asked if she ever recorded things.

Never, no. I'm not that inclined, or that interested really . . . there aren't many programmes that interest me really that's why I've never involved myself in it really. (Kay)

Her husband, as we have seen, was a very keen television watcher and used the VCR as an extension of television, recording one programme whilst watching another and consequently watching more television than before. He would plan very carefully.

Is he very methodical about it?

Yes.

He records things and then watches them?

Yes, definitely . . . I mean he might have them for a very long time, but he'll always watch them. (Kay)

Kay was reluctant to talk very much about this and appeared to begrudge the fact that her husband watched more television as a result of having the VCR. As we have seen elsewhere, she resented it and felt that it 'kept them in' more than she would like.

For Sheila and Shirley the marginality was more by default than a positive decision, mainly due to lack of planning.

I miss an awful lot of things, erm . . . simply because I happen to be upstairs and get carried away and I come down and whatever it is is on or my husband has been watching . . . I don't really . . . well I don't look through the books to see what's on, so if I find out later I'm a little bit annoyed and it's a case of 'Why didn't you remind me, I should have watched this' you know, erm . . . and he says 'Well the books are there you know . . . you choose your programmes.' This is why we have the other television, you know, so that we can each watch what we want or record something, but then again, the recording part . . . it's finding time to watch it when you've recorded it and that can cause problems, you know. (Sheila)

Sheila did, however, record programmes for her children. Did she ever record anything for herself?

No, not really for myself, it's mostly for . . . I might put it on for the children really. (Sheila)

Her lack of opportunity to plan an evening's viewing for herself meant that she tended to 'watch what's on'.

Well, it's on on an evening, but I wouldn't say that I really watch. I can't really concentrate. I haven't a lot of power of concentration, the slightest thing distracts me, you know . . . I could do to take a little television and go up into my own bedroom if I really want to watch something, you know . . . that would be the only way to do it because if one of them comes in with a boyfriend or girlfriend, that's it, you know . . . because I'm not one that . . . I'm very easily distracted and erm . . . so I suppose out of a full evening I don't really watch, to actually say I watch and devour much more than an hour of it really. (Sheila)

Sheila 'serviced' her husband and family and her sick mother, leaving little or no time for herself. This is reflected in her inability to engage with both television and the VCR, although she does engage with the VCR on her children's behalf, offering them yet another domestic service.

Shirley sometimes used the VCR to record something on one channel whilst watching another, but this did not happen very often. Like Sheila, this woman was not really aware of what was on television, so she rarely planned what she was going to watch.

We don't buy the *Radio Times*, you see, and I don't know what's on television until the evening because we don't get the paper in the morning. I see it when he comes home from work at night, then the first chance I get in the evening I'll sit down and skim through the paper, and look at the television page, so really unless it's something regularly that's coming up I don't decide until I'm there, really. (Shirley)

Alison did not feel that the VCR had enabled them to settle disputes about watching.

> No, not really, it's added to it because sometimes I feel as if I'm saying to them [her children] 'you can't record it' and there's no apparent reason, it's just because Brian doesn't want them to.

Do you ever tape anything?

> No, no. I suppose if there was something on that I'd like I probably would, but without sounding too . . . if the children wanted to tape something in preference I'd let them have it, it's not that important . . . it's more important for them than it is for me. You know, I wouldn't insist on watching something if they wanted to watch . . . but Brian would and has done.

Does he tape things?

> Yes, mainly late at night, if there's a film he wants to watch . . . he'll tape it, he taped the football on Sunday because his two little ones were here and he can't sit down and watch it. Boxing, he tapes that. (Alison)

The VCR was a site of conflict in this household and its use was controlled by the adult male.

TAPE MANAGEMENT AND ARCHIVING (LONG-TERM RECORDING)

This section will consider those households in which the video recorder is used to build up a 'library' or achive of tapes. I asked the women how many blank tapes they had and about their distribution between members of the households, trying to establish which members of the household were responsible for archiving as well as what was recorded on these tapes and the circumstances under which they were watched.

Very few of the women in the study had their own tape for recording off air, although their children usually did.

> The children have a tape each.

Do you have a tape?

Well, my husband and I just swap the others, we share the others out, and I mean, if they've run out of their tapes, they'd use one of ours, and then we'd use one of theirs. It's not a rigid thing, but they have a tape each and if they want to record something and we've put something on it, well, that's our tough luck. (Hilary).

The number of tapes in a household is an indication of intended use of the VCR. Thus, the households with twenty plus tapes had often originally planned on building up a library of good films, rather than using the VCR to time-shift. Caroline observed that the system had broken down.

I think we must have about thirty tapes, but it's virtually impossible to tell what's on them. There's horrible, scruffy-looking, crossed-out, you know . . . James's capacity to maintain the system over any length of time has long since collapsed. He knows little bits of what's on what tapes . . . the kids have tapes and they know what's on theirs. The early tapes are all beautifully recorded, you know, full of Marx Brothers films, and things like that and they're still there. (Caroline)

There is no doubt that this woman's partner is responsible for the archiving of tapes in this household, and this is not surprising given that it was his decision to purchase the VCR.

One household had around fifty tapes and were serious archivers, mainly of movies, although the dominant user was Jim, Jenny's husband. I asked her which tapes they watched a lot.

I'll get the list [laugh] . . . because there are a lot, the girls get to see them as well, then all of a sudden it becomes 'ours' . . . the girls get addicted to them . . . *High Society* was originally mine and now I'm quite happy to wipe it, I've seen it so many times . . . but the girls won't wipe it. Erm . . . *Network*, I think is mine and that's been on for ages, *Klute* . . . that's my great favourite, and that's been on almost since we've had the video. *Reds*..there's stuff on here that's ancient, and it's Jim's. *Close Encounters* . . . *Jaws, The Duellists*, and we've got so many of them, we don't watch them very often, but he'd never dream of wiping them. (Jenny)

I asked if there was any problem in getting 'her' films recorded for the archive.

> Oh, there's no problem, because I think Jim's the main user, so if I say I want something or other, that's fine. Yes, if I actually stick to something, then we definitely have it . . . I don't feel the same need to record that Jim does. As long as I can watch it there and then, that's fine. I mean, I wouldn't record all the Ealing comedies and Jim does . . . I would make sure that I saw it. Now, on the other hand, knowing that he's going to record it, I think, no I won't bother. Almost every film that Jim's interested in, if he wants to watch it once he wants to watch it again, so we record it, whereas it's got to be a bit special for me to watch it.

Does he ever wipe off the films he's recorded for himself?

> Yes, it's . . . this is very delicate . . . because I'm not . . . if I've seen it a few times, then I'm quite willing to wipe it, with several exceptions, probably half a dozen exceptions . . . whereas Jim won't wipe for ages and ages; the girls seem to be taking the same tendencies as him I think, we've now got fifty videos. (Jenny)

Jenny reiterates what many of the women in the sample said about their husband's desire to record, archive and re-view films. This is partly due to the fact that many of the men establish themselves as the dominant users of the VCR, that they generally have more time in the home to watch films and tape, and also that they consider their choice of films as superior to those that their partners would choose.

However, Rene, who instigated the purchase of their VCR, when asked which of them knew most about the content of their tapes, said,

> Oddly enough, my husband. Yes, because, this is what I mean, he didn't want the video, but he's the one that is really in charge of it. (Rene)

We saw earlier that Kay's husband was methodical about recording off air and watching the tapes, and Shirley's husband also organized the spare tapes for off-air recording use. Kay and Rene found that their husbands were much more keen on re-viewing films than they were. I asked Kay if she kept movies on tape.

Erm . . . I don't think we've got any recorded that I . . . for
me. Because, there again, I don't like to see anything twice –
I know I watched *Gremlins* twice, but once I know what's
coming you've lost my interest, it's got to be an element of
surprise to keep my interest going. Whereas, my husband can
watch a film over and over again, and love it every time he
sees it. And I go, 'How can you? You know what's coming
next!' (Kay)

Rene reported that her husband had kept a recording of *Casablanca*. What kinds of things did she keep?

Well I don't. Now this is where it's come into its own for
Bill. I have recorded things to keep, then I've thought 'oh no,
this is silly'. But we've got *Flight of the Condor* – that three-
hour documentary – now that again is Bill's. And we've got
a Spencer Tracy film, we both like that one – *Inherit the Wind*.
I have recorded things – I've kept *The Sound of Music*, actually,
because I think Emma, my granddaughter will like that . . . I
sort of recorded *Funny Girl* to keep, but I've let that go now.
I tend to think 'Oh yes, I definitely want to keep that' and
then it becomes unimportant because there's something else I
prefer, and I haven't got a spare tape. I think 'Oh well, that
can go, I'm going to record this' – but certainly those three
things will be there forever. (Rene)

Two of the three things that will be 'there forever', *Casablanca*
and *Flight of the Condor*, belonged to her husband and she had to
be flexible with her tapes if she ran out of recording space. She
also seemed to be less keen on archiving in general than he was.
I asked her how often they watched *Casablanca*.

Well, frankly, I'm sick of watching it. I mean, yes my husband
does, he really thinks it's marvellous. In fact, he went to the
cinema a couple of years ago – they had *The Maltese Falcon*
and *Casablanca* on, he paid money to go and see them again,
you know, which, well . . . I thought that was ludicrous. But,
however, yes, I . . . I think 'Oh no, I just can't watch it, not
again' . . . then Bill's getting quite involved in it, and yes I
do watch it. (Rene)

We have seen that, much to their dismay, Kay's and Rene's
husbands would watch a film over and over again, whereas they

themselves were much less enthusiastic. Whilst Susan was a fan of television and films, her attitude to re-viewing films was different from that of her husband.

> Films John records . . . erm . . . like *The Godfather* and all the larger films. I mean, we've still got them, he would watch them a million times [laugh] when I was out [laugh], he'd watch them over and over again, certain films he can watch a million times – ridiculous.

Are there any films you can watch again?

> Erm yes . . . erm . . . not a million times – about two or three times I could watch them. But, hang on . . . *Superman* – *Superman*, I could watch all day, he's my hero, I love him [laugh]. (Susan)

Although the reasons given for questioning the value of keeping tapes are different, there is a general feeling of not wanting to watch films or programmes repeatedly. This could also account for the relatively small number of purchased films in the entire sample.

Caroline and Hilary had recorded Shakespeare productions, and kept them, but often these went unwatched.

> I remember for a long time we had Laurence Olivier as *King Lear*, taking up one and a half hours of tape time and there was a sort of puritanical feeling that it ought to be watched, and it eventually gave place to something else, I forget what. (Caroline).

> I think we haven't watched *Cymbeline* again, to be honest – we've watched *Macbeth* a lot, but I suspect that's because Peter was doing it for O level and we've watched *Love's Labour's Lost* more, perhaps because it's lighter, or perhaps because I know it better. But I didn't keep *Hamlet* and regretted it. (Hilary)

For Caroline and Hilary, items considered to be of cultural value should be recorded, serving, in Hilary's case, a clear educational function for her children, but with some reservations.

> I keep them because I think the children might want them, but I also have a feeling that they're less . . . Although it is

the play, it's not the same as reading the play. You feel limited by the visual pictures much more, so that we actually have discussed whether they are worth keeping because it isn't the same as a piece of music. My husband agrees – he thinks that visual things you tire of more quickly. (Hilary)

Shirley and her husband were creating their own tape of *MASH* 'highlights' for archiving, and had considered doing the same with *Fawlty Towers;* these were two programmes they considered to be television 'classics'. I asked Susan what kinds of things they kept long-term.

Most of them are movies and there's a couple of tapes that have got bits of everything on, bits of this and that. Old films, very old films, you know, Bing Crosby films – I love those. A lot of musical shows and things, big ones, what's his name? . . . Frank Sinatra, any of the shows he was on. We were making our own tape of all the big stars, the big, big stars, old stars and we were combining tapes to keep forever, until I went over them.

Oh . . . accidentally?

Yes [laugh], we'd been doing it for two and half years, and we had a fabulous tape set up and I went over it with *Coronation Street* [sigh . . . laugh]. (Susan)

Compiling special tapes as referred to by Susan and Shirley is unusual in the sample and was not reported by many of the women, although, of course, other members of the household could well be engaged in this kind of practice without their knowledge.

Edna used her stored tapes to pass the time when her newsagent's shop was quiet.

Very convenient. I must agree, it's very convenient . . . erm . . . it's nice to be able to pick up a film, pop it in the video and have it on in here and, sort of lunch-time, we have an hour and a half for lunch, so if it goes on when we first start lunch and carries on afterwards, it doesn't really matter, because when we open the shop at half past two we're never busy 'til the kids come at quarter past three; so we've usually time to watch whatever you want . . . including my video of Neil Diamond [laugh]. (Edna).

This woman had already mentioned her passion for Neil Diamond and had purchased a copy of *The Jazz Singer* when they first bought the VCR. She observed that their use of the VCR had changed.

> We used to get films from the video library at first because we hadn't got a stock of things that you wanted to watch again and again. Er . . . we have one or two things that we won't ever wipe off . . . erm . . . I've got Al Jolson in *The Jolson Story* and *Jolson Sings Again* and those are two that I won't ever wipe off because I don't think they'll ever be on the television again. Erm . . . my boys are very much into, not martial arts, it's a different kind of thing, it's called Akido – it's something rather special I believe so they wanted *Shogun* so that's all on video and that won't be wiped off. Then something, a rather light-hearted programme, but we think it's lovely, it was a play, a Play for Today on BBC and they did one and not long afterwards they did a follow up to it and it's called *Dominic Hyde*, and that won't ever be wiped off I don't think, because we loved the story and the music particularly is very good. So, those are the things that won't be wiped off. Then, er . . . what else have we got, oh, *Mame*, the musical *Mame*, that's something that we all seem to like to pick up . . . er . . . so that might not be wiped off for quite a while, but apart from that we swop and . . . (Edna)

What is worth noting here is the way in which some of the archived tapes seem to be enjoyed by all the family, and the favourites were often watched on the rare times when the family were all in together. Jean, also a woman with a grown-up family still at home, spoke of their archiving of *The Boys from the Blackstuff*.

> Yes, we've got *Boys from the Blackstuff* which is fabulous. Jack's [husband] got almost every opera that's been on the television, he's a great fan and we can't stand opera . . . so he has taped all the operas and then when he's in on his own, quiet, he watches them. We all thought *Boys from the Blackstuff* was marvellous.
>
> *How often do you watch that?*
>
> I would say we've watched it four times . . . we watched it

when it was actually on, taping it at the same time . . . when
my sister and her husband came over from York, they don't
watch much television, and they hadn't seen it and they
thought it was great, so they watched a couple of episodes.
Then my eldest son came back from Saudi Arabia for Christmas and he watched the whole thing, but I think the favourite
episode was where there was a funeral . . . he died and they
ended up in the pub and they all have this sing–song and it
ends up with them flying through the window . . . we watch
that a lot more than the others. (Jean)

Clearly there is a tendency to ritualize the viewing of favourite
tapes, at Christmas and other times when the family are at home
together. However, as Jean has indicated, tapes can also be
archived for individual viewing when an enthusiasm is not shared.
Lesley's husband had an enthusiasm for boxing which she did
not share. She began by reporting how many tapes they had.

Lots . . . we usually have a few . . . which someone has taped
something, they haven't written what is on. They probably
have watched it or they have not . . . but you're allowed to
tape on any of those, and it's too bad . . . the ones in the
boxes belong to my husband, they're boxing . . . he keeps
those, the big fights, he has them all.

Do you keep any movies on tape?

I think he's got about three which he might watch again . . .
if I see something once I don't really want to watch it again.
(Lesley)

The boxed tapes belonging to her husband were kept separate,
and had a permanence which the other tapes did not, but apart
from these Lesley had very little knowledge of what the tapes
contained.

The women with younger children said that their archiving
was mainly films or programmes for the children who also had
their own tapes for recording purposes. Janet said they had twelve
tapes, but that three of those belonged to her three children. She
was asked whether they archived any tapes.

Well, this is the problem, they tend to tape on, and then you
can't . . . they want things, like they've got the tapes of their
own, and on each of them there's something they want to

keep, so therefore if there's another thing that's going to be on, a film or anything, they can't get it on there; so they've got *Kelly's Heroes, Sinbad* – I've just taped over that 'cos they've had it three years . . . they've got *Star Wars, Mary Poppins* is on the little girl's tape . . . erm . . . I don't know what's on Michael's . . . oh I think it was that one that's just been on with Burt Reynolds – *Cannonball* – and on Richard's there's one of them *Temple of Doom* ones . . . erm . . . and then one's my husband's with space and all sorts of bits on, you know, he's interested in . . . he likes computer programmes, and anything like that.

What about you, do you keep any films or anything like that?

No, I can't say I have, no . . . they'd probably tape over mine anyway [laugh], no I don't. My husband's got *Close Encounters of the Third Kind*, which he won't let me tape over, he likes anything like that and, erm . . . he's got bits of documentaries and things on . . . he likes anything like that . . . space . . . anything like that . . . but, as I say, I haven't got anything that . . . all mine I tape over, I tape anything, because it's mostly serials, you see.

Do you ever record a film from TV?

Erm . . . there again, mostly it's for . . . if the kiddies want to watch it . . . it's for them rather than for me . . . I wouldn't really think of recording something for myself. (Janet)

Janet, like Lesley, pointed to the archived video tapes which were in boxes with spines designed to have the appearance of books. In both cases, these were displayed on shelves in the living-room. I asked Janet who had purchased the boxes.

Oh, I did – I thought, well, if we're going to keep these things . . . I mean they're not very nice to look at are they? I think they look nicer on the shelves like that. (Janet)

Betty confirmed that they mainly kept films for their children.

We keep the children's ones. I've kept one that I taped about twelve months since – *My Fair Lady* – that's the only one that I've taped and kept. Course, many a time Derek'll say 'Oh, you don't watch it, might as well tape over it' – I say 'You're not'. (Betty)

This family purchased their tapes on family shopping expeditions, but Alison, whose children and partner were constantly at odds over the VCR, had a problem about this.

At Christmas, Brian bought four for Christmas.

Do the children have their own tapes?

No . . . not really, we got two tapes free with the video and I think those are really for the children. He more or less lets them do what they like on those . . . but now they've got films on . . . they keep saying when they get some money saved up they're going to buy their own, then they can tape what they like.

Have you ever thought of buying blank tapes?

[Laughing] I never have any money [laugh] I have no spare cash for blank tapes . . . as much as I would like to buy them something, my money's tied up. (Alison)

Alison's partner's desire to archive certain films caused conflict between him and the children, and she found herself in the middle of the dispute.

You know, there's no tape and they say, 'Well, why can't we tape over that film, we've seen it two or three times' . . . a couple of films we'd had them for months and months and we'd only watched them once or twice and, you know, they kept saying 'Can we tape over it?' and he'd say 'No, it's a good film we'll keep that'. But, as I say, at Christmas we bought four new tapes so we're not too bad now, but he'll say . . . I mean, my friends, they've got twenty-odd tapes, I feel as if I'm saying no to them all the time and I think, 'Why have we got the damned thing if they can't tape things?' It's as if Brian can't be bothered sometimes, it isn't that he doesn't want them to have it on, it's too much trouble, and that's why I think Mark, last week, wanted to know how to time it, because he feels that if he could time it he could do it without Brian knowing . . . you know, not deceiving or anything like that, but just so he wouldn't have to ask him. (Alison).

Here control is exercised over other members of the household by the person who purchases blank tapes for recording and determines how those tapes should be used. In this way archiving uses up tape-time and severely restricts the range of choices available to other members of the household. Alison herself had no financial means of increasing the availability of tape-time for her children.

Apart from Susan, the rest of the women did not consider themselves responsible for tape management or archiving. For two of the households, the only tapes that were archived were 'home videos': records of a wedding and, in one case, old home movies transferred on to video. These were usually viewed at Christmas time or when various different members of the family got together at other times.

SUMMARY

Half of the women had a problem with setting time aside either to watch tapes or to plan recordings. This was in part due to a declared lack of interest in either television, the VCR, or both. However, recording off air requires some forethought and planning in order to establish the time of the programme to be recorded and, if necessary, setting the timer, as well as locating a suitable tape. Quite simply, many of the women felt that they did not have the time during their day to indulge in this planning for themselves, although some would record programmes for either their partners or their children. A small number of women did not get access to the programme schedules until early evening, when their partners came home with their only newspaper. Only seven of the households took *Radio Times* or *TV Times* regularly. Other members of the household with access to schedules, and the time and inclination to plan ahead, would therefore tend to get their way with television and video choice.

On the occasions when women did make recordings, many of which were serials, these often had to be viewed during the day when the house was empty, because of lack of opportunity to view in the evening. We have seen that a very important part of the pleasure of television serials is to gossip about them the following day. Whilst VCR time-shifting allows more convenient and sometimes more pleasurable private viewing of these serials, it means sacrificing the shared experience of viewing at a regular time of day. Colin MacCabe suggests that 'much of television's appeal springs from the fact that viewers know they are watching

what others are watching' (MacCabe 1988: 31), but he does not
take time-shifting into account, a practice which shatters this
viewing 'community'. Viewing has to be carefully organized, as
we have seen, in order to keep up with a serial, but also in
order to keep up with television-related talk. The regularity and
immediacy of long-running serials like *Dallas* or *Eastenders* exert
a particular kind of pressure on the time-shifter. This draws our
attention to the appropriateness, or otherwise, of time-shifting for
particular types of product. We noted that Rene felt it necessary to
view live events and televised disasters 'as they happen' and we
could tentatively suggest here that catastrophes, for example, the
Brighton bomb, the Iranian Embassy siege and the sinking of the
Herald of Free Enterprise, all of which appeared on live television,
operate, in effect, as an open text. That is, the outcome is
unknown, both to the broadcaster and the viewers; we are literally
watching in suspense together and are given the status of eyewit-
ness, as Claus-Deiter Rath says (1989: 87). Christine Geraghty,
writing about long-running serials and soap operas, suggests that
one of their distinctive features is that 'the everyday quality of
narrative time and events, all encourage us to believe that this a
narrative whose future is not yet written' (Geraghty 1981: 11).
This is not to suggest that there is any confusion in the minds
of the viewers between a soap opera and the 'live' coverage of
an event, but it would seem that the soap opera's organization
of time and the way in which it presents itself as having an
unwritten future, its 'here and now' quality, interpellates the
viewer in similar ways.

We noted that watching video tapes during the day was often
due to absolute necessity and, in fact, Janet claimed that she felt
less guilty watching 'real' time television than she did when
watching a video tape. The television is transmitting whether she
decides to watch or not, but the use of a video tape implies a
guilty decision to view which is totally in her control. This would
seem to be an important difference between the experience of
broadcast television and time-shift video tapes for women at
home during the day.

Ever since Peter Fiddick confessed in *The Guardian* to recording
programmes he felt he ought to watch and then never actually
getting around to watching them, it has been a commonly-held
belief that, in general, people do not watch their recorded tapes.
However, on the evidence of this sample of women, it seems

that this is true only of the middle-class households, some of whom did report this kind of behaviour. Indeed, they claimed to record 'classic' television, concerts and productions of Shakespeare, some of which they had never watched. Conversely, most of the lower-middle- and working-class households did, in fact, watch what they recorded and very few indulged in the doubtful luxury of accumulating self-improving videos which they felt they ought to watch.

It can be seen that the distribution of tapes within the households tended to favour children and partners, with very few of the women owning a tape of their own or archiving tapes for themselves. The organization and maintenance of an archive would seem to be a predominantly male and middle-class activity. The limit which economic circumstances place on the number of tapes is significant here, but the gendered nature of this practice requires some examination. Obviously the question of available time as well as inclination is important, but some of the women reported their partner's concern to re-view tapes, especially movies. The women themselves did not share this preference. The whole concept of an archive is based on the assumption that there will be more than one viewing of the product, something that would appear to be a predominantly male activity. Even those women who did have archived films of their own, for example Susan and Jenny, reported that they were much more prepared to 'wipe' than their partners. In Jenny's case there was a distinct reluctance by her partner to wipe anything once it had been recorded. A significant number of the women reported that their children of both genders would constantly return to a familiar text in rather the same way. This, of course, can partly be accounted for in terms of available time to indulge in this re-viewing, but this is not a sufficient explanation. It does seem to be evidence also of their pleasure in the film *as a film*, rather than simply as a vehicle for narrative. As we have seen in chapter 4, story was an extremely important textual element for women. Once this is known, there seems little point in re-engaging with the text.

Chapter 7

The VCR: hiring tapes

> I know this girl – she comes into the shop where I work, and she goes to me 'Oh, there's a new "three parter" coming out.'
>
> (Megan)

The main use for the domestic VCR, other than off-air recording, is playing pre-recorded tapes, purchased or hired from a video rental outlet. The majority of the tapes available for purchase or hire are movies. 'Movies' in this context include films made specially for video distribution, films made for television, both British and American, as well as feature films produced primarily for the cinema. In Britain in the early 1980s, the beginning of the consumer boom in domestic VCR ownership or rental, a feature of almost every high street was a new phenomenon known as the 'video library'. These were often hastily converted small shops. The tapes were boxed and displayed on shelves or stands; their covers took their references and graphic artwork from movie posters, showing the title of the movie, eye-catching images, and, where appropriate, its 'stars'. A brief description appeared on the reverse. In the larger outlets tapes were shelved in categories, for example, Action/Adventure, Horror, Comedy, Family, Adult, etc. In these early days, usually in order to finance their purchase of new material, these under-capitalized libraries demanded a membership fee, often as high as £40, as well as a nightly fee for the hiring of tapes. At the time of the interviews, 1985–6, it was possible to join a video library free of charge, and pay a nightly rental fee of £1.00 to £1.50 per tape, although the purchase price of pre-recorded movies averaged about £40.[1] Other outlets for video tapes were the corner shop and garages, but notably not supermarkets or chain stores whose organizations were not flexible enough to respond to this new retailing opportunity nor to process a rental system. These outlets existed in the 'twilight zones' of shopping, attracting the impulse buy or an unplanned extra when going to buy a pint of milk or filling the car with petrol.

This new market spawned several magazines, most notably *Video Today* and *Video World*, with circulations of 38,000 and 30,000 respectively at the time of the interviews, although none of the households in the study subscribed to either magazine. Both magazines were consumer orientated, with features and lists of new software as well as information on hardware, and both attracted advertisers from both areas.

The video industry – and this term is used to describe the distributors and retailers of pre-recorded tapes for purchase or hire – has experienced major change. Many of the smaller outlets have gone by the board, forced out by the larger and well-established distributors, who moved in once the market had been tested. The industry has established its own quasi-professional organizations in order to protect itself against video piracy (the illegal copying of films for distribution) and to professionalize and improve its image, which has not been good. The 'moral panic' which resulted in the Video Recordings Bill of 1984,[2] providing for every film on hire to be censored for home viewing, had a devastating effect on the public image of the video libraries. This was fuelled enthusiastically by the popular press. On 1 September 1982 the *Sun* carried the headline 'Fury over video nasties' and referred to the video distributors and retailers as 'the merchants of menace', who were threatening the well-being of our children.

This was the general climate of public debate about the video industry at the time of my interviews, a period when the term 'video nasty' had become commonplace. The project was interested in the general use which the women made of video libraries and went far beyond concerns about the so-called, and rather hazily defined, 'video nasties'. I did not introduce this term into the discussions, allowing the women themselves to bring it up, should they see fit. Surprisingly few did, but some talked of their worries about their children's viewing of unsuitable video tapes and their attempts at control. As it was the intention to allow the women themselves to raise issues which they felt to be of importance this was then taken up and discussed.

In order to explore this aspect of VCR use, we will first deal with visits to the video library, and other outlets where appropriate, and the women's impressions of them, and then detail who hires the films and with what frequency. The second section deals with the kinds of tapes that are hired, and for whom, and what the women feel about these choices. As I am once more dealing with cultural preference, I have again grouped the women according to their educational background, as in chapter 4.

THE VIDEO LIBRARY

Group A: early school leavers

All the women in this group had been into a video library, but mostly these visits were with either partner, children, or both. Lynne's use of the video library was fairly typical of those households with young children.

> We all go together, usually on Sunday and take it back Monday . . . erm . . . sometimes the girls will have some money of their own and we let them choose one of their own and then we choose one that's not suitable for them to watch. Other times we get something that's suitable for everybody to watch. (Lynne)

Rene spoke of her favourite category in the video shop:

> I like a good melodrama, but they don't put them in terms of that. I don't like science fiction . . . I can't . . . it leaves me cold, it's not my cup of tea at all . . . war films, I'm not keen on . . . No. A good fictional romance I enjoy. (Rene)

She said that if there wasn't much on television and she and her husband were up-to-date with viewing their recorded tapes, they would go down to the corner shop together to choose a video. I asked her if the selection was wide or limited.

> Well, limited, for what I want it is, yes it is. But he's very good with me, he knows the kind of films I like, he's never gone wrong yet . . . we get a lot of milk . . . if I run out of milk or whatever, Bill – I don't drive you see – but he goes down in the car, so we've been a customer in the shop and he knows Bill, and he'll say 'Your wife will like this film . . .'

and Bill will often on a Monday night or Tuesday night when I'm working for instance, this Monday night he went out and got *Fawlty Towers*, 'cos he knows that I wouldn't want to sit there for an hour and a half and watch it. (Rene)

This is a good example of casual video rental; purchasing essential food supplies from the corner shop leads to renting a video. In these circumstances customers' tastes become known to the shop owner or manager, who recommends appropriate titles.

Betty's first impression of a video library was rather typical of many of the women.

They hadn't many that appealed to me [laugh] . . . you know, all this blood and guts and everything which I'm not really into. (Betty)

Alison was much more interested when she first went into the video library, but became worried after they had hired a few tapes.

Erm . . . when I first went in well . . . again, there were five of us and we were just looking for a film . . . I was quite taken up with it . . . I was a bit worried about whether the films were suitable for the children . . . because one or two we've had out have been a little bit near the knuckle and they're not small children, we're quite open about things, but sometimes when they're swearing . . . I cringe . . . One or two we've had out that's looked really good when we've got them home they've been swearing . . . The first time we went in I wasn't really worried about that, but after we'd had one or two out . . . it made me a bit wary of what we were getting out. I usually read a bit of the story on the back, and keep away from 18 ones – I'll get up to 15. You see they're all mixed up really . . . and sometimes the labels come off. (Alison)

Janet shared Alison's worries about the suitability of video tapes available for children's viewing. She accompanied her children when hiring videos, and said, 'We mainly hire for the kiddies.' She was asked if she looked around the shop when she went in with them.

Yes, I normally do – like, if I go up with them all, they're generally showing me films anyway that are way out of what they should have – you know, 'cheeky' ones and . . . and I

go *no*, definitely not . . . *no*. You know, I just won't . . . I
don't know, you don't know if you're doing right or not –
I've no idea . . . I'm not prudish with them by any means,
but I don't think a lot of this violence is. . . . I was adamant
that they weren't going to have that *Exorcist* – I wasn't going
to go up to the video shop and get them that, you know . . .
to me it's an X and that's why it's an X – because it's not fit
for them to see – so I was mean and horrible [laugh]. (Janet)

This woman's husband spent long periods away from home and
she was very conscious of her role as a single parent on these
occasions. The question of parental control of viewing is interesting in all its aspects, but here we can see that the video outlets
present these women with an often bewildering range of titles
which they feel they have to assess and, to a certain extent,
censor. The women themselves often have no knowledge of
current titles and the kinds of films the video shops offer, and
often their children know more about the films on display than
they do.

Some women were more confident in their dealings with the
video library and this was largely because of their wider knowledge of films. This could be general knowledge of genres as well
as an awareness of new films in circulation. Megan was typical
of this kind of consumer. Although she referred to the video
shops as 'mind-boggling', she often knew which films she wanted
and, although her son was the same age as one of Janet's children,
there was no mention of the problems of censorship which
emerged in Janet's talk. Again, like Rene, she and her tastes were
well known enough for the assistant in the shop to alert her to
new titles.

Julie, as the only driver in the household and the dominant
VCR user, always went to hire movies.

I was surprised at the amount of films that they had for rental.
They've got some that I'd never watch, that I'd never think
about watching, but there's a lot we watched, at first, when
we first got it, we hired one every day. (Julie)

I asked Susan, another enthusiast, what her first impressions of
the video library were.

Oh, it was wonderful [laugh], absolutely wonderful. At first

I knew exactly what I wanted to watch. I knew straight away what I wanted.

How did you know that?

Well, because I wanted to watch a lot of nasty horror films [laugh] so I just dived into the horror movies, you know . . . it was wonderful [laugh]. (Susan)

For Kay and Sheila, however, the libraries had little or no impact.

Well . . . I mean . . . I can look at titles and they mean absolutely nothing to me . . . the title gives nothing away, whereas my husband will say . . . 'oh yes, that's supposed to be very good', or 'that's not' . . . it's just water over my head really.

You wouldn't ever go and hire a film for yourself, then?

No, I shouldn't think so [laugh] . . . I mean I can always think of something else to do. (Kay)

Sheila said that she had never hired a film, but had been into the video library a few times to take her daughter's tapes back. I asked her what she thought of it.

What did I think of it . . . [pause] . . . it didn't have much impact, I'm afraid. I wasn't terribly, you know, I wasn't sufficiently interested to even look if there was anything I wanted. (Sheila)

Like Kay she had no interest in the films and also no knowledge of current titles.

Group B: later school leavers and graduates

In general, tape hire was not a regular feature of VCR use in this group. However, all the women had, at some time, been into a video library. Lack of transport, which could have some effect on access to a video library, was not a major problem for this group, apart from Maureen, whose husband was sometimes away on business. Would she hire a video for herself on these occasions?

No . . . Because I can't get . . . well I suppose I could, but it's at Dewsbury you see, which is three or four miles . . . I mean if I asked him he would get me one and then he'd take it back, but it would mean we would have it for two or three days, which is really defeating the object of hiring one. (Maureen)

I asked Jean what her first impressions had been of their local video library.

I vaguely remember all these horror things and ghost things, like *Halloween*, and I'm not interested in those . . . like *Earthquake;* there was very little that attracted me. (Jean)

Shirley had been to their video library once, with her husband. Were there a lot of films she would have liked to have watched?

No, not a lot, a few. I suppose we are aware of films coming out on release and think we'd like to see that . . . but we never actually get to the cinema. So maybe in a couple of years, when they get into the video shop . . . I missed *Out of Africa* which I can see myself getting . . . something like that. (Shirley)

Jenny's household belonged to six video clubs and she would quite often go to the video library to hire a film for joint watching, either with all the family or with her husband. She generally knew which film she was looking for before she went.

It tends to go that, about every few months, there'll be a batch of videos come out that we want to see because we don't go to the cinema any more. I'm always saying, 'let's go see such and such' . . . 'oh no, we'll wait until it comes out on video', he says . . . I would like to go see *Room with a View*, but then when I think of how much it's going to cost the pair of us, I think, well it'll be out in a few months, I might as well wait . . . So consequently, about every four to six months or so, you're aware there's a whole batch come out which you wanted to see at the pictures and which are waiting. The girls had a video out recently for them and whilst I was in there, you know, I found *Purple Rose of Cairo*, a list of them I wanted to see . . . so I know when the World Cup finishes we'll be off to the video, getting out one or two a week until we've seen them all.

Do any of them organize the films on display?

Some do, and some are hopeless . . . well I suppose in general they're all hopeless really, er . . . no, it's very much a question of looking. (Jenny)

WHO HIRES AND WITH WHAT FREQUENCY

Although almost all the women had been to a video library and had watched rented movies, there were many times when they watched movies on video which had not been their own choice. In recognizing that they are involved in the hiring of videos, we must not overlook the fact that often their choices were conditioned by the fact that they were selecting films for their children, films which they could watch with their partner, or simply going along with the majority decision. On other occasions their partners selected the tapes alone, either because they were keen viewers, or because the video shop was on their way home from work, or because they had money to spend on videos. Such films are often not enjoyed by the women.

Group A: early school leavers

Although most of the households in this group hired tapes on a regular basis, only three of the women claimed to hire tapes for themselves. The majority of the tapes, therefore, were hired either for family viewing or hired by the male partner for 'adult' viewing. Lynne's family went to the video library together and I asked her what kind of films they hired.

Not usually the ones I want [laugh] . . . my vote's usually cast way down the list.

It's rarely your choice?

Well usually when I choose one it turns out to be a flop anyway [laugh]. They say 'who chose this?' . . . *me* [laugh]. (Lynne).

The 'flop factor' identified by Lynne was a very significant element in the reluctance of some of the women in imposing their choice on their partners and children. Audrey spoke about the kinds of films that were mostly hired in her household:

Oh, well, they do tend to be war – back to the war – which isn't always received well from the other person in the family.

You know . . . it's time we let it die sort of thing, you know.
(Audrey)

Whose main selection is that?

Father's . . . mm . . . mm. (Audrey)

I asked her if she had ever chosen a film herself. Whilst she had
never selected one to watch on her own, she had chosen, from
the video library's list of tapes, a film to watch with her husband
and son on their regular Sunday evening viewing session. I asked
her what she had chosen.

The Deer Hunter, and that turned out to be a war film as well
[laugh] . . . but it was all the awards it was bringing . . . I
thought, well, it must be good for something. (Audrey)

Ironically, this woman had inadvertently chosen a film about war,
a genre of films which she did not enjoy and which dominated
her husband's selection of tapes for hire. But, as we saw in
chapter 4, the double irony was that her husband did not enjoy
the film, and the fact that her choice had been a 'flop' as far as
her husband was concerned had undermined her confidence in
attempting to assert her choice again. Similarly, many of the
women recognized that their choice would not be popular with
the rest of the family. And most were prepared to go along with
their husband's or children's selection.

Well, there's not really many that I would say 'Yes, we'll go
and get that'. Occasionally I pick a few, but more often than
not Derek'll say 'Shall we get so and so?'. . . . 'Well, if you
want' . . .'cos, I mean, I know he's going to watch it more
than I am anyway. (Betty)

It's normally Michael that gets tapes and I'm not . . . you
know, I'm not bothered . . . I'll watch it but I'm not . . . I
won't say, 'Oh, I'll get this one' . . . I don't really pick them,
he does . . . and he likes all war and horrors . . . he'll sit and
watch ones about prisons, and war and blood, he's not
fussy . . . I'm not bothered, he's working all week so he
deserves it doesn't he? (Cathy)

Kay's husband was an avid video fan and hired every week,
mainly at the weekends. Kay, as we have seen, would never hire

anything for herself and wasn't very interested. Her husband was apparently keen for her to become involved in watching videos with him, to the extent of pressing her to choose a title.

> My husband does try very hard, I mean I am terrible, I really am . . . he'll say 'What do you want to see, what would you like, what shall I get for you?' . . . and I'll say . . . 'well' . . . I'm not up . . . you see he's so up-to-date on things, he's read all the papers, he's seen all the film things, he seems to know what's going on, what's the latest films. I know nothing because I'm not interested in that area, so erm . . . he'll say . . . 'You might like so and so, and so and so', I say 'Well get that then', and he'll get it and he'll say 'Do you like it?' and I say [shrugs . . . laugh] . . . he does so want me to watch these things . . . erm . . . but no. (Kay)

Rene indicated the changing use of the VCR over their period of ownership.

> We use it a lot, oh, absolutely . . . the films from the library have worn off because there's only so many, erm, films out at one given time and we only like certain films anyway . . . now that has certainly worn off, we don't rent as many films as we did, but the machine now is probably being used more. (Rene)

For the small number of women who hired tapes for themselves there was still an awareness of 'their' choice not being shared by their partners, and vice versa, with significant differences as to what kinds of films are given priority for joint viewing.

> I don't like science fiction and I don't like cowboys.

Do you ever hire those kinds of film?

> Not science fiction, but a cowboy – if it were for Andrew, not for myself.

Would you watch it?

> No – it might be on, but I wouldn't particularly watch it.

What kind of film would you both like, what would you choose?

> Comedy, action adventure, all of the popular ones, like the *Rockys*, something like that – we've watched those. (Julie)

Susan's partner did not like her favoured genre – horror – so she tended to watch those on her own, either when he was away or after he had gone to bed. What kinds of films did her husband like to hire?

He hires a lot of erm . . . ooh . . . what would you call them? Again, new films, but ones I wouldn't want to watch, like, erm . . . boxing films, Al Pacino, tough guy films like that . . . that's more his cup of tea. Violent films, action films, something happening all the time.

So, what happens on a Saturday evening? Whose tape gets watched?

Both of them – I will watch his . . . just in case I'm missing anything, so his goes on first. Then I watch my horror movie after he's gone to bed. (Susan)

As we have seen earlier in this chapter, Megan used the video library regularly and I asked her if she thought she hired a lot of films.

Yes . . . more when my husband's at home, he's the one that goes and thinks nothing of getting four or five at a time. If he's home on a Saturday, he'll probably go and get four, even through the week, on a night, if there's nothing on the TV he wants to watch, he'll go and get three or four videos, he does more hiring. I mean we have had them over this last weekend, about five or six. I mean he's the one that goes up and he's stupid with them to an extent. Sometimes we get them and we don't really have time to sit down and watch them all . . . we do hire quite a lot of films.

What kind of films does he bring?

Well, a variety really . . . he brings a lot of horror, he likes horror and so does Matthew [son], but he doesn't bring all horror, he looks for things that he thinks I might enjoy watching . . . you know . . . he brings a . . . what I call a family film, and if he sees a tear-jerker . . . I'm into them . . . I like to be depressed . . . but he does, he brings a variety home. He's not one for westerns a great deal, but he goes for anything else. (Megan)

Although her husband brought her tear-jerkers, this woman regularly hired tear-jerkers and 'family sagas', or 'three-parters' to watch with female friends during the day, when their husbands and children were out, thus ensuring that they could watch without interruption or distraction.

Most women in this group reported that their households hired fairly regularly, but for some, frequency of hiring had declined as the novelty had worn off. However, hiring tapes was still a significant option for an evening's entertainment, particularly at weekends, and especially for those households who had small children or limited disposable income.

Group B: later school leavers and graduates

Hilary was asked under what circumstances a movie might be hired.

> We would do it if we thought we were going to have an evening in and we'd exhausted what we had, but we wanted to watch. Or more often it is I myself who hires them if my husband's away. I quite often hire one if he's away and watch it. (Hilary)

This woman was keen on cinema and was often the instigator of visits to the cinema with her husband. However, this was not possible very often because of their work and so she would catch up with films she had missed when he was away. This was a planned event and she knew in advance which film she wanted. For Beth, this forward planning was not part of her routine.

> Well, I might hire a movie, but it's something you don't think about until you sit and realize there isn't one on TV, then it's too late, you see. (Beth)

Maureen, whose husband generally chose the videos they hired, said that her husband was the one who knew about films.

> We've seen a few films. My husband usually reads the *Sunday Times* write up, that's where he gets all the gen from. (Maureen)

The knowledge which her husband had gained about films, his awareness of new titles, and whether they were 'good' or not, placed him in the position of an expert and therefore the most obvious person to select the tapes. Hilary, on the other hand, kept herself up to date with current films and was able, as a result, to exercise her own choice in hiring.

Beth was asked if they had ever hired a movie to watch.

Yes. I think about three, ever. That's only because in the past year a video shop has just opened up around the corner so I could hire them.

What kind of circumstances might you hire one?

Well . . . if it was a Saturday and there was nothing on we might hire one, or, I mean . . . George [husband] hired *Brazil* because he went into the shop to buy something – it's a computer and video shop, and he saw *Brazil*, and brought it home. I wouldn't have hired it. (Beth)

Further evidence is here of the casual nature of renting videos, but this group, in general, did not hire very frequently at all. Even for Maureen, hiring had become less frequent, although this was the main reason for purchasing the VCR.

We hired videos until we found they were coming on the television at Christmas, or whatever . . . erm . . . we used to get one every Friday night to watch instead of going out, and then we got we'd either been to the cinema and seen them when we were courting . . . or else when we'd been married . . . now we seem to have seen them all, and they're coming on to the television – so we just wait until they come on to the television. (Maureen)

She indicates a fairly critical period of time when movies can be hired, that is, between exhibition, when they might have been seen at the cinema, and their transmission on broadcast television. Hilary and Shirley made similar points when they talked about hiring films for their children.

I mean there's only a limited market in things like *Star Wars* . . . *Superman* has been on TV, we have hired those before they were on television, but there's only a limited range of those. (Hilary)

Fairly early on, when we first had it [VCR], we thought, oh yes, now we've got the video we'll be able to go out and get films and I think it was a Bank Holiday weekend and we went out and got this film, only to find it was shown on the Monday on television [laugh]. (Shirley)

They have all identified the critical gap between exhibition and transmission and recognized that eventually this leads to a decline in tape hiring. Their perception of this particular use of the VCR is stimulated by cinema and the films which are, in general, defined as mainstream, a point which has been discussed.

Although conflict about the choice of video to hire was not really emphasized in this group, Jean was simply outnumbered in her household of four men. I asked if she had been to hire a tape for herself.

> I've only been about twice . . . I'm not a very dominant person really. I tend to watch what they choose rather than impose my choice on them, because with me being the only female in the house, and there's four 'giants' around you, their choice isn't really mine . . . what I choose they wouldn't watch. (Jean)

Jenny's practice was much more typical in terms of agreement about choice of film in this group.

> That's purely a matter of convenience. It'll be decided beforehand what we're going to have, and I'll probably go and get it because I've got the car. (Jenny)

WHAT IS HIRED

In the last section I touched upon the kinds of tapes which were hired. This is obviously closely linked with the person who actually does the hiring, but we will now go into the actual selection in more detail. This section will examine how the women approach the selection of films, particularly for adult viewing, and the terms they used to describe this. As we have seen, some video libraries displayed their tapes under categories, and these category headings informed some of the discussion about films. The concept of genre is obviously of relevance here. Neale suggests that genres are 'systems of orientations, expectations and conventions that circulate between industry, text and subject' (Neale 1981: 19), and we can see the home video market as opening up new demands for popular genres. But the video library is a particularly interesting site for the circulation of meanings about genres, and we are more specifically concerned with the ways in which the women use their knowledge of different genres in their selection of tapes. Andrew Tudor reminds us that 'a genre exists in the conceptions of its audience as much as in the artefacts of which it is apparently composed' (1989: 6).

The first point to make about genre as a criterion for selection is that the Group B women implicitly rejected it. Andrew Tudor suggests that within mainstream film criticism, genres, as opposed to film movements, are seen as part of popular cinema and therefore mass culture (Tudor 1974: 182) and it is this assumption which the women in Group B seem to be making. They do not compare popular genres displayed in the video library under appropriate headings with the so-called 'art' films which have been organized by film historians into 'movements', but with the named film of which they have heard and about which they have read. John Ellis, in analysing the distinctiveness of cinema and broadcast television, indicates that cinema marketing sells the 'single film in its uniqueness' (Ellis 1982: 25) and it is this notion of the unique text which we will now extend to the organization of movies in the video libraries and the perceptions of Group B about the kinds of films they would select. The unique text is such by virtue of the fact that it has already stimulated critical acclaim and been established as a text of value and therefore worth watching, the kind of text that Hilary referred to as a 'quality' film.

> Well, I want to hire *The Spiderwoman* because I haven't seen it, but it depends at that moment in time . . . a lot of the ones you want to see aren't available on video of course, and it depends what's come out of the, what I would call quality films, that I would like to see. I've missed, for example, and I think it is on video now, *Letter to Brezhnev*, and I would quite like to see that.
>
> *So you tend to hire films that you've read or heard about?*
>
> Oh yes. I would never hire a film I didn't really know. (Hilary)

Lesley, whose husband and daughter tended to dominate the television and VCR, had a similar response:

> I don't hire films, my husband does sometimes, and my

daughter does . . . I don't really, unless there's something particular that has been advertised that I was interested in . . . I don't go to the shop . . . I don't ask for anything in particular unless I've read about something and I'm interested in it. (Lesley)

Three of the women in this group seemed to suggest that the kinds of films which they would choose didn't fit into any particular genre or category, and it seems that certain video libraries have created their own hierarchy of texts, reflected in the display lay-out, and the price.

There were these horror things – I didn't need to have looked at those, they were on a separate rack – and I went straight away to . . . it's about a year since I've been . . . there's these films that you have to pay extra for . . . Warner Brothers videos, those are more my choice I think . . . I looked there, I think I chose those. (Jean)

They do have some decent films, yes . . . there are the obvious new ones that are in the window that are advertised, I would go for one of those if there was something I hadn't seen. I wouldn't go in and just choose from a section, no. (Michelle)

The 'Warner Brothers' and newer films are usually separated out from the rest of the stock, even if the tapes are not displayed in sections, but the point is that these women have got some knowledge of the film itself as a unique text which they would not, themselves, see as belonging to any specific genre. Jenny expressed this feeling in an interesting way:

They have very loose areas, you know, comedy, horror, but I mean the main bulk of films you might be interested in don't come under those categories, you know . . . they're just films [laugh]. (Jenny)

'They're just films' seems to express most clearly what these women would see as their choice, critically acclaimed unique texts, which do not belong with the popular genres that constitute the rest of the video library stock. The unique text also tends to eliminate the significance of gender differences in the viewing subjects. With the exception of Jean, who was outnumbered by adult males with a penchant for horror and pornographic movies, all the women in Group B claimed that their partners had similar tastes in films to themselves. They would sit down and watch a unique text together. This is not to say that their tastes in films were totally shared. Some partners enjoyed genres traditionally associated with a male audience, for example, science fiction, a preference not shared by their female partners. However, there was a tendency for them to agree on the quality of the canon of unique films. Hilary told me that she and her husband enjoyed watching 'quality' films and Jenny's partner shared her tastes.

> We both know what films we're interested in, what got good reviews or had been recommended, or what we're just plain interested in. (Jenny)

These women's selection of films was much more narrowly prescribed than that of those women who had a relatively open approach to the video library and what it had to offer.

Just as the notion of a 'quality' film seemed to minimize gender differences in the viewing groups in Group B households, categorization of films into genres by the Group A women whose responses I now wish to consider seemed to highlight gender differences. The women often used genre categories when speaking about their male partner's hiring preferences.

> Horror [laugh], but I don't watch those because I hate horror, I can't bear horror; but, there again, my husband likes it and my two older children like it so . . . they all watch that.

What kind of film might he get for you?

> Erm . . . well, I liked *On Golden Pond*, I loved that, that type of film, you see I hate horror, I hate cowboys and he loves space, science fiction. Well, I can't get involved in science fiction . . . he gets the odd war one, but I find that quite depressing really, I don't like to watch that sort of thing . . . I'm very flippant I think, with my . . . I like things that make me laugh, that are funny . . . I like comedies or a good love story. (Kay)

Several of the women told me what their partners selected from the video library.

> Oh, the science fiction. . . . action adventure . . . he'd rather see action than story. (Lynne)

Well they do tend to be war. (Audrey)

Erm . . . well my husband likes space and goodness knows what and things like that. (Janet)

He likes all war and horrors . . . he'll sit and watch ones about prisons, and war and blood, he's not fussy. (Cathy)

If I say he'll watch anything, I'm not far wrong [laugh]. Erm . . . as I say, bloodthirsty ones, horror films, space, you know. (Betty)

The women referred not only to their husband's preferences in terms of genre, but also to their own, often using rather pejorative terms, such as 'tear-jerker'.

Love stories and things like . . . erm . . . these weepy ones, you know. (Julie)

Erm . . . [long pause] . . . *Who Will Love My Children?* . . . my husband brought that home for me; one of his mates at work had told him it was a bit of a weepy one [laugh]. (Brenda)

I think I would go for weepies first, then comedies. (Christine)

As we have noted, it was the 'unique' texts chosen by Group B in this section that provided for joint male-female viewing. In Group A the presence of particular 'stars' was both a criterion for selection, and a guarantee of suitability for joint viewing.

I'm trying to think what the last one was that we got . . . I just can't remember . . . it might have been a Clint Eastwood because I like Clint Eastwood films and so does my husband . . . now we do tend to get any of his that are out, we've had most of his, *Firefox* and things like that, we've had quite a few of his . . . I like that type of film. (Janet).

He likes Michael Caine, he thinks he's a good actor and he thinks he's a very serious actor . . . and he doesn't seem to get into movies that are really too make-believe . . . He'd probably watch anything with him in. (Jackie)

If I'm going I've usually in mind what I want. You know, what sort of film I want, er . . . I suppose if I didn't know what I wanted and I've no idea and I saw, say, a Clint Eastwood film that I'd never heard anything about, I would get a Clint Eastwood because we like him. Or Sylvester Stallone . . . mind you, I once got caught – I got a Sylvester Stallone and it was a dirty one [laugh]. (Julie)

But also some male 'stars' were chosen, especially by the younger women, because of their admiration for them. Richard Gere was favoured, but his films were not necessarily enjoyed by their male partners.

Oh, I liked him in *Officer and a Gentleman* . . . oh I liked that . . . that was a romantic film . . . you know, you're sat there and you're her and you're being swept off your feet . . . you know, and it's very nice . . . carried away.

Did your husband enjoy that one?

Oh . . . no . . . he thought it was a load of rubbish. (Lynne)

No female 'stars' were mentioned by the women, either in terms of selection or description of films which had been hired.

SUMMARY

It is clear that those women who had any interest at all in the hiring of video tapes approached their selection of movies with certain preconceptions. These can be ordered into two main categories: that of the unique text with a strong narrative image which has successfully marked it out from the popular genres of mass culture; and that based on generic familiarity which, conversely, tends to locate films in their similarity rather than in terms of their distinctive difference from other texts. Familiarity is an important element in the use of genre as a criterion for selection, as it provides a set of expectations about the film. But, of course, those women who select the unique text are also very familiar with its narrative image, which has been constructed and circulated through various media. They will know the 'history' of the making of the film, any literary connections which it has, the actors, the director and, in many cases, the context of its making. This is a different kind of knowledge from generic knowledge, and it creates for the spectator a distance from the text which already has been given the stamp of critical acclaim and 'quality'.[3] Of course, the marketing of blockbuster films, especially those addressed to the child audience, creates a certain kind of unique text which would determine choice for renting right across my sample. But in general there is a real distinction between those women who, like Hilary, would not hire a film of which they did not already have some knowledge, and those who would select a film because it belonged to a specific and favourite generic category.

In the main, the women who had received some form of higher education were those who used the unique text criterion and, incidentally, who also referred to 'classic' and 'quality' television. Furthermore, the majority claimed that their partners shared their tastes in these quality products, although there is evidence of tolerance, rather than a positive shared pleasure, in some of their statements. The fact that these women claimed a consensus of taste and standard with their husbands with regard to these products is significant and indicates their access to cultural capital provided by their education. It is also an indication that, in these cases, higher education has blurred gender categories in terms of cultural appreciation, with the emphasis on shared individual tastes rather than differences.

The women who used generic categories for their own selection and who referred to their partner's generic tastes as being very different clustered in Group A. Here we see the strongest evidence of gendered preferences for particular kinds of cultural products, which is reflected in the different preferences for hired movies. The use of stars as criterion hovers somewhere in between these two strategies, but stars themselves are potent signifiers operating within the pre-film world, setting up predisposition and anticipation in the potential spectator.[4] We noted that only male stars were mentioned by the women. It would be naïve and simplistic to equate this directly with a gendered audience in which the female section was being ill-served; some of the women, as we have noted, expressed their liking for some male stars. But what it does indicate is that the films they remember watching with their male partners, and which they would select for joint viewing, are identified with the male star.

There is evidence in the accounts of an unwillingness on the part of the women to impose their choice on the rest of the household. As we have seen, on the reported occasions when the women have chosen movies, they have not been seen as a success by their partners and children; this 'flop factor' has further undermined these attempts. As we saw in chapter 3 the consequence of this is that women often find themselves watching movies which they do not like in order to avoid conflict and the disapproval of husband and children.

Chapter 8

Gender and class in the household

The ethnography which forms the main body of this work has been organized so as to cover as comprehensively as possible those factors which have a bearing on women's use of the VCR. This includes the domestic division of labour, organization of and differential access to spare time, technology in the domestic environment, as well as the more immediately related activities of television and VCR viewing. It is now necessary to reflect on this description of household cultures in order to extend our understanding of them in terms of the wider social structure. This is not, and cannot be, a conclusion in the conventional sense; but it will raise questions for further work in the area. An important part of this enterprise has been to mobilize available theories in so far as they appeared to have explanatory power. In the event, however, the interview data has revealed weaknesses and limitations in some theories which could not account for the kinds of social and cultural patterns which emerged.

At the most general theoretical level the tendency towards exclusiveness of some theories proved unproductive. Theoretical accounts of society and its subjects often engender an either–or dualism which even the briefest excursion into the 'real world' of human practice will begin to challenge. For example, in relation to social structure, theories of capitalism and of patriarchy, with their often opposing concepts of class and gender, have been twin contenders in the debates about Marxism and feminism. In terms of the constitution of the subject, however, especially in relation to reading and viewing, the division has been one of psychological versus social. The focus here has been on how gendered subjectivity is achieved and to what extent this can account for differences in viewing pleasures between men and women. This conceptual configuration of class and gender, psychic and social, provides us with an interconnecting network whose combined elements will help account for the overarching concern of this study: the ways in which symbolic life and gender interact within the domestic sphere. In this context it is important to ask how certain cultural competencies are distributed through divisions of gender, as well as about the more material aspects of household culture such as the division of labour and the designation of 'appropriate' gender roles. However, it is also clear that class is an important factor, albeit not consistently so, in influencing the social activities which concern this study. It should therefore be possible to suggest some areas of women's lives where gender and class intersect and make some judgement as to their relative significance.

All this is somewhat complicated by the fact that this study addresses diverse topics. Questions such as 'Who does the washing up?', on the one hand, and 'What is it that you like about *Dynasty?*', on the other, are obviously dealing with very different kinds of human activity and experience. It is necessary therefore to make some more systematic distinction between the two areas of concern. I will therefore discuss issues of household structure; division of labour, organization of spare time and 'male' as against 'female' territories in the household geography under the heading 'Domestic social environment', and ideological and cultural questions under the general heading 'Domestic cultural environment'.

DOMESTIC SOCIAL ENVIRONMENT

Although three-quarters of the sample had paid work outside the home, few were in full-time employment; the majority therefore were to some extent dependent on the male salary. The aspects of the social environment that women have most in common are seen in the domestic division of labour, in apparent gender differences in the right to spare time within the routine of the household, in the use of gender-specific household technology, and in the existence of 'pink' and 'blue' territories. Although class and education were significant in the ways in which the women accounted for their domestic position, they were not significant in that almost all the women claimed major responsibility for domestic work and child care. Where class, and particularly education, became significant was in determining the extent to which the women could distance themselves sufficiently to reflect on their position and to recognize that this was not necessarily the only way of living. Most of the women in the lower education group seemed to accept the traditional division of labour as the norm and felt themselves lucky if their husbands helped with the housework. However, in the higher education group, although the women recognized their roles as 'traditional' they felt unable to change them, since the household structures depended on everyone knowing their place and performing their role.

A combination of female employment outside the home and absence of children led to the most egalitarian households, but if this situation was changed (for example, by the birth of children) the balance tended to shift towards a more traditional division of labour. In this event, the tendency for women right across the sample was that adjustments were made to their lives, either by their giving up work or by employing someone to take care of the children or clean the house. In these cases the women were responsible for the recruitment of domestic help. Once a woman is at home with small children, whatever her education or social background, it seems inevitable that she will be involved in domestic labour and that this will become the pattern for the future of the household. Her domestic role then becomes a constraint on her availability for any future paid employment, which is most likely to be part time or work which offers her the flexibility necessary to fulfil her child-care and domestic responsibilities. This was true of almost half of the women in paid employment.

Feminists have considered the family to be one of the major sites of women's oppression and have explored the institution from a number of different perspectives. These are usefully identified by Chris Weedon as liberal-feminist, radical-feminist and socialist-feminist approaches (Weedon 1987: 16). The liberal-feminist position is that the family is a universal norm, and the appropriate response to its oppressive character lies in equality of opportunity, of women's right to choose to have children and to the provision of child-care facilities. This approach focuses on the creation of material circumstances conducive to the individual's right to be self-determining, regardless of gender. The radical feminist argues that there is an essentially female consciousness and culture, biologically determined, which is oppressed by patriarchy in general and the family in particular. The 'life-giving' qualities which men lack, according to this theory, can only be developed and allowed to flourish outside the male structures in a separate female world. The individualism of liberal feminism and the essentialism of radical feminism are challenged by the third perspective, socialist feminism, which begins from the Marxist assumption that human beings are socially and historically produced. Patriarchy is not a straightforward universal but takes historically variable forms. This position is an investigation of the interrelation between the oppressive structures of capitalism, patriarchy and racism as they bear on the family. Whilst taking account of the psychological dimensions of gender, socialist feminists insist on locating it historically, thus resisting the universalizing inclinations of many psychoanalytic approaches. The family and its typical gender relations must therefore be seen in relation to the wider structure of society, a structure which would require transformation if women and men were to be released from the conjoint oppression of capitalism and patriarchy. Weedon argues that none of these feminist accounts attempts to explain what she sees as the crucial aspect of women's oppression: their seeming complicity in that process. It is clear from my interview material that many women had seen little or no alternative to marriage and family life, but, significantly, also had desired this goal of the feminine career. Furthermore, there were many examples of female deferral to male authority, particularly in relation to viewing choices, and of female self-sacrifice with regard to the needs of other members of the family. Weedon suggests,

> In order to understand why women so willingly take on the role of wife and mother, we need a theory of the relationship between subjectivity and meaning, meaning and social value, the range of possible *normal* subject positions open to women, and the power and powerlessness invested in them.
>
> (Weedon 1987: 18–19, original emphasis)

This conceptualization in terms of the range of subject positions available to women is important in that it encourages us to investigate differences between women within patriarchy, but also lays emphasis on the social construction of subjectivity through a variety of discourses which, in turn, exist within relationships of power. Whilst Weedon's poststructuralist feminism breaks with the individualism of liberal-humanist feminism and the essentialism of radical feminism, the break she makes with socialist and

Marxist feminism runs the risk of losing sight of the economic and material factors which contribute to sexual divisions in our society. Barrett criticizes such theories of discourse where 'men and women themselves represent discursive categories in which differences are produced', and suggests,

> Masculinity and femininity obviously are categories of meaning in one sense, but men and women occupy positions in the division of labour and class structure which, although not pre-given, are historically concrete and identifiable.
>
> (Barrett 1980: 253)

Weedon, however, clearly believes that the subject is the product of discourse when she points out,

> A poststructuralist position on subjectivity and consciousness relativizes the individual's sense of herself by making it an effect of discourse which is open to continuous redefinition and which is constantly slipping.
>
> (Weedon 1987: 106)

Positions of femininity and masculinity are never inevitable, but, according to Weedon, men and women are 'not the mere objects of language, but the sites of discursive struggle, a struggle which takes place in the consciousness of the individual' (ibid.: 106). The individual, in this formulation, is not merely a product of discourse, but has a potentially active role in resisting the interpellation of particular discourses. What is not clear from poststructuralist feminism is why specific discourses combine to produce different feminine subject positions within our society, and what particular combination of circumstances might lead to resistance to one or other of the discourses. Theories of language and discourse are not sufficient in themselves to explain the 'complicity' of the women interviewed in this study. Whilst the role of ideology is obviously crucial, the consequences of their positions within the division of labour and the class structure cannot simply be explained away by reference to discourse. An over-emphasis on the ideological and the construction of subjects through discourse is criticized by Michelle Barrett, although she also argues that

> It is only through an analysis of ideology and its role in the construction of gendered subjectivity that we can account for

the desires of women as well as men to reproduce the very familial structures by which we are oppressed

(Barrett 1980: 251)

However, Barrett also insists that the meaning of gender within our society is in many important aspects related to a household structure and division of labour which in turn occupies a particular place in the relations of production. For this reason, she argues, the ideology of gender does have a material base, and she points to the impossibility of seeing economic and ideological categories as distinct and exclusive.

An important dimension of household structure for this study relates to leisure. In our discussion of the organization of spare time in the home it was noted that most of the males of the households seemed able to claim their 'own time' once at home. This was often justified in terms of their being the major earner, but even where both partners worked the man was more likely to be able to relax at home whereas his female partner would have to engage in domestic labour. Many of the women reported that they found it difficult, if not impossible, to justify taking time out to do something for themselves, and that if they did sit down during the day and read or watch television they were constantly haunted by the unfinished tasks with which they were surrounded. Thus, as well as being responsible for household work, the women are continually guiltily conscious of their responsibilities, a fact which often militated against their becoming involved in leisure activities which required concentration. The men in the study, however, appeared to be able to switch off from the domestic environment and pursue their hobbies and leisure activities.

Differential distribution of time available in the household for leisure activities would seem to be a crucial factor in understanding VCR use. As we have seen, the decision to purchase or rent a VCR was mainly the prerogative of the adult male, although he often had to win the consent of his female partner for this investment. The reasons for this can be seen as a combination of the masculine address of VCR advertising, the relative freedom of male leisure time in the home, and male economic power. However, the consequence is that the male of the household quickly becomes adept in the operation of the machine and from this position of knowledge can command some control over its use. Those members of the household who have few obligatory duties in the home, both adult and children, are likely to have time to spend in watching material and planning ahead for recording and hiring of video tapes. Many of the women, however, considered television and video to be a 'last resort' leisure activity. For them leisure and the opportunity to relax was identified with going out, as this provided essential distance from domestic duties and the obligations that were always present at home. These women often spoke of television and video with resentment, as if they considered them an intrusion into family life and a distraction from more appropriate uses of leisure time. Women from different social positions across the sample described their partner's use of television as a way of switching off from domestic life, the television screen legitimating non-communication within the household. We can see, therefore, that the men and women in the sample take up very different positions in relation to their domestic environment. Men are able to be singular, remote, and maintain a relatively autonomous position, whereas women's experience is more likely to be non-unified and fragmented, in which they are continually responding to the demands of others, their attention always available for someone or something else. If, as this research suggests, this is a consistent difference between men and women within the domestic context, it is important to find some way of accounting for this naturalized pattern.

This can be approached through Nancy Chodorow's object–relations theory of gendered subjectivity (Chodorow 1978) which has been used by Tania Modleski and Janice Radway to account for the particular appeal of women's genres and their structures of identification (Modleski 1982; Radway 1984). Radway has also used Chodorow's theory in suggesting that women consume popular romantic fiction as an act of resistance to the patriarchal family within which they are positioned as wives and mothers. However, Chodorow usefully relates her psychoanalytic explanation of gender reproduction to a sociological account of the sex–gender system[1] and in particular to the kind of family unit in which the majority of my sample live. Her subsection, 'Family and Economy', begins thus:

> Women's relatedness and men's denial of relation and
> categorical self-definition are appropriate to women's and

men's differential participation in nonfamilial production and familial reproduction.

(Chodorow 1978: 178)

In our society, she notes, women's roles are basically familial and concerned with the personal, while men's roles are not defined by the familial but by what they do. Women are located first in the sex–gender system, men first in the organization of production. While many men do live in families and are fathers, they are not primarily defined by this fact. The very existence of the phrases 'family man' and 'career woman', which define those who transgress these traditional divisions, indicates how deeply rooted these assumptions are in our society. Within the sex–gender system of contemporary capitalism, the role of wife and mother draws on women's subjectivity in specific ways:

> The activities of wife/mother have a nonbounded quality. They consist . . . of diffuse obligations. Women's activities in the home involve continuous connection to and concern about children and attunement to adult masculine needs, both of which require connection to, rather than separateness from, others.

(Chodorow 1978: 179)

Conversely, Chodorow notes, work in the labour force, that is, 'men's work', is 'likely to be contractual, to be more specifically delimited, and to contain a notion of defined progression and product' (ibid.: 179). The particular value of Chodorow's theory is that she begins with a psychoanalytic account of the construction of gendered subjectivity within the family but she then relates it to the wider structures of capitalism and patriarchy. This is obviously important in understanding the sexual division of labour in the home, and it is clear that for many of the women in this study their concern for the needs of their children and male partners extends into leisure time. Chapter 3 outlines the social organization of different viewing contexts, revealing that women are most likely to defer to their partner's or children's choices of viewing material both for broadcast television and hired tapes. Different positions within the household occupied by men and women have their effect in relation to modality of viewing. As we saw, the male is able to switch off and view in a concentrated mode, and, as Morley's work shows, prefers to view in this way. Many of the women in this study viewed distractedly, often knitting or sewing while they were in front of the television and video.

Time-shifting created some problems for the women in terms of when to watch a recording. For example, factors such as limited tape availability and a tendency for the rest of the household to record over any tape which happened to be around, meant that women had to find a time to view a programme before it disappeared. But there was also a felt pressure to view when the material was an episode of a long-running serial, such as *Dallas*, a pressure which became acute when there was a risk of missing neighbourhood or work-place gossip, or worse, of story developments being revealed prior to viewing. For these reasons some of the women were forced into watching late at night or early morning. For those who were 'guilty viewers', especially during the day, recorded tapes seemed to compound the guilt. Janet reported less guilt watching broadcast television as against prerecorded tapes, either time-shift or hired, the implication being that the choice of watching tapes was hers entirely, whereas scheduled broadcasters have taken responsibility out of her hands by transmitting programmes at particular times. The time-shift facility was used for individual viewing by all members of the households where particular tastes were not shared, but the occasions when women organized this kind of viewing for themselves seemed to be infrequent.

Accumulation of large numbers of tapes occurred across the whole sample, but this was, in general, a male practice, both in terms of responsibility for organizing the collection and re-viewing tapes. This male activity, as has been noted, was often mystifying to their female partners, who preferred not to see a film repeatedly. Their commonly articulated reason was that once the conclusion of the narrative was known then there was little point in watching a film again. However, there were exceptions to this. Re-viewing of favourite horror movies was noted, but in general this was practised by viewing 'fans'. Second, some re-viewing of favourite tapes as a collective family enterprise was reported.

In terms of use of leisure time, the one area where women did take the initiative was in instigating 'family outings'. Many men appeared either to positively dislike these outings or simply didn't think about them and had to be persuaded into them by their partners. The women who were most keen were those who identified most fully with their roles as wives and mothers, but this also extended to women who worked outside the home. Images of the ideal family saturate a wide range of media output and Clarke and Critcher note that these images are both encountered during leisure time and are about leisure:

> As the family, together or separately, relax and enjoy themselves they will soon encounter distortions of their own images, as others would like them to be.
>
> (Clarke and Critcher 1985: 166)

Again, women's familial work takes the form of reproducing 'the family' symbolically through supposedly unifying leisure activities.

We can see from the ethonography that women are 'positioned' in the domestic environment and that this has profound effects on their use of spare time as well as on their viewing of television and video. Those women with children who were full-time family managers often had difficulty in carving out any spare time for themselves, and when they did were often guiltily conscious of this 'indulgence'. However, even women who worked outside the home and those who had time on their own in the home rarely used that time to pursue their own activities, such as reading or viewing. This sample of women were almost all living in a particular kind of domestic unit, with male partners in full employment, and with children. It appears that the kinds of female and male subjectivities which this particular living unit engenders are continually reproduced across the different rituals of domestic work and leisure.

DOMESTIC CULTURAL ENVIRONMENT

The importance of perceptions of VCRs as complex technology emerged from the interviews, which raises questions about prevailing gender divisions in the acquisition of technological knowledge. The low reported use of the VCR does not represent a straightforward lack of competence on the part of the women. After all, domestic technology presents few problems for women, who quickly become adept at using cookers, washing machines, sewing machines, etc. Some of the women claimed to be generally resistant to technology, dismissing the VCR as yet another gadget in the household. Some were simply not interested in television and, therefore, in video. In some cases there was also an element of calculated ignorance whereby women resisted becoming involved in the VCR simply to avoid yet another domestic servicing function.

This rather complicated web of cultural and social factors serves to indicate the kinds of negotiations which women are likely to be involved in, often from an already determined position, in order to establish their relationship with this particular item of entertainment technology. Their male partners and children would seem to have a much more direct and less conditional relationship with the machine. The territories so often marked out through the domestic division of labour – 'pink' kitchen and 'blue' garage – are further established through ideologies of technological competence. With the increased technologization of the sitting-room, particularly in relation to leisure and entertainment, this potentially neutral area of relaxation is also becoming 'colour coded'.

VCR operating modes, for example, can be appropriately colour-coded; the 'record', 'rewind' and 'play' modes are generally lilac, but the timer switch is nearly always blue, with women having to depend on their male partners or their children to set the timer for them. The blueness of the timer is exceeded only by the deep indigo of the remote control which in all cases was held by the male partner or male child. This observation was also confirmed by David Morley and Peter Collett (Collett 1986: Morley 1986).

The VCR obviously offers potential for expanded cultural consumption. In this context it is important to establish the cultural preferences and competencies which the women bring to their use of the video recorder, and their expressed preferences for specific kinds of cultural products need to be understood in relation to a wider social and cultural environment. It is clear that it is in the area of cultural preference and competence that major differences emerge *between* the women, thereby blurring the more distinct gender divisions manifest in other areas of daily life. The most important differentiating factor in expressed cultural preference is higher education, which is, in turn, significantly associated with class. In David Morley's study of East End families, he found that those women in his sample who had engaged in higher education – two were mature students at the time of the interviews – or who had a higher educational standard than their husbands, were exceptions to the perceived preferences in gendered types of programme. These differences were expressed in terms of a liking for factual programmes, in one case, and in the others a dislike of soap operas. Both these stated preferences were in direct contrast to the rest of the sample, but as Morley suggests,

> the exceptions to the rule are themselves systematic. This occurs only where the wife, by virtue of educational background, is in the dominant position in terms of cultural capital.
>
> (Morley 1986: 163)

Only one woman in my sample (Jean) was in this position, and her education had distanced her taste from that of her husband and sons. The rest of the educated women were with partners whose standard of education was the same if not higher than their own. These women claimed to have similar preferences in programmes and films to their partners, and the majority of them were keen to distance themselves from soap opera, particularly American products. It would seem, then, that access to cultural capital through education produces an alliance of male and female preferences for 'quality' texts while also placing women in that group in alliance with men in the lower education group in their shared dislike for soap opera. It is important not to take these apparent alliances at face value, and during the interviews I explored the specific pleasures and displeasures which particular texts or genres offered to the women. It is clear from the interview material that women in the higher education group had a stated preference for 'quality' products, which they shared with their male partners. However, it also appears that the texts which gave most pleasure to these women, whether novels, films or television programmes, shared certain essential elements. These were expressed as follows: a strong story line, well developed characters, and a 'believable' setting. In many cases, the women insisted that their partners did not require these particular elements to find a text pleasurable. Science fiction was given by some of these women as an example of a male genre which did not fulfil their criteria for enjoyment and none of the women expressed a liking for this genre. The reasons given by two of the 'educated' women focused on the lack of developed characters in the genre:

I'm interested in people . . . I think that's why I don't like horror films and science fiction, because I can't relate to it at all. (Clare)

Jenny went further in her description of the viewing of films in general with her partner:

> If it's caught you up sufficiently, I will get very involved with the story and very involved with the characters in a way that Jim won't. (Jenny)

What Clare and Jenny expressed is their desire for a certain form of 'emotional realism' in their preferred genres as well as the portrayal of a particular kind of world with which they feel familiar. Science fiction does have strong story lines, developed characters and is 'believable' to its consumers, but the women were not convinced by these texts and took no pleasure in them. Their criticisms of this and other male genres are evidence of a lack of the reading competence and genre familiarity required in order to make sense of the text.

In Chodorow's terms, these women require identification with characters, emotions and human relationships in their consumption of fiction in a way that they feel their partners do not. Educated women share the same cultural capital as their partners, and this produces a desire for texts with a high cultural evaluation. This can be explained through their access to education, and indirectly in class terms. However, the 'complex, relational self' of the feminine subject as it is produced within the patriarchal family is expressed through her desire for connectedness and emotional identification with a text, and therefore must be understood in relation to gender. In Clare's case the contradiction that this particular subject position produces is evidenced in her reluctance to become involved in soap opera. Although she recognizes that the genre foregrounds human relationships and as such would appeal to her 'relational self', its low cultural evaluation means that she cannot, given her cultural capital, comfortably engage with this genre. This is further compounded by the fact that she considers television itself to be of low cultural status, but does listen to *The Archers*, the Radio 4 soap.

Turning to the other 'alliance' we see that dislike for soap opera is shared by the 'educated' women in the group and almost all the male partners across the sample. This suggests that the women in the higher education group have more in common with men, regardless of class, than they have with the rest of the women. However, if we explore the reasons for disliking soap opera we see that the situation is again more complex. The men in David Morley's study, none of whom had engaged in higher education, claimed, in general, not to like fiction, regarding its consumption as a 'feminizing' activity, and many saved their most dismissive remarks for soap opera. The 'educated' women's dislike for soap opera is not primarily because it is a female genre, but because it is perceived as having low cultural value. Both want to distance themselves from the product because it challenges an important element of their subjectivity. For the men, their masculine subjectivity resists involvement in the emotional world demanded by soap opera. For the women, access to education and cultural capital has constructed a subjectivity which places itself at a distance from the products of low culture. To use Bourdieu's term, they have achieved an 'aesthetic disposition' which, as he argues, is based on the adoption of an individual position of distanced objectivity with regard to cultural products. Thus, in the hiring of tapes and the criteria used for selection, we can see that educational and cultural capital becomes a factor in explaining differences between the women. The 'educated' women used their notion of a unique text as the major criterion, whereas the other women would opt for a favoured genre irrespective of their knowledge of the particular film. The 'educated' women who rejected soap opera spoke of the dangers of addiction and the risks of becoming enmeshed to the extent that soap operas might 'take over your life'. These are very telling phrases, indicating their reluctance to lose themselves in a popular text. To do so would represent a challenge to the self-control essential to the 'aesthetic disposition' as outlined by Bourdieu, and upon which their education insists.

As suggested in the summary of chapter 4, those women who had not been the subjects of higher education saw the possibilities of abandonment to a text not as a danger but as an essential part of the pleasure; 'I like to be taken out of myself', as Rene put it. Many similar expressions, indicating their much more direct involvement with the text, echoed Bourdieu's description of the 'popular aesthetic' as marked by 'the desire to enter into the game, identifying with the characters' joys and sufferings' (Bourdieu 1980: 238). Bourdieu equates the popular aesthetic with the working class, but it is clear that in relation to different popular genres gender differences are also significant. Working–class men do not share their female partner's enthusiasm for soap opera, romance, family saga, etc., and conversely, those popular genres enjoyed by men – action and adventure, war, science fiction, spy thrillers, etc. – do not pleasurably engage the women in this group. For working-class women, or at least for those with no higher education, their relational selves are not compromised by their engagement with preferred cultural products. The working-class male, however, may be the self-less subject of the popular aesthetic, but he is the 'separate self' of the masculine subject. His position is therefore contradictory in this respect, as is the educated female position. However, his 'masculine' preferences give him cultural power over his female partner. The strongest gender and genre division emerged in the C category (see Appendix), and particularly in those households where both partners had a limited education. But even in this group, the female-preferred genres were considered by both women and men to be of a lower order than the male-preferred genres, which texts would always take priority for shared viewing. The tensions in the woman's position, therefore, result from the low cultural value which her preferences carry, both publicly and domestically. We can see that the least contradictory subject is the educated, middle–class male whose sense of self-control marks his masculine subjectivity and his aesthetic disposition.

The social and cultural aspects of the domestic environments within which the VCR takes its place are crucial to an understanding of the determining factors surrounding women's reported use of the machine and the opportunities for and choice of viewing material. The implications of this study are that new entertainment technology enters the existing household structures and familial ideology, and these structures and traditions, particularly in relation to gender, become encoded in the new technology both in terms of its physical use and choice of software. Theories of the construction of gendered subjectivity within specific social contexts, and of the acquisition of unequally distributed cultural capital, enable us to shed some light on the operation of gender and class in the daily routines of domestic work and leisure.

Appendix

SAMPLE DETAILS BY SOCIO-ECONOMIC CATEGORY

Code	Age	Age left education	Occupation	Ages of children at home	Home status	Partner's occupation
A/1	44	U*	p-t ESL teacher	13, 16	owners	Professor
A/2	43	U	f-t Research fellow	5, 12	owners	Architect (SE)
A/3	46	17	f-t Nursery nurse	13, 15	owners	Clinical psychologist
A/4	37	U	f-t Lecturer–Architect	6, 8, 11	owners	Lecturer–Architect
B/1	39	15	p-t Nursery assistant	10, 15, 17	owners	Pensions consultant
B/2	35	U	p-t Careers advisor	2, 4	owners	Grammar school teacher
B/3	25	18	f-t Family manager	4 mths	owners	Company Secretary
B/4	48	15	p-t Clerical assistant	18, 20	owners	Sales executive
B/5	50	14	p-t Wine bar assistant	–	owners	Leisure executive
B/6	36	U	Vol. ESL tutor	2, 5	owners	Solicitor
C1/1	29	15	p-t Plant displayer	4, 7	owners	Plumber (SE)
C1/2	40	16	p-t Book-keeper	18, 21	owners	Chef
C1/3	29	15	p-t Hairdresser's receptionist	–	owners	Motor accessories distributor

Code	Age	Age left education	Occupation	Ages of children at home	Home status	Partner's occupation
C1/4	51	15	p-t Doctor's receptionist	27	owners	Haulage contractor (SE)
C1/5	34	15	f-t Family manager	7, 10, 12	owners	Electrical engineer
C1/6	33	TT**	f-t Primary teacher	–	owners	Actor
C1/7	44	TT	f-t Middle school teacher	19, 23	owners	Fire officer
C1/8	52	16	Newsagent	17, 17, 25, 25	owners	–
C1/9	31	16	Temp. school assistant	7, 9	owners	Area manager, oil co.
C2/1	21	15	Packer (eve)	2	owners	Maint. engineer
C2/2	32	15	Domestic (eve)	4, 7	owners	Electrician
C2/3	34	15	p-t Cashier	12, 15	owners	Sheet metal worker (SE)
C2/4	35	15	f-t Family manager	0, 10, 12, 15	owners	Sheet metal worker
C2/5	27	16	f-t Family manager	2	owners	Fitter– engineer
D/1	36	U	p-t Clerical admin.	8, 10	tenants	Process worker
D/2	30	15	f-t Family manager	3, 6, 8	tenants	Asphalter
D/3	21	16	f-t Shop assistant	–	tenants	–
D/4	48	15	p-t Textile mender	17, 21	tenants	Warehouse-man
E/1	19	17	Unemployed	–	tenants	–
E/2	38	15	Casual worker	17, 19	tenants	Jobbing builder

* university education
** teacher training qualification

The coding represents identification by class. The location of class was established through consideration of education and housing as well as occupation of the male partner.

Notes

INTRODUCTION

1 Time budget studies have shown that women are responsible for most of the household work, especially that of a routine nature; see, for example, Pahl 1985. An ethnographic study (Hunt 1980) reaches the same conclusion.

2 Deem 1986; Dixey and Talbot 1982; Green, Hebron and Woodward 1985a and 1985b; Griffin 1981, 1985; Stanley 1980.

3 This is discussed in Deem 1986, McIntosh 1981, Roberts 1981 and Stanley 1980.

4 For summaries of this tradition see Halloran 1970 and Klapper 1960.

5 See, for example: Lundberg and Hulten 1968; McQuail, Blumler and Brown 1972; Katz, Gurevitch and Haas 1973; Rosengren and Windahl 1973; and for an overview of the approach see Katz, Blumler and Gurevitch 1974.

6 See Women's Studies Group 1978 and Hall et al. 1980 for papers exploring these areas.

7 This term was first used by Sean Cubitt in Masterman 1984, p. 46.

8 Morley also draws on the work of Brodie and Stoneman 1983, Goodman 1983, and Lindlof and Traudt 1983, all of whom are concerned with the role of television in family interaction.

9 This term was used by Stuart Hall in Hall et al. 1980 and he notes that 'screen theory' draws extensively on French theoretical writing across a number of fields: 'film theory (early semiotics, the work of Christian Metz, the debates between the journals Cahiers du Cinéma and Cinétique), the theory of ideology (Althusser), the psychoanalytic writings of the Lacan group, and recent theories of language and discourse (Julia Kristeva, the 'Tel Quel' group, Foucault)' (ibid.: 157). Hall also notes the influence of the critique of 'realism' on this body of work.

10 Hall et al. 1980 notes that the visual metaphors in the work of Freud and Lacan (e.g. the 'mirror phase', voyeurism, scopophilia, Lacan's work on the 'look' and the 'gaze') lend themselves to the application of the relationship between the spectator and visual media.

11 Brunsdon, 'Text and audience' in Seiter et al. 1989.

12 Chodorow, quoted in Radway 1984, p. 94.
13 See Cockburn 1983 and 1985. In the latter text she addresses questions of domestic technology. Zimmerman (1986) also raises the issue, but mainly in relation to domestic labour.

1 METHOD AND SAMPLE

1 The IBA (1988) estimates that nearly 7 out of 10 people with children have now acquired a VCR, and they indicate that penetration since 1980 has occurred most rapidly and extensively amongst this group.
2 See Gray 1987.
3 Morley, however, set out to interview families together. Although aware of the problems of individual interviews (e.g. respondents' freedom to say what they choose without fear of contradiction from others and to tell me what they think I want to hear), I would argue that these personal accounts are significant in themselves and that the extended interview or discussion allows for contradictions to emerge and for questions to be approached in different ways. See Gray 1988.
4 For discussions of feminist research methods, see: Bell and Roberts 1984; McRobbie 1982a; Roberts 1981; and Stanley and Wise 1983.
5 This has often taken the form of an attack on all theory as being a masculine form of discourse, its application to the understanding of women's expression of their experience would therefore maintain male dominance over women and suppress the 'feminine'.
6 Coding for identification in Appendix.

2 ORGANIZATION OF SPARE TIME

1 Interview extracts are verbatim. Pauses are indicated thus: . . . .
2 I am grateful to Cynthia Cockburn for this idea, which she shared at a seminar at the University of York in June 1985.
3 This term was used by McRobbie (1982b) to describe the 'ideal career' for women which progressed through romance to marriage and family.
4 I am following the women in using 'Mills and Boon' as a generic term for short romantic novels.

3 VIEWING CONTEXTS AND RELATED TEXTS

1 I am using this term with reference to books, TV programmes and movies.
2 The exceptions to this are Collett 1986 and Morley 1986.
3 This point is also made by Bausinger in relation to male use of TV where switching on does not mean ' "I would like to watch this", but rather "I would like to see and hear nothing" or "I don't want to talk to anybody" ' (Bausinger 1984: 344).

4 VIEWING AND READING PREFERENCES

1 This refers to the marital problems of Ken and Deirdre Barlow, the subject of much speculation at the time.
2 Seiter *et al.* 'Don't treat us like we're so stupid and naive' in Seiter *et al.* 1989.
3 Barbara Taylor-Bradford's *A Woman of Substance* and *Hold the Dream* are examples of this generic sub-category.
4 A video retailer of *The Evil Dead* was prosecuted under the Obscene Publications Act in Leeds in 1984.
5 The distinctive narrative structure of soap opera is outlined by Geraghty 1981, pp. 9–26.

5 TECHNOLOGY IN THE DOMESTIC ENVIRONMENT

1 Collett's research involved placing a video camera into a specially-designed TV cabinet which began recording when the TV was switched on. The recordings made showed that the remote control was often held by males and occasionally there were physical attempts by other members of the family to gain possession.

7 THE VCR: HIRING TAPES

1 The market for pre-recorded tapes has now increased dramatically, according to the British Video Association quoted in the *Guardian*: 'The sale of pre-recorded video cassettes, almost unknown in this country five or six years ago, has reached around £250 million a year. Forecasts suggest that 25 or 30 million units will be sold in 1989 compared with just a million in 1985' (*Guardian*, 11 March 1989).
2 For a discussion of the 'video nasties' moral panic, see Petley 1984, Kuhn 1984b, and see also Barker 1984.
3 Although these 'unique' films are set apart from popular genres, as far as the women are concerned this should not disguise the fact that, as Tudor (1974) suggests, 'their social dynamics are similar to those of genres. They develop a particular cultural pattern and an audience educated in their special characteristics' (ibid.: 181).
4 Ellis, speaking of cinema, says, 'Stars have a similar function in the film industry to the creation of a "narrative image": they provide a foreknowledge of the fiction, an invitation to cinema' (1982: 91), and we can see that their function has been transferred to the selection of video tapes.

8 GENDER AND CLASS IN THE HOUSEHOLD

1 The sex–gender system is defined by Gayle Rubin as 'a set of arrangements by which the biological raw material of human sex and procreation is shaped by human, social intervention and satisfied in a conventional manner' (Rubin 1975: 157–210).

Bibliography

Allen, R. C. (1985) *Speaking of Soap Operas*, Chapel Hill, N.C. and London: University of North Carolina Press.

Ang, I. (1985) *Watching Dallas: Soap Opera and the Melodramatic Imagination*, London: Methuen.

—— (1991) *Desperately Seeking the Audience*, London: Routledge.

—— and Hermes, J. (1992) 'Gender and/in media consumption', in J. Curran and M. Gurevitch (eds) *Mass Communication and Society*, rev. edn, London: Edward Arnold.

Armistead, N. (1974) *Reconstructing Social Psychology*, Harmondsworth: Penguin Books.

Baboulin, J., Gaudin, J. and Mallein, P. (1983) *Le Magnetoscope au quotidien: un demi-pouce de liberté*, Paris: Aubier Montaigne.

Barker, M. (ed.) (1984) *Video Nasties: Freedom and Censorship in the Media*, London: Pluto Press.

Barrett, M. (1980) *Women's Oppression Today*, London: Verso.

Bausinger, H. (1984) 'Media, technology and daily life', *Media, Culture and Society* 6(4): 343–51.

Bell, C. and Roberts, H. (eds) (1984) *Social Researching*, London: Routledge & Kegan Paul.

Bennett, T., Boyd Bowman, S., Mercer, C. and Woollacott, J. (eds) (1981a) Popular Television and Film, London: British Film Institute.

Bennett, T., Martin, C., Mercer, C. and Woollacott, J. (eds) (1981b) *Culture, Ideology and Social Process*, London: Batsford.

Berelson, B. (1949) 'What missing the newspaper means', in P. F. Lazarsfeld and F. M. Stanton (eds) *Radio Research, 1942–43*, New York: Duell, Sloan & Pearce.

Bordo, S. (1990) 'Feminism, postmodernism, and gender-scepticism', in L. J. Nicholson (ed.) *Feminism/Postmodernism*, London: Routledge, pp. 133–56.

Bourdieu, P. (1980) 'The aristocracy of culture', *Media, Culture and Society*, 2(3): 225–54.

Brodie, J. and Stoneman, L. (1983) 'A contextualist framework for studying the influence of television viewing in family interaction', *Journal of Family Issues*, June: 330–44.

Brunsdon, C. (1981) 'Crossroads: notes on a soap opera', *Screen* 22(4): 32–7.

—— (1984) 'Writing about soap opera', in L. Masterman (ed.) *Television Mythologies: Stars, Shows and Signs*, London: Comedia, pp. 82–7.

—— (1989) 'Text and audience', in E. Seiter, H. Borchers, G. Kreutzner and E. Warth (eds) *Remote Control: Television, Audiences and Cultural Power*, London: Routledge, pp. 116–29.

Brunsdon, C. and Morley, D. (1978) *Everyday Television: 'Nationwide'*, London: British Film Institute.

Buckingham, D. (1987) *Public Secrets:* EastEnders *and its Audience*, London: British Film Institute.

Burgin, V., Donald, J. and Kaplan, C. (eds) (1986) *Formations of Fantasy*, London: Methuen.

Burman, S. (ed.) (1979) *Fit Work for Women*, London: Croom Helm.

Chodorow, N. (1978) *The Reproduction of Mothering. Psychoanalysis and the Sociology of Gender*, Berkeley, Calif.: University of California Press.

Clarke, J. and Critcher, C. (1985) *The Devil Makes Work: Leisure in Capitalist Britain*, London: Macmillan.

Cockburn, C. (1983) *Brothers: Male Dominance and Technological Change*, London: Pluto Press.

—— (1985) *Machinery of Dominance: Women, Men and Technical Know-how*, London: Pluto Press.

Collett, P. (1986) 'Watching the TV audience', paper presented to International Television Studies Conference, London.

Cubitt, S. (1984) 'Top of the pops: the politics of the living room', in L. Masterman (ed.) *Television Mythologies: Stars, Shows and Signs*, London: Comedia, pp. 46–8.

—— (1988) 'Time shift', *Screen* 29(2): 74–81.

—— (1991) *Timeshift: on Video Culture*, London: Comedia Routledge.

Daly, M. (1979) *Gyn/Ecology*, London: The Women's Press.

Deem, R. (1986) *All Work and No Play? A Study of Women and Leisure*, Milton Keynes: Open University Press.

Dixey, R. and Talbot, M. (1982) 'Women, leisure and bingo', Leeds: Trinity & All Saints.

Dyer, R., Geraghty, C., Jordan, M., Lovell, T., Paterson, R. and Stewart, J. (eds) (1981) *Coronation Street*, London: British Film Institute.

Elliott, P. (1974) 'Uses and gratifications research: a critique and a sociological alternative', in J. G. Blumler and E. Katz (eds) *The Uses of Mass Communications: Current Perspectives on Gratifications Research*, Beverley Hills, Calif.: Sage.

Ellis, J. (1982) *Visible Fictions: Cinema, Television, Video*, London: Routledge & Kegan Paul.

Faulkner, W. and Arnold, E. (eds) (1985) *Smothered by Invention*, London: Pluto Press.

Feuer, J., Kerr, P. and Vahimagi, T. (eds) (1984) *MTM 'Quality Television'*, London: British Film Institute.

Finch, J. (1984) ' "It's great to have someone to talk to": the ethics and politics of interviewing women', in C. Bell and H. Roberts (eds) *Social Researching*, London: Routledge & Kegan Paul, pp. 70–87.

Frith, S. (1988) 'Fast forward', *Screen* 29(2): 90–3.

Geraghty, C. (1981) 'The continuous serial: a definition', in R. Dyer, C. Geraghty, M. Jordan, T. Lovell, R. Paterson and J. Stewart (eds) *Coronation Street*, London: British Film Institute, pp. 9–26.

Gershuny, J. I. (1982) 'Household tasks and the use of time', in S. Wallman and associates, *Living in South London*, London: Gower.

Giddens, A. (1976) *New Rules of Sociological Method*, London: Hutchinson.

—— (1979) *Central Problems in Social Theory*, London: Macmillan.

Golding, P. and Murdock, G. (1983) 'Privatising pleasure', *Marxism Today*, October: 32–6.

Goodman, I. (1983) 'Television's role in family interaction: a family systems perspective', *Journal of Family Issues*, June.

Graham, H. (1984) 'Surveying through stories', in C. Bell and H. Roberts (eds) *Social Researching*, London: Routledge & Kegan Paul, pp. 104–24.

Gray, A. (1987) 'Reading the audience', *Screen* 28(3): 24–35.

—— (1988) 'Reading the readings', paper presented to the International Television Studies Conference, July, University of London, Institute of Education.

Green, E., Hebron, S. and Woodward, D. (1985a) 'A woman's work', *Sport and Leisure*, July–August: 36–8.

Green, E., Hebron, S. and Woodward, D. (1985b) 'Leisure and gender: women's opportunities, perceptions and constraints', unpublished report to Economic and Social Research Council and Sports Council Steering Group.

Griffin, C. (1981) 'Young women and leisure', in A. Tomlinson (ed.) *Leisure and Social Control*, Brighton: Brighton Polytechnic, School of Human Movement.

Griffin, C. (1985) *Typical Girls*, London: Routledge & Kegan Paul.

Griffin, S. (1981) *Pornography and Silence: Culture's Revenge Against Nature*, London: The Women's Press.

Grossberg, L. (1988) 'Wandering audiences, nomadic critics', *Cultural Studies* 2(3): 377–91.

Gubern, R. (1985) 'La antropotronica: neuvos modelos tecnoculturales de la sociedad mass-mediatica', in R. Rispa (ed.) *Neuves Tecnologias en la Vida Cultural Española*, Madrid: FUNDESCO.

Hall, S. and Jefferson, T. (1976) *Resistance Through Rituals*, London: Hutchinson.

Hall, S., Hobson, D., Lowe, A. and Willis, P. (eds) (1980) *Culture, Media, Language*, London: Hutchinson.

Halloran, J. (ed.) (1970) *The Effects of Television*, London: Panther.

Hammersley, M. and Atkinson, P. (1983) *Ethnography Principles in Practice*, London: Tavistock Publications.

Heath, S. and Skirrow, G. (1986) 'An interview with Raymond Williams', in T. Modleski (ed.) *Studies in Entertainment*, Hamden, Conn.: Indiana University Press.

Hebdige, D. (1979) *Subcultures: The Meaning of Style*, London: Methuen.

Hermes, J. (1991) 'Media, meaning and everyday life', paper presented to the Fourth International Television Studies Conference, July, London.

Herzog, H. (1944) 'What do we really know about daytime serial listeners?', in P. F. Lazarsfeld and F. M. Stanton (eds) *Radio Research, 1942–43*, New York: Duell, Sloan & Pearce.

Hobson, D. (1978) 'Housewives: isolation as oppression', in Women's Studies Group, *Women Take Issue*, London: Hutchinson.

—— (1980) 'Housewives and the mass media', in S. Hall, D. Hobson, A. Lowe and P. Willis (eds) *Culture, Media, Language*, London: Hutchinson, pp. 105–14.

—— (1982) *Crossroads: The Drama of a Soap Opera*, London: Methuen.

Hunt, P. (1980) *Gender and Class Consciousness*, London: Macmillan.

Independent Broadcasting Authority (1988) *Attitudes to Broadcasting*, London: IBA.

Irigaray, L. (1977) 'Women's exile', *Ideology and Consciousness*, 1.

Kaplan, E. A. (ed.) (1983) *Regarding Television*, Los Angeles: American Film Institute.

Katz, E. and Lazarsfeld, P. F. (1955) *Personal Influence: The Part Played by People in the Flow of Mass Communications*, New York: The Free Press.

Katz, E., Gurevitch, M. and Haas, H. (1973) 'On the use of the mass media for important things', *American Sociological Review* 38: 164–81.

Katz, E., Blumler, J. G. and Gurevitch, M. (1974) 'Utilization of mass communication by the individual: an overview', in J. G. Blumler and E. Katz (eds) *The Uses of Mass Communications: Current Perspectives on Gratifications Research*, Beverley Hills, Calif.: Sage.

Keen, B. (1987) ' "Play it again, Sony": the double life of home video technology', *Science as Culture* 1: 7–42.

Klapper, J. (1960) *The Effects of Mass Communication*, Glencoe, Ill.: The Free Press.

Kuhn, A. (1984a) 'Women's genres', *Screen* 25(1): 18–28.

—— (1984b) 'Reply to Julian Petley', *Screen* 25(3): 116–17.

Lazarsfeld, P. F. and Stanton, F. M. (eds) (1949) *Radio Research, 1942–43*, New York: Duell, Sloan & Pearce.

Levy, M. (ed.) (1989) *The VCR Age: Home Video and Mass Communication*, Newbury Park, London and New Delhi: Sage.

Levy, M. and Gunter, B. (1988) *Home Video and the Changing Nature of the Television Audience*, London: John Libbey.

Lindlof, T. and Traudt, P. (1983) 'Mediated communication in families', in M. Mander (ed.) *Communications in Transition*, New York: Praeger.

Lull, J. (1980) 'The social uses of television', *Human Communications Research* 6(3).

—— (1990) *Inside Family Viewing*, London: Comedia Routledge.

Lundberg, D. and Hulton, O. (1968) *Individen och Mass Media*, Stockholm: Norstedts.

MacCabe, C. (1988) 'Those golden years', *Marxism Today*, April: 24–31.

McIntosh, M. (1979) 'The Welfare State and the needs of the dependent family', in S. Burman (ed.) *Fit Work for Women*, London: Croom Helm.

McIntosh, S. (1981) 'Leisure studies and women', in A. Tomlinson (ed.)

Leisure and Social Control, Brighton: Brighton Polytechnic, School of Human Movement.

McQuail, D., Blumler, J. G. and Brown, J. R. (1972) 'The television audience: a revised perspective', in D. McQuail (ed.) *Sociology of Mass Communications*, Harmondsworth: Penguin Books.

McRobbie, A. (1978) 'Working class girls and the culture of femininity', in Women's Studies Group, *Women Take Issue*, London: Hutchinson.

—— (1981) 'Settling accounts with subcultures: a feminist critique', in T. Bennett, C. Martin, C. Mercer and J. Woollacott (eds) *Culture, Ideology and Social Process*, London: Batsford.

—— (1982a) 'The politics of feminist research: between talk, text and action', *Feminist Review* 12: 46–57.

—— (1982b) '*Jackie*: an ideology of adolescent femininity', in B. Waites, T. Bennett and C. Martin (eds) *Popular Culture: Past and Present*, London: Croom Helm, pp. 263–83.

Mander, M. (ed.) (1983) *Communications in Transition*, New York: Praeger.

Marks, E. and de Courtivron, I. (1981) *New French Feminisms*, Brighton: Harvester.

Masterman, L. (ed.) (1984) *Television Mythologies: Stars, Shows and Signs*, London: Comedia.

Mead, M. (1962) *Male and Female*, Harmondsworth: Penguin Books.

Modleski, T. (1982) *Loving with a Vengeance*, Hamden, Conn.: Archon.

—— (1983) 'The rhythms of reception: daytime television and women's work', in E. A. Kaplan (ed.) *Regarding Television*, Los Angeles: American Film Institute.

—— (ed.) (1986) *Studies in Entertainment*, Hamden, Conn.: Indiana University Press.

Moores, S. (1988) 'The box on the dresser: memories of early radio and everyday life', *Media, Culture and Society* 10(1).

—— (1991) 'Dishes and domestic cultures: satellite TV as household technology', paper presented to the Fourth International Television Studies Conference, July, London.

Morley, D. (1980a) *The 'Nationwide' Audience*, London: British Film Institute.

—— (1980b) 'Texts, readers, subjects', in S. Hall, D. Hobson, A. Lowe and P. Willis (eds) *Culture, Media, Language*, London: Hutchinson, pp. 163–73.

—— (1981) 'The "Nationwide" audience: a critical postscript', *Screen Education* 39: 3–14.

—— (1986) *Family Television: Cultural Power and Domestic Leisure*, London: Comedia.

Morley D. and Silverstone, R. (1988) 'Domestic communication: technologies and meanings', paper presented to International Television Studies Conference, London.

Neale, S. (1981) 'Genre and cinema', in T. Bennett, S. Boyd Bowman, C. Mercer and J. Woollacott (eds) *Culture, Ideology and Social Process*, London: British Film Institute, pp. 6–25.

Nicholson, L. J. (ed.) (1990) *Feminism/Postmodernism*, London: Routledge.

Oakley, A. (1974) *The Sociology of Housework*, London:Martin Robertson.
—— (1981) 'Interviewing women: a contradiction in terms', in H. Roberts, *Doing Feminist Research*, London: Routledge & Kegan Paul, pp. 30–61.
O'Sullivan, T. (1991) 'Television memories and cultures of viewing, 1950–65', in J. Corner (ed.) *Popular Television in Britain*, Studies in Cultural History, London: British Film Institute.
Pahl, R. (1985) *Divisions of Labour*, London, Blackwell.
Parkin, F. (1973) *Class Inequality and Political Order*, London: Paladin.
Paterson, R. (1980) 'Planning the family', *Screen Education* 35.
Petley, J. (1984) 'A nasty story', *Screen* 25(2): 68–74.
Radway, J. A. (1984) *Reading the Romance*, Chapel Hill, N.C. and London: University of North Carolina Press.
—— (1988) 'Reception study: ethnography and the problems of dispersed audiences and nomadic subjects', *Cultural Studies* 2(3): 359–76.
Rath, C.-D. (1989) 'Live television and its audience: challenges of media reality', in E. Seiter, H. Borchers, G. Kreutzner and E. Warth (eds) *Remote Control: Television: Audiences and Cultural Power*, London: Routledge, pp. 79–95.
Reiter, T. T. (ed.) (1975) *Toward an Anthropology of Women*, New York: Monthly Review Press.
Roberts, H. (ed.) (1981) *Doing Feminist Research*, London: Routledge & Kegan Paul.
Roberts, K. (1981) *Leisure*, London: Longmans.
Roe, K. (1987) 'Adolescents' video use: a structural cultural approach', *American Behavioral Scientist* 30(5): 522–32.
Rosengren, K. E. and Windahl, S. (1973) 'Mass media use: causes and effects' (mimeo), Lund.
Rubin, G. (1975) 'The traffic in women: notes on the "political economy" of sex', in T. T. Reiter (ed.) *Toward an Anthropology of Women*, New York: Monthly Review Press, pp. 157–210.
Scannell, P. (1986) 'Radio Times: the temporal arrangements of broadcasting in the modern world', paper presented to International Television Studies Conference, London.
Segal, L. (1987) *Is the Future Female?*, London: Virago.
Seiter, E., Borchers, H., Kreutzner, G. and Warth, E. (1989) 'Don't treat us like we're so stupid and naive', in E. Seiter, H. Borchers, G. Kreutzner and E. Warth (eds) *Remote Control: Television, Audiences and Cultural Power*, London: Routledge.
Stanley, L. (1980) 'The problem of women and leisure: an ideological construct and a radical feminist alternative', paper presented to 'Leisure in the 80s Forum', sponsored by Capital Radio, London.
Stanley, L. and Wise, S. (1983) *Breaking Out: Feminist Consciousness and Feminist Research*, London: Routledge & Kegan Paul.
Taylor, L. and Mullan, B. (1986) *Uninvited Guests: the Intimate Secrets of Television and Radio*, London: Chatto & Windus.
Tudor, A. (1974) *Image and Influence*, London: George Allen & Unwin.
—— (1989) *Monsters and Mad Scientists: A Cultural History of the Horror Movie*, London: Blackwell.

Turkle, S. (1984) *The Second Self: Computers and the Human Spirit*, London: Granada.

Waites, B., Bennett, T. and Martin, C. (eds) (1982) *Popular Culture: Past and Present*, London: Croom Helm.

Walkerdine, V. (1986) 'Video replay: families, films and fantasy', in V. Burgin, J. Donald and C. Kaplan (eds) *Formations of Fantasy*, London: Methuen, pp. 167–99.

Weedon, C. (1987) *Feminist Practice and Poststructuralist Theory*, Oxford: Blackwell.

Williams, R. (1974) *Television: Technology and Cultural Form*, London: Fontana.

Willis, P. (1977) *Learning to Labour*, London: Saxon House.

Women's Studies Group (1978) *Women Take Issue*, London: Hutchinson.

Zimmerman, J. (1986) *Once upon the Future*, London: Pandora.

Index

43, 44, 49, 77, 78